101 Tax Loopholes for the Middle Class

101 Tax Loopholes for the Middle Class

▼
▼
▼

SEAN M. SMITH, E.A.

▼
▼
▼

BROADWAY BOOKS   NEW YORK

BROADWAY

101 TAX LOOPHOLES FOR THE MIDDLE CLASS. Copyright ©
1998 by Sean M. Smith. All rights reserved. Printed in the United
States of America. No part of this book may be reproduced or
transmitted in any form or by any means, electronic or mechanical,
including photocopying, recording, or by any information storage and
retrieval system, without written permission from the publisher. For
information, address Broadway Books, a division of Bantam
Doubleday Dell Publishing Group, Inc., 1540 Broadway, New York,
NY 10036.

Broadway Books titles may be purchased for business or promotional
use or for special sales. For information, please write to: Special
Markets Department, Bantam Doubleday Dell Publishing Group, Inc.,
1540 Broadway, New York, NY 10036.

BROADWAY BOOKS and its logo, a letter B bisected on the diagonal, are
trademarks of Broadway Books, a division of Bantam Doubleday Dell
Publishing Group, Inc.

Library of Congress Cataloging-in-Publication Data
Smith, Sean M., 1956–
   101 tax loopholes for the middle class / by Sean M. Smith.
      p. cm.
   Includes index.
   ISBN 0-7679-0149-5
   1. Income tax—Law and legislation—United States—Popular works.
2. Tax planning—United States—Popular works. I. Title.
KF6297.Z9S577   1998
343.7305′2—dc21   97-31541
                                                    CIP

FIRST EDITION

Designed by Ellen Cipriano

98 99 00 01 02 10 9 8 7 6 5 4 3 2 1

For my father, Carl,
and my son, Liam

▼

▼

▼

Contents

Your Home: A Shelter—and a Tax Shelter

Withholding Strategies for Maximum Income—Without Underpayment Penalties

Your Investments and Taxes

Get the Most from Your Retirement Plan

You Don't Have to Be Wealthy to Save on Estate Taxes

Business Tax Angles for Any Business

Three Payroll Tax Savers for a Small Business Employer

Small Business Fringe Benefits

Special Tax Savings for the Self-Employed

Running Your Business as a Regular C Corporation

▾

▾

▾

Running Your Business as an S Corporation

The Limited Liability Company—New Kid on the Block

Up Against the IRS

✳ **Denotes new tax savers for '97**

Acknowledgments

Special thanks to my mother, Lucille Smith, for the gift of words; to my editor and friend, Richard Spencer, for wrestling with every sentence; to my friend Tom Flynn, for reminding me to accomplish; to my agent, Nina Graybill, for jumping into the fray on my behalf; to Charles Conrad and Ted Sammons at Broadway Books, for always asking for more; and finally, special thanks to my wife and friend Pamela, for her infinite patience and constant support from the first blank page to the last typed page.

Disclaimer

The information contained in this book is intended to provide general guidelines on matters of interest to taxpayers. The application and impact of tax laws can vary widely from case to case, however, based upon the specific or unique facts and circumstances of each taxpayer. Accordingly, this book is not intended to serve as legal, accounting, or tax advice for individual taxpayers. Furthermore, the information contained in this book is based on the Internal Revenue Code of 1986 amended as of August 5, 1997, and tax rules and regulations change frequently. Readers who require advice or assistance regarding their specific situations should seek the services of a qualified professional.

The author and publisher cannot be held responsible for positions taken or losses incurred as a result of the application of any information contained in this book.

Introduction

ABOUT THIS BOOK

During my 15 years as a tax accountant to middle income clients, the most frequent advice I give is: When it comes to taxes, saving money is a matter of being informed. The trouble is, becoming informed can be a challenge. There are laws that can be used to the advantage of middle income taxpayers. More often than not, though, they are obscured by tax code technicalities, which make them virtually inaccessible to anyone who's not a tax accountant. With this in mind, I have assembled *101 Tax Loopholes for the Middle Class* in a format that is accessible and easy to understand and use. Unlike the many books published annually to help ease the burden of filing tax returns, *101 Tax Loopholes* is not a tax preparation guide. This book will not walk you line-by-line through tax forms nor will it bring you face-to-face with the legalese of the tax code. Instead I present straightforward and legal strategies for minimizing the taxes you pay.

HOW TO MAKE THIS BOOK WORK FOR YOU

This book is organized according to specific circumstances you may be facing as a middle income taxpayer. At the beginning of each chapter, you'll find a short summary outlining the important aspects and requirements of the particular tax-saving strategy. Allowing you to quickly determine the loopholes that suit you best, these summaries are followed by a concise description, real-world examples, important planning pointers, and a checklist.

WHAT YOU WILL FIND INSIDE

101 Tax Loopholes for the Middle Class is a compilation of specific tax-saving strategies in the following categories, all updated to include changes resulting from the Taxpayer Relief Act of 1997:

- Personal income tax savers

- Using your home as a tax shelter

- Paycheck withholding strategies

- Tax strategies for investments

- Retirement plan tax savers

- Estate tax loopholes

- Tax angles for any sized business

- Payroll tax savers for the small business employer

- Loopholes for the self-employed

- Small business fringe benefits

- Loopholes for small business C corporations

- Loopholes for small business S corporations

- Loopholes for small business LLCs

- Tax audit strategies

As you will see, the loopholes I offer apply to a wide range of taxpayers and situations. Consider the following:

- Working late? Loophole #67 points out that your company can buy you a deductible dinner.

- Stuck with almost worthless stock? Loophole #30 explains four different ways to write it off.

- Own a home computer? Loophole #63 reveals a way to make it tax deductible.

- Planning a wedding? Loophole #7 shows you how to let Uncle Sam help pay for your honeymoon.

Until now, the only thing that has kept you from realizing tax savings has been a lack of information. The strategies and explanations I present in *101 Tax Loopholes for the Middle Class* give you the information you need to start saving now. Paying taxes is inevitable, but prudent use of the information in this book will ease the burden.

Personal
Income Tax
Savers

▼
▼
▼

1 Borrow to Pay Your Child's College Tuition and Enjoy Up-Front Tax Benefits (Then, Deduct the Interest You Pay on the Student Loan)

$ This tax loophole is for taxpayers paying their children's college tuition expenses.

$ Two new education tax credits are now available.

$ Take out a student loan to pay tuition expenses and enjoy the education tax credits now—not later, when you repay the loan.

$ When you repay the student loan, deduct the interest paid, even if you don't itemize deductions.

$ The new education tax credits and the deduction for student loan interest are available only to low- and middle-income taxpayers.

The Taxpayer Relief Act of 1997 establishes two important education benefits for the middle class: the HOPE scholarship credit and the lifetime learning credit. For many parents, the real benefit of these new education credits is that they can take out a student loan for their child, use the loan proceeds to pay for tuition expenses, and benefit from the new education tax credits in the year the loan proceeds are spent for tuition—not in a later year, when the loan proceeds are repaid.

The HOPE scholarship credit, effective for qualified tuition expenses paid beginning in 1998 for education received in 1998, allows for a 100% tax credit for the first $1,000 of qualified expenses incurred and a 50% credit for the second $1,000 of qualified expenses incurred during the first two years of postsecondary education (after high school). Thus, the credit is limited to $1,500 for each student.

The lifetime learning credit, effective for qualified tuition expenses paid after June 30, 1998, allows for a 20% credit of up to $5,000 (the dollar cap is scheduled to be raised to $10,000 for the year 2003 and later years) in qualified lifetime tuition expenses. The lifetime learning credit is available per taxpayer—not per student—but can be used for undergraduate, graduate, and professional degree expenses. Assuming the full $10,000 cap after the year 2002, the lifetime learning credit will allow for total tax savings of $2,000.

As a parent paying for your child's tuition, it will be important to maximize the tax savings provided by these education credits. If you have to borrow to pay for the education expenses, you can enjoy the tax benefits long before you repay the student loan. The new tax act also provides for the deductibility of interest paid on student loans. Beginning in 1998, you can deduct up to $1,000 in student loan interest paid. The allowable deductible amount rises to $1,500 in 1999, $2,000 in 2000, and $2,500 in 2001 and the years thereafter.

☞**EXAMPLE:** Mr. and Mrs. Smith plan to pay for their daughter's college tuition expenses. In 1998 the Smiths will have an adjusted gross income of $60,000 and are thus able to benefit from either the HOPE scholarship credit or the lifetime learning credit.

(For married taxpayers filing jointly, the available credits are phased out for adjusted gross incomes between $80,000 and $100,000. The credits are not available to married taxpayers filing jointly with adjusted gross income in excess of $100,000. For single taxpayers, the phase-out occurs for adjusted gross incomes between $40,000 and $50,000, with no credits available to single taxpayers whose adjusted gross income is in excess of $50,000.)

During 1998, Ms. Smith's qualified tuition expenses equal $2,500. As she is carrying at least one-half the normal full-time class load, her qualified tuition expenses are eligible for the HOPE scholarship credit. Mr. and Mrs. Smith take out a student loan and pay the tuition expenses. They can take the full $1,500 HOPE scholarship tax credit for 1998, even though they have paid for the tuition expenses with the proceeds from a loan. The $1,500 HOPE scholarship tax credit reduces their federal income tax liability for 1998 dollar for dollar—they save $1,500 in federal income tax.

Because the lifetime learning credit cannot be taken in the same year the HOPE scholarship credit is taken, the Smiths are unable to use the lifetime learning credit for 1998. However, they can use it in 1999. If their daughter's tuition again equals $2,500, they can use part of the lifetime learning credit to save $500 ($2,500 times 20%) in federal income tax. Again, they can take this credit even if the tuition expenses are paid with the proceeds of a student loan.

When the Smiths begin to repay the student loan, they will be able to deduct the interest paid on the loan subject to the annual deduction limits (see above).

♀**PLANNING POINTERS:** It is important to remember that the HOPE scholarship credit is available only for the first two years of postsecondary education. Be certain to maximize your benefit from this credit before using the lifetime learning credit. Only one of the two education tax credits can be used in a single tax year.

If the level of your income will rise above the adjusted gross income phase-out levels within the next few years, you should encourage your child to take a full-time course load so that you can maximize your tax savings before your income grows too high and thus makes you ineligible to take the credit.

The income phase-out level for deducting student loan interest is lower than the income phase-out level for taking the education tax credits. If you expect your income to grow, you should maximize interest payments on the student loan before your income is too high for you to enjoy the deductible benefit. For married taxpayers filing jointly, the allowable tax deduction for student loan interest paid is phased out for adjusted gross incomes between $60,000 and $75,000, with no deduction allowed if your adjusted gross income exceeds $75,000. For single taxpayers, the allowable tax deduction for student loan interest paid is phased out for adjusted gross incomes between $40,000 and $55,000, with no deduction allowed if your adjusted gross income exceeds $55,000.

☑ CHECKLIST:

- Determine whether you are allowed to take one of the two education tax credits per the amount of your adjusted gross income for the year.
- If you take out a student loan to pay the qualified tuition expenses, the education credits are available to you for the years you pay the tuition—not in later years, when you repay the loan.
- Reduce your federal income tax, dollar for dollar, by the amount of the allowable education tax credit. Remember, you cannot use both tax credits in the same tax year.
- If your adjusted gross income does not exceed the applicable phase-out levels, deduct the interest paid on the student loan up to the dollar limits allowed for the year. The deduction is an "above-the-line" deduction. This means you do not have to itemize deductions on your federal income tax return to take the deduction.

2 Use the New Lifetime Learning Tax Credit for Your Business-Related Education Expenses

$ This loophole is for employees and self-employed taxpayers who pay for business-related education costs.

$ Determine who should deduct qualified tuition expenses and who should take the new lifetime learning tax credit.

$ Only qualified tuition expenses paid after June 30, 1998, are eligible for the new lifetime learning credit.

The new lifetime learning education tax credit is not limited to the tuition expenses you incur on behalf of your children. Maybe you do not have children, or your children are already grown and educated. You can use the new tax credit to help pay for your own education. The question is: Should you use the new tax credit?

- If you are self-employed and incur business-related continuing education costs, you should NOT use the new lifetime learning credit. Because you can deduct business-related education costs from your self-employment income, you save income tax and self-employment tax. If you are in the 28% federal income tax bracket and have to pay 15.3% in self-employment tax, a deduction for $1,000 in business-related education costs will save you $433 in combined federal income and self-employment tax. On the other hand, taking the new lifetime learning credit for the same $1,000 will save you only $200 in federal income tax.

- If you are an employee in the 28% or 31% federal income tax bracket and can deduct unreimbursed business-related education expenses as an itemized deduction, you should NOT use the new lifetime learning credit. If you are in the 28% federal income tax bracket, a deduction for $1,000 in business-related education costs will save you $280 in federal income tax. On the other hand, taking the new lifetime learning credit for the same $1,000 will save you only $200 in federal income tax.

- If you are an employee in the 28% or 31% federal income tax bracket and cannot deduct unreimbursed business-related education expenses as an itemized deduction, you should use the new lifetime learning credit. Since you cannot deduct the expense, the credit is the only way to save tax.

- If you are an employee in the 15% federal income tax bracket, you should use the new lifetime learning credit. It does not matter whether you can deduct unreimbursed business-related education expenses as an itemized deduction. In the 15% federal income tax bracket, a tax deduction for $1,000 in business-related education costs saves you only $150 in federal income tax. On the other hand, taking the new lifetime learning credit for the same $1,000 will save you $200 in federal income tax.

(*Note:* If you are an employee living in a state with high state income tax rates and you are in the 15% federal income tax bracket and can deduct the business education costs, the combined federal and state income tax savings from the deduction may outweigh the benefit of the new lifetime learning credit. Measure the state income tax savings generated by the deduction before deciding on the new lifetime credit.)

☞**EXAMPLE:** Mr. Smith is an employee in the 28% federal income tax bracket. In the fall of 1998, he incurs and pays $1,000 in tuition costs that qualify as business-related education expenses.

Even though he itemizes deductions on his personal income tax return, Mr. Smith cannot deduct the expenses. This is because unreimbursed employee expenses are categorized as miscellaneous itemized deductions subject to the "2% rule." Mr. Smith can deduct only miscellaneous itemized deductions in excess of 2% of his adjusted gross income. Assuming his adjusted gross income for 1998 is $50,000 (on a married-filed-jointly tax return), Mr. Smith can deduct only miscellaneous itemized deductions in excess of $1,000 ($50,000 times 2%). Assuming also that Mr. Smith has no other miscellaneous deductions, the $1,000 in unreimbursed business-related education expenses cannot be deducted.

Since Mr. Smith cannot deduct the education expenses, he uses the new lifetime learning education tax credit and saves $200 ($1,000 times 20%) in federal income tax.

♀**PLANNING POINTERS:** The lifetime learning credit is effective for qualified tuition expenses paid after June 30, 1998, and allows for a 20% tax credit up to $5,000 in qualified lifetime tuition expenses (the dollar cap is scheduled to be raised to $10,000 for the year 2003 and later years). Assuming the full $10,000 cap after the year 2002, the lifetime learning credit will allow for total tax savings of $2,000 ($10,000 times 20%).

If you expect to have tuition expenses in 1998 that you cannot deduct as a business-related education expense, you should wait (if possible) until after June 30 to pay the expenses. By waiting, the qualified tuition expenses you incur will be eligible for the lifetime learning credit.

If you are a married taxpayer filing jointly, the lifetime learning credit is phased out if your adjusted gross income is between $80,000 and $100,000, with no credit available if your adjusted gross income is in excess of $100,000. If you are a single taxpayer, the lifetime learning credit is phased out if your adjusted gross income is between $40,000 and $50,000, with no credit available if your adjusted gross income is in excess of $50,000. The credit is not available in any amount to married taxpayers who file separately.

☑ CHECKLIST:

- Determine whether you will save more tax by deducting business-related education costs or taking the lifetime learning credit for those costs. Then take either the deduction or the lifetime learning credit—whichever saves you more tax.
- If you expect to have qualified tuition expenses in 1998 and cannot deduct the expenses for whatever reason, you should wait (if possible) to pay the costs until after June 30, 1998. Qualified tuition costs paid prior to July 1, 1998, are not eligible for the new lifetime learning credit.

3   Claim Head-of-Household Status When Your Adult Child Lives at Home

$ Recent Tax Court ruling allows single taxpayers with an adult child living at home to claim head-of-household status.

$ Taxpayers can qualify for this status even if they cannot claim a dependency exemption for the adult child.

$ Amend previous years' tax returns if applicable.

If you are a single taxpayer and have an adult child living in your home, you may have missed out on a big tax break. The tax break in question involves whether you can file as a head of household on your Form 1040 or whether you must file as a single individual. The IRS has always held that to claim head-of-household status, you must be able to claim a tax exemption for the relative living with you. Therefore, single adults whose grown children lived with them and earned a living were denied this benefit. The Tax Court has recently ruled against this IRS limitation, and you may be able to benefit for this year and the last three years.

This may not sound like much, but consider the benefits:

- For 1997, the standard deduction for head of household—if you don't itemize deductions—is $6,050. It is only $4,150 if you file as a single taxpayer.
- For 1997, a person filing as a head of household has to pay only 15% in federal income tax on taxable income up to $33,050. A single taxpayer can use the 15% tax bracket on taxable income only up to $24,650; after that, the taxpayer must pay at the 28% tax bracket. This tax rate benefit is true of all the "bracket jumps"—head-of-household taxpayers pay less in income tax all the way up the line. Single taxpayers have to start paying tax at higher rates for lower levels of taxable income.

Obviously, filing as a head of household rather than as a single individual can save you a chunk of tax change. And now the Tax Court says that an adult child living at home, even if he or she has too much income for you to list as a tax exemption, will qualify you to file with the more favorable head-of-household status if you meet the other head-of-household rules.

To qualify, (1) you must be unmarried on the last day of the year, (2) you must maintain a household and contribute more than half the cost of maintaining the home, (3) you must not be a nonresident alien at any time during the year, and (4) your home must be the principal residence for a relative—now including adult children—for more than half the tax year.

EXAMPLE: Mr. Smith is a widower and still owns his family home. His son is an adult, has his own contracting business, and still lives at home with his father. As long as Mr. Smith is unmarried on the last day of the year, he is not a nonresident alien at any time during the year, he contributes more than half the cost of maintaining the home, and his son lives under his roof for more than half the year, he is able to file his Form 1040 as a head of household and take advantage of an increased standard deduction and more favorable tax rates.

PLANNING POINTERS: To take advantage of this tax break, you must contribute more than half the cost of maintaining your home during the year. The cost of maintaining your home includes rent, mortgage interest, property taxes, property insurance, maintenance and repair costs, utility costs, and the cost of food eaten in your home. The cost of maintaining your home does not include clothing costs, medical costs, life insurance costs, transportation costs, and other costs such as the cost of a vacation.

If you split expenses with an adult child living in your home, be careful to pay the larger share of the expenses that qualify as a cost of maintaining your home; let the adult child cover the smaller part of these costs and pick up the tab for costs that do not qualify. And make sure to document who pays for what. In this way, you can ensure the favorable head-of-household status and protect it if it is challenged by the IRS.

IMPORTANT: If you qualify for this tax break but have filed as a single individual in previous years, you should amend those previous years' tax returns (you can generally go back and amend for the three previous years) and receive a refund for the taxes you have overpaid. Use IRS Form 1040X. And don't forget to file amended state income tax returns, as well, if applicable.

CHECKLIST:
- Determine whether you qualify for head-of-household status under the new Tax Court ruling.
- Keep records during the year documenting that you have paid more than half the cost of maintaining your home.
- File as head of household on your Form 1040. In the section

listing dependents, write in "Head-of-household status allowed without dependent exemption per Huff TC Memo 1995-200."

- If you qualified for this beneficial status in previous years, amend your tax returns for those years using Form 1040X. Amend state income tax returns for the same years if applicable.

4 Adoptive Parents: Save More with the Adoption Credit Than with Your Employer's Adoption Assistance Program

$ Adoption credit under new tax law will save you more than an adoption expense reimbursement from an employer-provided adoption assistance program.

$ Amount of adjusted gross income determines availability of adoption credit.

$ Unused adoption credit can be carried forward to future tax years.

The 1996 tax law gives new support to adoptive parents, offering them two options: either a tax credit or a paycheck exclusion. It takes very little number crunching to see that the tax credit will save the adoptive parents more than will the paycheck exclusion.

Both options cover adoption expenses. The first option is a tax credit for up to $5,000 of certain adoption expenses incurred with each child adopted ($6,000 for each child with special needs). With the tax credit, you pay for the adoption expenses yourself. The second option is an exclusion of up to $5,000 ($6,000 for each child with special needs) in gross income from your employer-provided adoption assistance program, set up to cover adoption expenses you will incur. With the second option, your employer sets up an employee benefit plan and you can exclude from taxable income the monies paid to you from the plan for the qualified adoption expenses.

At first glance, both options may seem to offer equal tax savings, but this is not the case. When you pay for adoption expenses without an employer-provided plan, you receive a tax credit for the amount of the adoption expenses you incur. This means you can offset your income tax with the credit on a dollar-per-dollar basis. On the other hand, when you exclude the adoption expense from your income by way of a reimbursement from an employer adoption assistance program, you will save only a percentage of the adoption expenses incurred. This percentage will depend on your federal and state income tax bracket and the amount of money you save in FICA tax (Social Security and Medicare). No matter how much you would save with the employer-provided adoption assistance program, you will always save more by taking the adoption credit instead.

☞**EXAMPLE:** Mr. and Mrs. Smith are adopting a child in 1997. The child does not have special needs as defined under the new tax law, so the Smiths benefit from a maximum of $5,000 in adoption expense support. Since their adjusted gross income for 1997 does not exceed $75,000, they are eligible for the full $5,000. And because the adoption is finalized in 1997, they can use the adoption expense to lessen the tax burden on their 1997 income tax return. Instead of participating in an employer-provided adoption assistance program, they take the adoption credit.

To generate the $5,000 needed to pay the adoption expenses out of pocket, they have to earn $8,424.58 in gross taxable salary. This gross salary is reduced by 7.65% FICA withheld ($644.48), by 28% federal income tax ($2,358.88), and by 5% state income tax ($421.22). Thus, paying for the adoption expense out of pocket requires that the Smiths pay $3,424.58 in combined tax before they have the $5,000 to spend on adoption expenses. But because they can take the dollar-for-dollar tax credit, they also save $5,000 in federal income tax. Their net benefit is $1,575.42 ($5,000 tax credit less $3,424.58 combined taxes paid).

If they had opted for the employer-provided adoption assistance program and received reimbursement for the adoption expenses, the reimbursement would have been excluded from their gross income.

Assuming they were in the same 28% federal income tax bracket, 5% state income tax bracket, and 7.65% FICA tax bracket, the $5,000 exclusion from gross income would have saved them only the $3,424.58 in combined taxes calculated above.

By taking the adoption credit instead of a reimbursement from an employer-provided adoption assistance program, the Smiths save an additional $1,575.42 in tax ($5,000 less $3,424.58).

♀PLANNING POINTERS: If you have the option to take expense reimbursements from an employer-provided adoption assistance program, attempt instead to take the benefit as a salary increase. If you have a choice of benefits—but not cash—take another benefit and pay for the adoption expenses out of your own pocket. You'll come out ahead.

Qualified adoption expenses include reasonable and necessary adoption expenses such as attorney fees, court costs, adoption fees, and any other necessary expenses related to the adoption. Qualified adoption expenses do not include fees for a surrogate parent or fees incurred in adopting a spouse's child.

If your federal income tax liability for the year is less than the available credit, you can carry forward and use the unused portion of the credit for up to five years.

You cannot take the full $5,000 (or $6,000) tax credit or gross income exclusion from an employer adoption assistance program if your adjusted gross income for the year the adoption is finalized is more than $75,000. The $5,000 ($6,000) is phased out for adjusted gross incomes of $75,000 to $115,000. For adjusted gross incomes of more than $115,000 there is no adoption tax benefit available.

☑ CHECKLIST:
- Determine, based on your level of income, whether the adoption expense tax saving benefit is available.
- If so, keep records of all adoption-related expenses.
- If you are able to do so, take the adoption credit rather than an exclusion from gross income with an employer-provided adoption assistance program.

5 Caring for a Friend? Deduct Their Personal Exemption

$ This tax break is for taxpayers who financially support a friend.

$ For 1997, you may be able to deduct your friend's personal exemption of $2,650 on your own income tax return.

Have you taken in a sick or elderly friend with little or no financial resources? Even though he or she is not related to you, you can include your friend's personal exemption on your income tax return if all the following requirements are met:

■ You provide more than half your friend's financial support during the year.
■ Your friend is a member of your household for the entire year.
■ Your friend's total gross income for the year is less than the personal exemption amount. For 1997, your friend's gross income must be less than $2,650.
■ Your friend is a U.S. citizen or resident.

Why should your friend let you use his or her personal exemption on your income tax return? Because when people have little or no income, their standard deduction by itself is large enough to wipe out any income tax they might owe. By giving their personal exemption to someone else, they prevent it from going to waste.

☞ **EXAMPLE:** Mr. Smith, a single taxpayer, is taking care of an old friend who is suffering from a terminal illness. His friend has some assets that generate earnings but not enough to exceed the personal exemption amount of $2,650. Since becoming ill, Mr. Smith's friend has been unable to work and so has no earned income. During 1997, Mr. Smith's friend lives in Mr. Smith's house the entire year, and Mr. Smith pays for more than half his friend's "support" items.

Because his situation meets the requirements of the tax code, Mr. Smith can take his friend's personal exemption deduction on his own 1997 income tax return. If Mr. Smith is in the 28% federal income tax bracket, taking his friend's personal exemption of $2,650 will generate $742 in federal income tax savings.

PLANNING POINTERS: Items that qualify as financial support for your friend include payments for food, shelter, medical and dental bills, church contributions, child care, and large items such as a car or a stereo.

Even though friends may want to contribute their small assets to the support pot, they should limit their contribution to less than one-half the total amount expended for support. Instead, they should pay directly for nonsupport items. Friends who are terminally ill should name their care-giving friends as beneficiaries in their will.

Ill friends do not need to give up their ownership of assets to give their personal exemptions to their care-giving friends—but they cannot use them to provide for half their own support.

If you want to deduct your friend's personal exemption, your friend must be a member of your household for the entire year. However, you can still take the personal exemption if your friend passes away during the year, but only if your friend lived exclusively with you during that portion of the year.

Watch out for these limitations:

- Tax-exempt Social Security benefits cannot be counted as part of gross income (to determine whether your friend earned $2,650 for 1997); however, if the Social Security benefits (no matter if they are tax-exempt or taxable) are used to pay for support items, they will be counted in determining whether you provided more than half your friend's support.
- On the other hand, Medicare (basic or supplemental) and Medicaid payments will not be considered support payments. The bottom line is that you don't have to take Medicare or Medicaid payments into account when you determine

whether you paid more than one-half your friend's support. But if your friend uses Social Security benefits to pay for support items, they would count in determining whether or not you paid more than half.

- If you are a single taxpayer and you care for a friend, you cannot file your personal income tax return using the more favorable "head-of-household" filing status. You can file as head of household only if you provide care for family members.

- You cannot take a personal exemption for a friend if your relationship is against the law in your state.

☑ CHECKLIST:

- Carefully document general household support payments.
- Carefully document direct support payments you make on behalf of your friend.
- Allocate to your friend his or her portion of the general household support payments and combine this with the direct support payments you make on his or her behalf. This will give you the total amount of support you provide for your friend.
- Document the amount of self-support your friend has.
- Check these totals before year-end. If your friend has managed to be more than 50% self-supporting for the year-to-date, you should have him or her stop spending, and you should continue to pay for support items. By doing this, you can be certain that you provide more than half the support for the year.
- Keep your support records for as long as your income tax return is subject to audit—generally, three years.
- If you have failed to take a friend's personal exemption in previous years and are able to document that you met all the requirements for taking the exemption in those years, file an amended return for the years in question. Generally, you can file an amended income tax return for the three years previous to the current tax year. Use IRS Form 1040X to amend a previous year's income tax return.

6 | Support Your Elderly Parents by Giving Money to Your Children

$ This is for taxpayers who contribute to the support of their elderly parents and also plan to provide a nest egg for their adult children.

$ Save income tax on monies used to support your elderly parents by shifting assets to lower-tax-bracket adult children.

If you intend to help your adult children by providing them with a financial nest egg but are also faced with the duty of providing for your elderly parents, there is a way you can accomplish both goals and save income tax. All you have to do is give the money to your children now, and then let them provide for their grandparents. Your elderly parents receive the current financial assistance they need, and, after a while, your children can use the nest egg for themselves. In the meantime, you save income tax.

Here's how it works. You make a complete (no strings attached) gift to an adult child who is in a lower federal income tax bracket than you are. This child, concerned for the welfare of his or her grandparents, banks the money and then gifts the earnings from the money to them.

What makes this strategy work is that your children will be taxed on the earnings in a tax bracket that is lower than yours. You save the difference between what you would have paid in income tax and what your children pay in income tax.

EXAMPLE: Ms. Smith is in the 28% federal income tax bracket and 5% state income tax bracket. Over the years she has managed to set aside $45,000, which she planned to give to her son when he became an adult. But now, Ms. Smith's elderly parents also require supplemental support.

Let's say Ms. Smith earns 5% in interest income each year on the $45,000. This comes to $2,250 annually. Ms. Smith has to pay combined federal and state income tax of $743 on the interest earnings, leaving $1,507 available after tax for her to give to her elderly parents.

Instead of keeping the money, Ms. Smith makes a complete gift of the $45,000 to her eldest son, who is 22 years old and in the 15% federal income tax bracket and 3% state income tax bracket. On the same annual earnings of $2,250, her son will pay combined federal and state income tax of only $405, leaving $1,845 available after tax for distribution to his elderly grandparents. This means an extra $338 can go to Ms. Smith's elderly parents each year instead of going to the IRS.

And, of course, Ms. Smith can give her son $405 each year to pay the tax. Effectively, Ms. Smith pays the government only $405, not $743.

♀PLANNING POINTERS: You should consider this income tax saving strategy only if you have been planning to give your child a sum of money as a financial nest egg. To shift the income tax, control of the gifted money must pass completely out of your hands. You cannot make the gift contingent on your child gifting the earnings to the grandparents—the gifts to grandparents must be made voluntarily after your child has control of the funds.

Unless you have a sizable estate, the money you give to your child will be free of any gift tax. If you are married, you and your spouse can gift up to $20,000 per donee each year without paying gift tax, or without using your lifetime gift tax exclusion. For any amounts above $20,000 gifted to one donee in a single year, you can use a portion of your lifetime exclusion of $600,000 to avoid gift tax (your spouse also has a lifetime exclusion of $600,000 for gift tax purposes).

If your oldest child's income begins to increase and he or she jumps into your income tax bracket, he or she may no longer feel a need for the nest egg. This older child may be inclined to pass the monies to a younger sibling, one still in a lower federal income tax bracket.

If the second child is similarly concerned with the welfare of his or her elderly grandparents, this second child can continue to gift the earnings on the gift proceeds to them—after paying income tax at the lower rates. And, of course, if you are so inclined, you can make the child a gift each year of the cost of the income tax.

Ultimately, the second child may decide that the older sibling should have given up only half the nest egg. The second child may then gift back half the gift proceeds to the older sibling. Of course, since the second child is concerned about the welfare of the elderly grandparents, he or she will probably not make this gift back to the older sibling until the elderly grandparents no longer require supplemental assistance.

☑ CHECKLIST:

- Make a complete gift to an adult child who is in a lower federal income tax bracket than you are.
- If the adult child is so inclined, he or she can use the earnings from the gift proceeds to help provide for the welfare of his or her elderly grandparents (your parents).
- The gift you make to your child cannot be contingent upon your child using the earnings for the benefit of the grandparents.
- During the years your child is providing for elderly grandparents from the proceeds of the gift, you can gift your child the amount of the taxes he or she has to pay on the earnings generated by the gift.
- For annual gifts of more than $10,000 per donee, including combined spousal gifts limited to $20,000, you are required to file IRS Form 709. This is a relatively straightforward form that you are also required to file if you use all or a portion of your annual lifetime gift tax exclusion to avoid gift tax on larger gifts.

7   Take a Charitable Deduction Now for a Contribution You Make Later

$ Contribute a bank letter of credit to a charity.

$ Deduct the full amount currently, even though the charity defers making withdrawals of the funds.

$ This is a good strategy for an "income jump" year.

If your income has increased this year and you are thus facing a big hike in your income tax, you will need all the deductions you can take. If you have a favorite charity, there may be a way for you to take a larger deduction this year without parting with the cash—at least not right away. You can do this by contributing an irrevocable bank letter of credit to the charity. You are allowed to take a current deduction for the full amount of the letter of credit, even if the charity does not actually take the funds until a later year.

☞ **EXAMPLE:** This year, apart from his regular earned income, Mr. Smith received a distribution from a retirement plan and sold some shares of stock, which generated a taxable gain. On top of this, beginning this year, he is no longer able to take an exemption for his youngest child. Because of these tax changes, Mr. Smith is facing a hefty increase in his income tax liability for 1997. He can use all the deductions he can take.

Mr. Smith contributes regularly to the small church he attends. He ordinarily contributes about $1,200 each year. He plans to continue contributing to the church but would like to accelerate his deductible benefit into this year. Instead of contributing the $1,200 for this year, Mr. Smith contributes an irrevocable bank letter of credit for $6,000 to the church.

Since the letter of credit is irrevocable, the church has the right to take the full amount immediately. However, the church leaders understand that Mr. Smith would "prefer" that they limit the church's withdrawals from the letter of credit to $1,200 per year. Of course, Mr. Smith's preference is strictly nonbinding. The church leaders can do as they please, but they see no reason why they should withdraw more than $1,200 per year.

For 1997, Mr. Smith can deduct in full the $6,000 value of the bank letter of credit.

♀PLANNING POINTERS: An accelerated charitable deduction is especially useful in a year when your taxable income has increased and pushes you into a higher income tax bracket. If you expect to be in a higher income tax bracket next year than you are this year, you may benefit more by waiting to take the accelerated charitable deduction in the later year. That is, it is probably better to wait until next year to make the contribution of the bank letter of credit.

For the entire amount of the bank letter of credit to be currently deductible, it must be irrevocable. This means that once you execute the letter of credit, you give up control of the funds. The charity receiving the benefit of the funds can access the benefit at any time. Before making the gift, you should communicate what your withdrawal preference is and feel confident that the charity will consider this preference. It is important to note, however, that you cannot take the charitable deduction if the contribution is contingent on your withdrawal preference. Although the charity can consider your preference, it must have the power to decide for itself when the withdrawals will be made.

In the IRS ruling that allows for this type of accelerated charitable deduction, the taxpayers in question were well known in their community and were not required by the bank to collateralize the letter of credit. If you enjoy this type of relationship with a bank, you can do the same as the taxpayers in the letter ruling. It is likely, however, that most banks will require you to set up an account at the bank and deposit at least the amount of the letter of credit. If you are required to do this, you should set up an account that generates the largest amount of interest earnings. In this way, while the money waits to be taken by the charity, you continue to earn interest on the account balance.

☑ CHECKLIST:

- To deduct a larger current charitable contribution, establish an irrevocable bank letter of credit favoring a specific charity.
- If the charity decides to defer making withdrawals, you will have an up-front deduction without currently parting with the cash.
- If you expect to be in a higher income tax bracket in the near future, wait until the higher-bracket year before making the contribution of the letter of credit.

---

8   Find a Credit Card with a Built-In Charitable Deduction

$ This involves charitable deductions for taxpayers who file Form 1040 Schedule A.

$ Purchase rebates offered as an incentive by credit card companies can be donated to a charity of your choice.

$ You can take the deduction without taking the rebate into income.

$ The designated charity can be changed at any time, or you can stop donating these purchase rebates at any time.

Your credit card can do more than charge purchases. Thanks to a recent IRS ruling, you can now use your credit card to make tax-deductible charitable contributions without spending a single dime. Because the IRS ruling is fairly recent, all credit card companies may not provide this option. So as you shop around for the best credit card, check to see whether this benefit is available.

Here's how it works. Many credit cards offer rebates on credit card purchases as an incentive to keep customers. When you make a purchase and charge it, the credit card company credits your account for a percentage of the purchase amount. You are basically receiving a sales discount for using that particular credit card. Now you can direct the credit card company to donate these rebates to the charity of your choice on your behalf. You haven't spent anything more than you would have to make the purchase, and you receive a tax deduction as well.

☞**EXAMPLE:** Ms. Smith applies for a credit card that offers the charitable deduction benefit. She designates the United Way Campaign as the charitable beneficiary of any purchase rebates she will receive on the credit card. At the end of each calendar quarter, the purchase rebates are paid to the designated charity. However, there is one exception that works in Ms. Smith's favor: The credit card company pays the accumulated fourth-quarter donations before the end of the year, instead of waiting until the fourth quarter is over. In this way, Ms. Smith can enjoy a bigger tax deduction for the year. She then takes a charitable deduction for the year's purchase rebate donations on her Form 1040 Schedule A when she files her income tax return.

💡**PLANNING POINTERS:** You can change the charitable beneficiary or stop the charitable contribution of your purchase rebates by writing to the credit card company.

If a single credit card donation—say, for the second quarter of the year—is more than $250, you must contact the charity for a written receipt or letter that documents the donation. This rule is true for any kind of charitable deduction you make.

Thanks to the IRS, these kinds of purchase rebates are not considered income. You can take the deduction without having to take the purchase rebate into income first.

Be careful if you use your credit card to make deductible business purchases. If you want to charge your business purchases and take a charitable deduction at the same time, you must reduce the original amount of the business purchase by the amount of the charitable contribution rebate. Otherwise, you will be double deducting the rebate, and that's not allowed.

If your credit card company is not familiar with this recently okayed charity deduction, refer it to IRS Letter Ruling 9623035. It won't be long before the company offers the benefit.

- When applying for a credit card that offers this charitable deduction benefit, designate your charitable beneficiary.
- If you currently use a credit card that offers purchase rebates, check to see whether it offers this charitable deduction option.
- Keep the credit card statements that show when a charitable contribution has been made. You will need this documentation if you are ever audited.

9 | Let Uncle Sam Help Pay for Your Honeymoon

$ This is a break for taxpayers who are planning a year-end wedding.

$ To save income tax, crunch the numbers and plan your wedding date accordingly. Even only one day can represent tax savings.

If you are planning a year-end wedding, be careful to plan for income tax savings as well. Whether you will save more in taxes by getting married before or after year-end depends on the individual tax situations of you and your prospective spouse. The difference between tying the knot on December 31 or waiting until January 1 could mean big savings. Take the time to crunch a few numbers before you set the date.

The tax rule is simple: Whatever your marital status is on the last day of the year is considered to be your marital status for the entire year. There's no such thing as filing part-year single and part-year married. So the trick is to determine what your combined income tax would be if you remain unmarried for the entire year, and then compare that with what your combined income tax would be if you get married before year-end. After you make the comparison, choose the least expensive option and plan your wedding date accordingly.

☞EXAMPLE: Mr. Smith and Ms. Jones are planning their wedding and need to decide whether to set the date for before or after year-end.

Ms. Jones is a computer consultant and will earn approximately $60,000 for 1997. She will not have enough personal deductions to itemize them and so will have to take the standard deduction. If Ms. Jones remains single for the entire year, she will have to file as a single taxpayer for 1997. After deducting her standard deduction of $4,150 and her personal exemption of $2,650, she will have taxable income of $53,200. Based on this taxable income and filing as a single taxpayer, she will have a total federal income tax liability of $11,692 for 1997.

Mr. Smith is a bookkeeper and will earn approximately $25,000 for 1997. Like his fiancée, he has too few personal deductions to itemize them, and, likewise, he will have to take the standard deduction. If Mr. Smith remains single for the entire year, he will have to file as a single taxpayer for 1997. After deducting his standard deduction of $4,150 and his personal exemption of $2,650, he will have taxable income of $18,200. Based on this taxable income and filing as a single taxpayer, he will have a total federal income tax liability of $2,730 for 1997.

If Ms. Jones and Mr. Smith set a wedding date for after year-end and both file as single taxpayers for 1997, their combined federal income tax liability for 1997 will be $14,422 ($11,692 plus $2,730).

On the other hand, if Mr. Smith and Ms. Jones wed before year-end, they will be required to file their 1997 income tax return as "married." Together they will have a joint income of $85,000 ($60,000 plus $25,000). Assuming that they will file a joint return, after they take their standard deduction of $6,900 and their two personal exemptions totaling $5,300, they will have taxable income of $72,800. Based on this joint taxable income, they will have a total federal income tax liability of $15,028.

To save income tax, Mr. Smith and Ms. Jones should set their wedding date after the end of the year. By filing as single taxpayers for 1997, and not as married taxpayers filing jointly, they will save federal income tax of $606 ($15,028 minus $14,422).

In short, waiting to marry until January 1 will save Mr. Smith and Ms. Jones $606!

💡**PLANNING POINTERS:** As a general rule, if there is a large difference between the incomes of the spouses-to-be, it usually works out to be less tax-expensive to be married before year-end. It is best, however, to ignore this general rule. Because each individual's tax situation is different, it is very important to crunch the numbers—taking into account all your individual tax variables.

What if one spouse-to-be currently has a dependent and qualifies for the favorable head-of-household filing status but will lose this status once married? What if one spouse-to-be currently qualifies for the earned income credit but will lose this credit once married? What if one spouse-to-be can itemize personal deductions and the other can take only the standard deduction?

Each detail of both individuals' tax scenarios should be taken into account before comparing their individual filing tax cost with their tax cost of filing as a married couple.

It is also wise to project the combined federal income tax liability based on filing "separately as a married couple." Although it is very rare that filing separately as a married couple saves more tax than filing jointly as a married couple, in your situation it just might work out that way.

☑ **CHECKLIST:**

- Assume that you will not be married before year-end, and determine your combined federal income tax liability based on your current filing statuses (usually this is a single filing status, but one or both of you could also be eligible to file as head of household).
- Assume that you will be married before year-end, and determine your federal income tax liability based on filing as a married couple for the year. Calculate whether it would be more beneficial to file married filing jointly or married filing separately (in most cases, it is more beneficial to file jointly).
- Compare the combined federal income tax liability you will have if you do not marry before year-end with the federal income tax liability you will have if you do marry before year-end.
- Use the option that generates the smaller tax to decide the wedding date.

10 Use Your Credit Cards for Year-End Tax Planning

> $ People who are self-employed should delay making deductible retirement plan contributions, should use available cash to make an estimated state income tax payment before year-end, and should use bank credit cards for business purchases.
>
> $ Employees should use cash to make an estimated state income tax payment before year-end and bank credit cards for business expenses.
>
> $ Employees should arrange to receive business expense reimbursement before year-end.

Since effective tax planning takes into account not only what you spend your money on but when you spend it, you should always think about the timing of your tax-deductible expenditures. When you look ahead to the end of the year, in addition to tax-deductible purchases you should also consider deductible contributions to retirement plans and estimated state income tax payments. The idea is to pay them in the order that minimizes your income tax and maximizes your positive cash flow.

Since timing is everything, don't overlook the use of a credit card. A credit card can give you the tax deduction you need at year-end. If you charge a tax-deductible purchase before year-end with a bank credit card—but not with a store credit card—you can take the write-off even though the credit card charges will be paid after the end of the year. But use your credit card as a last step—after you have planned your cash flow around other tax deductions.

If you are self-employed:
First, you can wait until August 15 of the following year to fund your Keogh or SEP retirement plan. Such a move frees up year-end cash for

other deductible expenditures like estimated state income tax payments and business expenses.

Second, although most states do not require the last estimated state income tax payment until the middle of January of the following year, you can make this fourth-quarter estimated state income tax payment before year-end. By giving the state the money two weeks sooner, you get a federal income tax deduction for this year instead of next year.

Third, since you are self-employed, you should estimate your taxable income for the year, make allowances for the payments to your retirement plan you will have to make eight months into the future, and then use any available cash to make your fourth-quarter estimated state income tax payment before year-end. After that, any cash you didn't use for the estimated state income tax payment you can use to make business purchases. If you don't have enough cash left to make all the deductible business purchases you want, that's the time to use your credit card.

If you are an employee:
First, you obviously will not be concerned with contributions to a retirement plan for the self-employed. However, you still should consider making an estimated state income tax payment before the end of the year. You don't have to be self-employed to make an estimated payment—anyone can.

Second, after making an estimated state income tax payment, you should use leftover cash to make whatever deductible employee business purchases you need to make. If you run low on cash, then you will want to use your credit cards.

If you make business purchases and are to be reimbursed by your employer, try to get reimbursement before year-end. Otherwise, the "2% limitation" may keep you from enjoying the tax-deductible benefit of your employee business expenses. According to the 2% limitation, unreimbursed employee business expenses when combined with other miscellaneous expenses on a tax return are not deductible for the extent of the first 2% of your adjusted gross income.

So, apart from improving your cash flow, reimbursement before January 1 will also "wash out" your expenses so that you will not be forced to deduct these unreimbursed employee business expenses as a miscellaneous itemized deduction (and possibly lose all or a part of the deduction due to the 2% limitation). What's worse, if your business expenses are not reimbursed until next year, not only can the 2% limitation keep you from the benefit of deductions this year, but the late reimbursement means that you will have to include the reimbursed money in your taxable income next year.

☞**EXAMPLE 1:** Mr. Smith is self-employed. He has $2,500 in cash that he can spend before year-end on tax-deductible items and needs to decide where the money will be best spent. He could fund his SEP retirement plan, but this would be a waste of cash. He can wait until August to fund his SEP and still take a tax deduction for this year. He could use the cash to purchase computer hardware components for his business, but this would not leave him any cash to make an early fourth-quarter estimated state income tax payment.

Consequently, Mr. Smith uses the $2,500 to make his fourth-quarter estimated state income tax payment before the end of the year. Since the payment exhausts his supply of cash, he uses his credit card to purchase the computer components for his business. Following this strategy, he will be able to currently deduct the $2,500 state income tax payment, the retirement plan contribution (yet to be made), and the purchase price of the computer components charged on his bank credit card.

☞**EXAMPLE 2:** Ms. Jones is an employee. She has $2,500 in cash that she can spend before year-end on tax-deductible items. Even though she has state income tax withheld from her paycheck, she can still make an estimated state income tax payment and then deduct it on her current federal income tax return.

Ms. Jones uses the $2,500 to make an estimated state income tax payment before year-end. She uses her bank credit card to pay for employee business expenses.

Since Ms. Jones's adjusted gross income equals $50,000, the IRS will not allow her to deduct the first $1,000 (2% of $50,000) of her unreimbursed employee expenses. Therefore, Ms. Jones applies for and receives reimbursement for these expenses from her employer before year-end, even though she will not pay for them until she receives her bank credit card statement in January. In this way, she avoids losing the deduction for $1,000 this year and also avoids having to list the $1,000 reimbursement as taxable income next year.

♀PLANNING POINTERS: People who are self-employed (but not employees) can deduct as business interest a portion of the interest their credit card company charges. The interest, allocated proportionately to the business purchases made with the credit card, can be deducted on Form 1040 Schedule C in the year they pay the interest.

☑ CHECKLIST:

- People who are self-employed: Do not use dwindling year-end cash to make retirement plan contributions. Instead, use the cash to make your fourth-quarter estimated state income tax payment early. Then use any excess available cash and bank credit cards to make deductible business expenditures.
- Employees: First use available cash to make an estimated state income tax payment before year-end. Then use any excess available cash and bank credit cards to make deductible business expenditures. If you will not benefit from unreimbursed employee business expense deductions because of the 2% limitation, have your employer reimburse you for the expenses before year-end, even though you will not pay for the expenses until you receive your credit card statement in January.

---

11 Use an Amended Return to Your Best Advantage

$ Amend income tax returns within three years for tax refund.
$ Check for previously overlooked tax-saving items and items that have become retroactively deductible.

$ Consider whether you should file a last-minute "gray area" amended return.

A tax year does not necessarily end when you file your income tax return. Generally, the IRS can audit your tax return any time up to three years after the date the original return was filed, or up to two years after the date the tax was paid for the year—if the two-year period ends after the three-year filing period.

Fortunately, taxpayers have the same period of time to file an amended income tax return. If you are like the majority of taxpayers who regularly file their tax returns and pay their taxes by April 15, then April 15, 1998, will be the last day that you can file an amended return for tax year 1994. Once the year closes, you will no longer be eligible to file a claim for a refund.

There are three reasons to use tax time to review your previous years' returns and possibly file an amended return:

- *Overlooked deductions.* In the bustle of tax preparation, taxpayers often overlook deductions, and other beneficial items, that could lower their taxes. With calm hindsight and a fresh perspective, taxpayers can often find these overlooked savings simply by reviewing their tax returns and documentation after they have filed.
- *Retroactive tax law changes.* On many occasions a beneficial tax change is instituted retroactively. When this occurs, taxpayers who filed returns prior to the rule change missed out on the benefit, since the rule was not in effect at the time they filed. A good example of this is the retroactive change that occurred a few years ago with regard to deducting points on the purchase of a principal residence. Taxpayers are now allowed to deduct points paid by the seller of the home. This change was made retroactively and offers savings for taxpayers who amend their earlier returns.
- *Last-minute "gray area" changes.* Just as April 15, 1998, is generally the last day the IRS can audit and assess a further tax for your 1994 income tax return, it is also the last day the IRS can deny a claim for a refund. Taxpayers who declined to take a last-minute tax deduction, or other tax-saving benefit, on

their original tax return may want to consider filing an amended return by certified mail on the last allowable day for filing the amended return. As the IRS will not receive this amended return until after the time has passed for denying the refund, it must pay the refund.

CAUTION: The three-year rule is not applicable when items taken on amended returns substantially understate the total tax due for the year or when civil or criminal fraud is involved. In last-minute amended return situations, taxpayers should carefully document their good-faith basis for taking the position they have taken.

☞**EXAMPLE 1:** Mr. Smith had a tax item in 1994 that would have saved him a considerable amount of federal income tax. After doing some research and then consulting a tax accountant, he decided that the tax-saving benefit was allowable. However, the IRS had yet to issue the pertinent regulations for the treatment of the item. Instead of taking the benefit on the original return, Mr. Smith decided to wait for regulatory guidance from the IRS. If future IRS regulations would clearly indicate that the benefit was allowable, he would file an amended return. Unfortunately, after almost three years, the IRS had still not issued regulatory guidance on the matter. To not lose what he considers in good faith to be an allowable tax-saving benefit, Mr. Smith files an amended 1994 tax return on April 15, 1998, sending it by certified mail. If the correction is ultimately not allowable but Mr. Smith has not substantially understated his total tax for 1994 in taking the benefit, and if he has not committed civil or criminal fraud in taking the benefit, then the year is closed and the IRS cannot deny him his refund.

☞**EXAMPLE 2:** Ms. Jones files an amended 1994 income tax return on April 15, 1998, and mails it to the IRS by certified mail. In amending her 1994 return, she takes a big deduction for home mortgage interest she never paid. The IRS calls her in and asks for documentation, which she cannot produce. It is clear that she knowingly filed a fraudulent amended return. She does not receive the refund. She is also in big trouble.

PLANNING POINTERS: You must file an amended return in a timely fashion or your refund will be denied. Be certain to retain supporting documentation for the items you amend, including your basis for last-minute benefits.

Always send amended returns by certified mail.

Don't forget to amend your state income tax returns if applicable.

CHECKLIST:

- Review previous years' income tax returns and documentation.
- If you have not previously taken a tax benefit to which you are entitled, amend your income tax return for the year by filing Form 1040X.
- Amend any related state income tax returns, if applicable.
- Send in the amended returns by certified mail.

Your Home:
A Shelter—and
a Tax Shelter

▼
▼
▼

'97
TAX
BILL

12 Plan Strategically When You Use an IRA Distribution to Help Purchase Your First Home

$ First-time home buyers can use an IRA distribution to help finance the purchase of their new home.
$ The IRA distribution avoids the 10% penalty tax, but federal income tax is still due.
$ Time your new home purchase so you can shelter your taxable IRA distribution with home-related tax deductions.

Beginning in 1998, the new tax act allows first-time home owners to use distributions from an IRA to help finance the purchase of their new home. If you purchase a new principal residence, and you have not owned another principal residence for at least two years prior to the purchase of your new residence, you are considered a "first-time home buyer." As a first-time home buyer, you are allowed under the new tax law to take lifetime distributions up to $10,000 from an IRA and use the proceeds to buy, construct, or rebuild a first home.

But be careful—there is a catch. This special IRA distribution escapes the so-called 10% early withdrawal penalty tax levied on withdrawals from an IRA when the withdrawals are made by a taxpayer before reaching age 59$^{1}/_2$, but it does NOT escape the ordinary income tax due on the distribution. So for a taxpayer in the 28% federal income tax bracket, a $10,000 distribution will cost $2,800 in federal income tax. The good news is that the taxpayer will avoid paying another $1,000 (on top of the $2,800 in federal income tax) for the 10% early withdrawal penalty tax.

If you wish to take advantage of this new benefit, you should try to do so in a manner that allows you to shelter as much of the IRA distribution as possible for federal income tax purposes. The easiest way to do this is to purchase your new home as early in the year as possible. Points you pay on the purchase of the new residence are deductible and will shelter a portion of the IRA distribution. Similarly, any real estate taxes and mortgage interest paid during the year are deductible. If you purchase your home earlier in the year, you will increase the number of mortgage payments you have to make during the year, thus increasing the deductible mortgage interest paid as part of the mortgage payments.

☞**EXAMPLE:** Ms. Smith is a first-time home buyer. She plans to take a $10,000 distribution from her IRA to help finance the purchase of her home. Because she is a first-time home buyer, she can avoid the 10% early withdrawal tax on the distribution from the IRA, but she will have to pay federal income tax on the distribution unless she can shelter the distribution with tax deductions.

If Ms. Smith goes to settlement in December and purchases her new home, she will be able to deduct $2,500 in points she is required to pay as part of the settlement. But since she will not have to pay real estate taxes or mortgage interest until the following year, the points are all she will be able to deduct. From the $10,000 IRA distribution, she can shelter $2,500, leaving taxable income of $7,500. If Ms. Smith is in the 28% federal income tax bracket, she will owe a tax of $2,100 ($7,500 times 28%).

On the other hand, if Ms. Smith waits and goes to settlement at the beginning of January (and also waits to take the IRA distribution until the beginning of January), she will still be able to deduct the points she has to pay. She will also be able to deduct any real estate taxes and mortgage interest she pays during the year. If she pays $800 in real estate tax and $7,500 in mortgage interest during the year, her total deductions for points ($2,500), real estate tax, and mortgage interest paid will come to $10,800. She will have completely sheltered the $10,000 IRA distribution from federal income tax and will have another $800 in deductions with which to shelter other income.

♀**PLANNING POINTERS:** If you use an IRA distribution to help finance the purchase of a new house and are unable to shelter the distribution with sufficient tax deductions (e.g., if you purchase your home at year-end), be careful to calculate and set aside the federal income tax due as a result of the distribution. Depending on the amount of your withholding and/or estimated tax payments for the year, you may be able to wait to pay the tax due until you file your income tax return for the year.

☑ CHECKLIST:

- Before taking an IRA distribution to help finance the purchase of your new home, determine the amount of home-related tax deductions (points, real estate taxes, mortgage interest) you will be able to generate before year-end.
- If the related tax deductions are insufficient to shelter the taxable IRA distribution and you can postpone settlement on the home purchase until after year-end, do so and wait until after year-end to take the IRA distribution. By postponing the IRA distribution until the beginning of the next year, you will have more new home-related deductions available during the year to shelter the IRA distribution.
- If you take an IRA distribution and have insufficient tax deductions with which to shelter it, be careful to calculate any federal income tax due. Determine the latest date you are required to pay this tax without incurring underpayment penalties.

13 Should You Prepay Your Mortgage This Year for an Extra Interest Deduction?

$ This strategy is available for all homeowners, not just first-year homeowners.

$ If you are a homeowner, decide whether you should prepay your January mortgage payment for an extra month's mortgage deduction.

$ Don't prepay when your standard deduction for

the current year is more than your total itemized deductions.

$ Don't prepay if you'll be in a higher federal income tax bracket next year.

$ Figure out the requirements for future years once you have prepaid your January mortgage payment.

You can deduct an extra month's mortgage interest this year by simply making your January mortgage payment before the end of December. Unfortunately, this deduction is allowed only if your mortgage payment is due on the first day of the month.

Ordinarily, the IRS will not allow you to take prepaid interest as a current deduction. But mortgage payments are customarily one month behind (your January 1 payment is for December). So for tax-deduction purposes, a mortgage payment made in December for a January 1 due date is not "technically" considered a prepayment.

But watch out: The allowable current deduction for "prepaid" mortgage interest rests on one day's time. If your mortgage payment is due sometime after the first of the month—say, by the 10th—you cannot prepay your January mortgage payment in December and take a tax deduction for this year. The reason is that part of this payment would include an overlapping prepayment for days in January, and the amount of interest allocated to January cannot be deducted from the current tax.

For those of you who can take the extra month's deduction, the question is whether you should. If you are a first-year homeowner and you purchased your home late in the year, you may not have enough deductions—even with a few months' mortgage interest and deductible points—to itemize your deductions for the year. For the current year, the standard deduction will more than likely give you a larger write-off than your combined itemized deductions. In a case like this, prepaying your mortgage for an extra interest deduction would be a waste. You would be better off not prepaying the mortgage, taking the standard deduction for this year, and taking the extra mortgage interest deduction next year, when your full year's mortgage interest payments plus your other personal deductions will allow you to itemize deductions.

Another instance in which you should not prepay your mortgage for an extra interest deduction is when you expect to be in a higher federal income tax bracket next year. If you are in the 15% bracket this year, each extra dollar you deduct will save you only 15¢ in federal income tax. On the other hand, if you expect to be in the 28% or 31% federal income tax bracket next year, every dollar you deduct next year will save you 28¢ or 31¢, depending on the bracket to which you jump. Obviously, it would be better to wait and save more.

A prepaid mortgage deduction is a one-time tax benefit. Because you prepay this year and receive an extra deduction, you will have to prepay in future years to receive your normal 12 months' interest deductions. To put it another way, if you accelerate January of next near into this year, you will be a month short next year unless you also accelerate the following year's January into the next year. So once you prepay you will have to continue to prepay in order to deduct 12 months of interest expense in future years.

☞**EXAMPLE 1:** Mr. Smith, a single taxpayer, purchases a home at the end of 1997. His total itemized deductions, including two months' mortgage interest, equal $3,000. If he prepays his January mortgage payment and gains an extra month's mortgage interest, he will increase his itemized deductions to $3,500. As a single taxpayer, Mr. Smith's standard deduction for 1997 is $4,150. Since his standard deduction comes to more than his itemized deductions—even with an extra month's mortgage interest deduction—it is better for Mr. Smith not to prepay his mortgage. Instead, he should take the standard deduction this year, and then take the deduction for the January mortgage payment next year when he will be able to save more.

☞**EXAMPLE 2:** Ms. Jones is a homeowner in the 15% federal income tax bracket for this year. Because of a salary increase, she will be in the 28% federal income tax bracket next year. If she prepays her mortgage, she will have an extra mortgage interest deduction of $500. In the 15% bracket, this will save her $75 in federal income tax this year. If she does not prepay but instead waits to make the payment and take the deduction next year, she will be in the 28% bracket and will save $140 in federal income tax. That's an extra $65 for the same deduction.

💡PLANNING POINTERS: Timing is crucial—so plan your prepayment accordingly. If your mortgage payment is due January 1 and you make your mortgage payment before year-end, you must take the extra deduction for the year you made the early payment. You cannot pick and choose later. If you later realize that it would have been better to wait, you cannot choose to take the deduction in the later year.

Similarly, if you wish to have the payment count for next year, make sure to make the payment next year. Do not inadvertently prepay when you intend for the deduction to be taken next year. The date of payment establishes the year the payment is deductible.

Whether you prepay or pay after year-end, use certified mail to prove timely mailing.

This prepayment strategy is available to any homeowner whose mortgage payment is due on the first of the month—not just first-year homeowners. You may have owned your home for a few years without prepaying the January mortgage. This year you can prepay the January 1 mortgage payment and take an extra tax deduction.

☑ CHECKLIST:

- Add up your itemized deductions for the year, including the extra mortgage interest deduction you would receive by prepaying your mortgage.
- Determine whether you will be in a higher federal income tax bracket next year than you are in this year.
- If your standard deduction this year is more than your total itemized deductions this year, or if you will be in a higher federal income tax bracket next year, you should not prepay your January mortgage payment.
- Be careful to make the January mortgage payment in the year you want to take the deduction—before year-end if you want the deduction this year, or after year-end if you want the deduction next year. Use certified mail for proof of timely payment.
- Once you prepay your January mortgage payment for an extra month's mortgage interest payment, continue to prepay your January mortgage payment in future years to ensure 12 months of deductions in each future year.

14   One Way to Increase Your Allowable Home Equity Interest Deduction

$ Borrow money against your home and use it for investment purposes.

$ Loan the proceeds to a family member starting a business.

$ Elect to treat your home equity loan as a "non-home-equity loan."

$ Deduct the interest paid as "investment interest expense."

$ Preserve your full home equity interest deduction for other uses.

Maybe your child has an idea for a profitable business but needs a loan from you to get started. If the easiest way for you to raise the money is to borrow against your home, there is a tax-deductible way you can do it without depleting your allowable home equity interest deduction, a deduction ordinarily limited to interest paid on $100,000 of home equity debt. Using this method, you can save your deductible home equity interest for other future use. The method is simple. After you use your home equity to secure a loan, elect to treat the loan as a "non-home-equity loan" on your tax return.

The IRS recently allowed this treatment by a father who borrowed against his home and elected to treat the loan as if it were not secured by his home. He had loaned the proceeds of the loan to a partnership owned by his sons, charging interest to the partnership at a rate 1% above the rate on the loan he had taken out against his home.

Because the father had investment income—the interest income received from his sons' partnership—he was allowed to deduct the interest he paid on his loan as "investment interest expense" instead of home equity interest. By characterizing the interest this way, he could still borrow another $100,000 against the equity in his house for some other purpose and deduct the interest in full.

☞ **EXAMPLE:** Mr. Smith owns a principal residence with a current fair market value of $150,000. He finished paying off the mortgage some years ago. Mr. Smith's daughter wants to open a beauty salon and needs $50,000 to get started. Mr. Smith borrows the money against his home equity at an 8% per year interest rate and loans it to his daughter, charging her 9% interest per year.

If Mr. Smith treats his home loan as home equity indebtedness, he can deduct the 8% annual interest he pays in full, but in doing so he limits any future deductible home equity borrowing to $50,000. This is because interest paid on home equity debt can be deducted only for $100,000 of home equity debt.

But what if Mr. Smith needs to borrow a further $75,000 against his home equity at some later date? His total home equity debt would be $125,000 (first loan of $50,000 plus second loan of $75,000) and only the interest paid on $100,000 of this debt would be deductible. The interest paid on the excess $25,000 would be nondeductible personal interest.

So instead of treating his home loan as home equity indebtedness, Mr. Smith makes an election on his income tax return for the year to treat the $50,000 home loan as "not from home equity indebtedness."

By doing this, the interest he pays on the loan is recharacterized as deductible investment interest expense. Since he has more investment income—the interest income from the loan to his daughter—than he has investment interest expense, he can deduct the investment interest expense in full.

At the same time, he has safeguarded his allowable home equity interest deduction. If he needs to borrow up to another $100,000 against his home equity, he can fully deduct the interest paid on this further borrowing. No portion of the interest paid on this $100,000 home equity loan will be treated as nondeductible personal interest.

💡 **PLANNING POINTERS:** If you use this strategy, you should ▾ take two protective measures: ▾
▾

- The non-home-equity loan should be a separate loan. Do not take it as part of another home equity debt—say, a home equity line of credit in which other amounts have been taken or will be taken for other purposes. The loan should be separately identifiable.

- To deduct the interest expense as investment interest expense, you have to earn at least as much income from the investment as you pay in investment interest on the loan (you cannot deduct investment interest expense for the year when it exceeds investment income for the year—the excess expense will have to be carried over to future years). As long as the relative to whom you have loaned the money pays you your interest, you will be set. But what if the relative gets behind on payments? Where this might happen, be certain to have investment income (interest, dividends, etc.) from other sources. That way, the full amount of investment interest you pay will be currently deductible.

  This strategy is not limited to loans made to family members. The proceeds can be used for unrelated investments. But make sure it's a good one—the income you earn should be greater than the interest you pay and should justify risking the equity in your home.

☑ CHECKLIST:

- Borrow money against your home and use it for investment purposes—loan it to a family member starting a business.
- Charge a higher interest rate on the loan you make to the family member than the one you are paying to the bank.
- Elect to treat the home equity loan as if it were not from home equity indebtedness. You do this by attaching a statement to your income tax return for the year, stating that an election is being made under Treasury Regulation 1.163-10T(o)(5) and identifying the debt that is not to be treated as home equity indebtedness. This election is effective for all future years that you have the debt and cannot be changed without IRS consent.
- Include the interest income you earn on Form 1040 Schedule

B and deduct the investment interest paid on Form 1040 Schedule A. You must also complete IRS Form 4952 and attach it to your Form 1040.

15   Get Around the Home Equity Interest Deduction Limits and Take a Larger Write-Off

$ This strategy is for taxpayers who use their home for business as well as personal use (e.g., home office use, renting out an apartment, etc.).

$ It allows the taxpayer to fully deduct home equity interest on home equity debt exceeding $100,000.

A deduction for the home equity interest you pay can mean big tax savings. Ordinarily, this deduction is limited to home equity debt of $100,000 or less. But don't shortchange yourself. Hidden in the IRS regulations is a way for you to increase your home equity interest expense and deduct more than is ordinarily allowed. You can take advantage of this benefit if you use a portion of your house for business purposes. If you have a home office, if you rent out a portion of your house, or if you use a part of your home for some other business reason, you can qualify for bigger tax savings.

There are two types of home mortgage interest expense that you are allowed to deduct. The first type is the interest you pay on the mortgage you incurred when you first bought or improved your personal residence. You can take a deduction for this interest. However, as you pay down the mortgage, your tax write-off for the decreasing interest expense also decreases.

If you wish to borrow more against your home, and write off all the interest paid, you can take out a second type of debt: home equity debt. The interest deduction for home equity debt is generally limited in two ways: First, for you to be qualified to deduct all the home equity interest, home equity debt cannot be more than the fair market value of your home less any existing original mortgage debt. Second, home equity debt cannot exceed $100,000 ($50,000 if you are married filing separately).

The bottom line is that most taxpayers are stuck with deducting home equity interest only up to this $100,000 debt limit. But you don't need to be stuck if you use some portion of your home for business purposes. All you have to do is make a special IRS election to treat home equity debt as something other than home equity debt, and you can take a bigger home equity interest deduction!

☞**EXAMPLE:** Mr. Smith owns a home with a $175,000 fair market value. He purchased the home several years ago, and the balance of the original mortgage he took out on the home is now down to $25,000. He therefore has $150,000 equity in his home ($175,000 fair market value less $25,000 existing mortgage). But because of the home equity loan limitations, if he wants to take out a home equity loan and write off all the interest paid, he is limited to borrowing $100,000.

Fortunately, Mr. Smith has also converted his basement—one-third of the overall space of the house—into a separate apartment, which he rents out. If Mr. Smith does not make the special IRS election and accordingly takes out a home equity loan for only $100,000, he will have to allocate two-thirds of the interest paid to his Form 1040 Schedule A (personal portion of home equity interest deduction) and one-third of the interest paid to his Form 1040 Schedule E (rental portion of home equity interest deduction). Let's say his total interest for one year comes to $9,000 ($100,000 loan at 9%). After making the required IRS allocations, his total deduction is still only $9,000. If he is in the 28% federal income tax bracket, this means a federal income tax savings of $2,520 (28% of $9,000).

On the other hand, if Mr. Smith takes advantage of the special IRS election, he can handle his home equity debt differently and reap bigger write-offs. Instead of taking out one home equity loan for $100,000, he takes out two separate home equity loans—one for $100,000 and one for $50,000. The sum of the two loans equals the current "real" equity in his home of $150,000. In taking the two loans, he has merely broken down his "real" equity into a personal-use portion (two-thirds) and a rental-use portion (one-third).

Mr. Smith then elects to treat the $50,000 rental portion loan as something other than home equity indebtedness. Since the $100,000 personal portion loan does not exceed the $100,000 home equity limit, he can write off all this interest paid on this loan on his Schedule A. The interest he pays on the $50,000 rental portion loan is deducted in full on his Schedule E.

By making the IRS election, Mr. Smith has increased his overall home equity interest deduction. Assuming the same 9% interest rate, Mr. Smith now has fully deductible interest expense of $13,500 (9% of $150,000). In his 28% federal income tax bracket, that means a federal income tax savings of $3,780. This special IRS election saves Mr. Smith an extra $1,260 in federal income tax the first year the home equity loans are outstanding. And he will continue to save more as long as the combined outstanding home equity loans exceed $100,000.

PLANNING POINTERS: The IRS election allows this special treatment for "any debt" but does not specifically allow for an election for part of a debt. For this reason, you should make an election for a separate, identifiable debt, not for part of a single debt. There should be two separate home equity loans, one of which will not be treated as home equity.

You make the election by attaching a statement to your tax return for the year of election that states that an election is being made under Treasury Regulation 1.163-10T(o)(5). You must also identify which debt is not to be treated as home equity indebtedness. The election applies for the election year and all subsequent years. It can be revoked only with IRS permission.

BE CAREFUL. There is no IRS guidance in this area when you convert the business-use portion of your home back to personal use. You should plan to pay down the "business portion non-home-equity loan" before you convert the business-use space back to personal-use space. Otherwise, the interest paid (after the conversion) on any of this outstanding debt will end up as nondeductible personal interest. In short, use the space for business purposes as long as you have the debt.

☑ CHECKLIST:

- Calculate your "real" home equity by subtracting the current balance of your original mortgage from the current fair market value of the property.
- If the "real" home equity is more than $100,000 and you use a portion of your home for business purposes, allocate the "real" home equity between two home equity loans. The home equity loan allocated to the personal-use portion cannot exceed $100,000.
- Take larger interest deductions due to the personal/business-use allocation.
- Make an election for this special treatment with your tax return for the first year the election takes effect.
- In the future, be certain to pay down the business portion home equity loan before converting the business portion back to personal use.

16   Defer Payroll Taxes with Your Principal Residence and Your Closely Held Corporation

$ Defer payroll tax liability on shareholder-employee of regular C corporation.

$ Use loan to shareholder secured by shareholder residence.

$ Corporation defers payroll tax until year-end.

$ Shareholder-employee has home equity interest deduction on personal income tax return.

As a shareholder-employee of your own closely held regular C corporation, you are paid a salary for the employee duties you perform. And since you are the boss, the timing of the salary payments is your decision. If you can postpone taking a salary until year-end, you also postpone having to pay to the IRS and the state tax authorities the required payroll taxes that are attached to your salary earnings.

These payroll taxes include the federal and state income tax withholding as well as the employee portion of FICA (Social Security and Medicare) taxes that are withheld from your paycheck. They also include the payroll taxes that your corporation, as your employer, has to pay. Your corporation must match any FICA taxes you pay as an employee, and it is also responsible for federal unemployment and state unemployment taxes.

When you add up all the taxes that have to be paid, obviously it would be nice if you could defer paying these taxes until year-end. Your corporation would have the use of the tax monies in the meantime and, if nothing else, could earn extra interest income on the funds by keeping them in the corporate savings account.

The problem is that you need cash for personal purposes during the year.

The solution is to establish a home equity credit line with your own corporation. The credit line is documented with a fair rate of interest in a loan agreement between you and your corporation and secured with your principal residence. Instead of taking paychecks during the year, you take loans from the corporate credit line. The interest due on the loans is accrued during the year and added to the loan balance due.

At year-end, you take a large enough salary so that after the income and FICA taxes have been withheld, the net income pays off the credit line loans—including the interest that has accrued during the year.

Here's the tricky part. The corporation has to take the interest it has earned on the credit line into income. But at the same time, because you have paid off the loan from your net paycheck, you have an interest expense. And as long as the interest expense qualifies as home equity interest, you can deduct the interest in full on your Form 1040 Schedule A as home equity interest.

The corporate income tax due because of the interest income is offset by the personal income tax savings due to the home equity interest deduction. Overall, the loan is interest and tax free!

☞**EXAMPLE:** Ms. Smith is the sole shareholder of Smith Company, a regular C corporation. Instead of taking salary payments throughout the year, she establishes and documents a credit line with her corporation and secures the credit line with her principal residence. In checking with various area banks, she determines and documents that the going fair rate of interest on a home equity loan is 8%. She uses this interest rate as the rate of interest being charged by the corporate credit line.

Ms. Smith borrows $45,000 from her corporation over the year in different monthly amounts. Just before year-end, the accrued loan interest for the year comes to $3,000. Ms. Smith's loan balance with the corporation is therefore $48,000 ($45,000 plus $3,000).

On December 30, Smith Company makes a salary payment to Ms. Smith of $62,000. Of this $62,000, $4,743 is withheld for FICA tax, $6,500 is withheld for federal income tax, $2,757 is withheld for state income tax, and $48,000 is left as net pay for Ms. Smith. The corporation cuts Ms. Smith a check for her net pay of $48,000, which she immediately signs back over to the corporation to pay off the loan.

As you can see, the corporation has deferred payment of $14,000 in various taxes withheld from Ms. Smith's paycheck. It has also deferred the $4,743 in FICA taxes the corporation has to match and pay out of its pocket. On top of this, the corporation has deferred payment of approximately $250 in federal and state unemployment taxes. All together, this is $18,993 deferred that would otherwise have to be paid during the year. Even if the corporation earns only 5% on this total amount during the year, that is still $950 more for the corporation—and less for the taxman.

At this point, the corporate credit line has a zero balance. The corporation has $3,000 in taxable interest income, and Ms. Smith has a $3,000 home interest deduction on her personal income tax return.

After deducting the salary payment to Ms. Smith and before taking the interest earned into taxable income, the corporation has net taxable income of $55,000 for the year. This puts it in the 25% federal corporate income tax bracket. Thus, the corporation will have to pay $750 in income tax on the $3,000 of interest income (25% of $3,000 is $750).

On the other hand, Ms. Smith is in the 31% personal federal income tax bracket. Because she can deduct the $3,000 in full as home equity interest expense, she will save $930 in personal federal income taxes (31% of $3,000 is $930).

Not only is the interest on the loan tax free overall, but there are even some further tax savings because Ms. Smith's personal tax bracket rate is higher than Smith Company's corporate federal tax bracket rate. The corporation has to pay only $750 on the "interest earned," while Ms. Smith is saving $930 by deducting the "interest paid."

♀PLANNING POINTERS: To be considered deductible home equity interest, interest paid must be for a debt that (1) is secured by either a principal residence or a second residence selected by the taxpayer and (2) is not more than the fair market value of the residence less any existing indebtedness or $100,000 ($50,000 if married filing separately).

Taxpayers using a residence as security on a loan of this type must record or perfect the loan as required by applicable state law. Also note that the term *residence*—if the place has sleeping space, a toilet, and a place to cook—could refer to a house, a condominium, a mobile home, a trailer home, or a boat. So if you elect a houseboat as a second home, you can use it as security for the corporate credit line and write off the interest as home equity interest expense.

☑ CHECKLIST:

- Research and document the going fair market interest rate for a home equity loan.
- Create a formal credit line agreement between the shareholder and the corporation. Use the shareholder's residence as security for the credit line.
- Make certain that the residence qualifies for home equity indebtedness treatment, and record or perfect the loan as required by state law.
- Keep records of the loan amounts and the accrued interest earned by the corporation on a month-to-month basis during the year.
- Prior to year-end, offset the loan balance—including accrued interest—with a salary payment to the shareholder.

- Include interest income earned in corporate taxable income, and deduct interest paid as home equity interest from personal taxable income.

17 Corporation Owners: Use Your Home to Save Twice on Taxes

$ Corporate shareholders can rent their home or other "dwelling unit" to their corporation to be used for bona fide business purposes.

$ Shareholder receives rent tax free.

$ Corporation takes tax deduction for rent paid.

If you own a C or S corporation, you can use your personal residence for a double tax write-off. This is especially useful if you are a shareholder of a closely held corporation and look for ways to take cash out of your corporation without having to pay the taxman.

The strategy is straightforward: Save the corporation's cost of renting a conference room or hotel room for corporate meetings or other business gatherings (e.g., the company Christmas party), and instead have the corporation rent your home for such business needs. If you, as a shareholder, rent out your home for fewer than 15 days each year, the rental income you receive is tax free. If the use of your home is for a bona fide business purpose and the rent paid is reasonable, the corporation can deduct the rent paid on its tax return.

Although this write-off is traditionally used by individuals who rent out their primary homes or vacation homes for fewer than 15 days and thereby collect tax-free income, there is nothing in the tax rules that prohibits this strategy from being used by shareholders who rent to their own corporation.

EXAMPLE: Mr. Smith is a shareholder in Smith Company, a closely held C corporation. He rents his home to Smith Company for

10 days. Smith Company will use it for corporate meetings and as lodging for several out-of-town business contacts in town for some of the meetings. Mr. Smith determines and documents that renting comparable accommodations from an area hotel would cost Smith Company approximately $2,000. Consequently, Mr. Smith charges Smith Company a slightly discounted price of $1,700 because he wishes to be reasonable in determining a fair rental value.

Mr. Smith receives the $1,700 tax free. If he is in the 31% federal income tax bracket, "tax free" means a savings of $527 in federal income taxes. Smith Company also gets a tax deduction for the $1,700 it paid. If Smith Company is in the 34% corporate federal income tax bracket, it will garner a corporate federal income tax savings of $578 (34% of $1,700).

The combined federal income taxes saved by Mr. Smith and Smith Company come to $1,105. This is what the IRS would have taken if the $1,700 Smith Company paid for rent had been characterized as a corporate dividend payment to Mr. Smith.

♀PLANNING POINTERS: This beneficial treatment applies to any taxpayer "dwelling unit." A dwelling unit must have plumbing, a kitchen, a place to sleep, and a living area. Houses, apartments, boats, motor homes, and mini motor homes all count as dwelling units. If you already treat a boat as a second residence (to deduct home mortgage interest), you may want to consider renting this "dwelling unit" to your corporation.

Be careful when determining the fair rental value, and make sure to document how you arrived at the fair rent figure. The IRS is not likely to question fair rent, unless the parties are related. If the corporation pays less rent than it would have at another location—say, a hotel—and documents this savings, the IRS should be convinced that the rent paid is reasonable.

☑ CHECKLIST:

- Determine the fair rental amount that would have to be paid by the corporation to a third party or different competing third parties for comparable services.
- Document these costs.

- Charge your corporation slightly less than what the third party or parties would have charged to ensure the characterization of the rent paid as reasonable.
- Consider using a boat, vacation home, or other bona fide dwelling unit as a place to rent to your corporation for bona fide business purposes.

18 Self-Employed: Use Your Home Office, Sell Your Residence After May 6, 1997, and Benefit from a Hidden Tax Shelter

$ This tip is for self-employed workers who use a home office.

$ Avoid tax on the home office portion of your principal residence when you sell your residence at a profit.

$ Distinguish between home office depreciation deducted before May 7, 1997, and home office depreciation deducted after May 6, 1997.

A new tax law change includes a hidden tax-saving benefit for self-employed taxpayers who use a home office in their business. Self-employed workers who sell their principal residence after May 6, 1997, will be able to exclude a large portion of the gain on the sale that is attributable to the business use of their residence.

Traditionally, self-employed workers who used a home office and then sold their principal residence could save income tax only on the sale of the personal-use portion of their residence. For the purposes of both the "roll over of gain" on the sale of a principal residence and the "lifetime exclusion of gain" on the sale of a principal residence, taxpayers were required to pay tax (when they sold their residence) on the portion of the gain related to the home office use.

The Taxpayer Relief Act of 1997 has repealed the so-called rollover rules and has replaced the lifetime exclusion rules. For principal residences sold after May 6, 1997, taxpayers who file a joint income tax return may now exclude up to $500,000 of gain on the sale of a principal residence ($250,000 if filing as a single taxpayer). This tax-saving exclusion is no longer limited to once in a lifetime but can be used every two years.

Also, the rules requiring separate treatment for personal and home office use of a principal residence have been replaced by a new rule requiring taxable recognition of gain for any depreciation taken or allowed to be taken after May 6, 1997. This change allows self-employed workers to enjoy increased tax savings when they sell their residence.

EXAMPLE: Mr. Smith is self-employed and has used a home office to run his business for several years. He uses 25% of his residence as a home office. The original purchase price of the residence was $60,000 and is now valued at $160,000. Over the years, Mr. Smith has deducted depreciation of $10,000 on the home office portion.

Under the old rules, if Mr. Smith wanted to sell the residence, he would have to allocate the gain on the sale between the personal-use portion of the residence and the home office portion. The gain allocated to the home office portion would be currently taxable. On the home office portion, he would have a tax basis of $5,000 (25% of $60,000 purchase price less $10,000 in depreciation deducted). This tax basis of $5,000 subtracted from the allocable sales price of $40,000 ($160,000 total sales price times 25%) would mean a currently taxable gain of $35,000.

Under the new rules, Mr. Smith can escape this tax completely. Let's say he sells his house on May 7, 1997—so that no depreciation is deducted after May 6, 1997. The old requirement for allocating between personal use and home office use is no longer applicable. The tax basis for the entire house is $50,000 ($60,000 purchase price less $10,000 depreciation taken). This tax basis of $50,000 subtracted from the total sales price of $160,000 creates a total gain of $110,000. Since, under the new rules as a single taxpayer, Mr. Smith can exclude up to $250,000 of his gain from tax, no part of Mr. Smith's total gain of

$110,000 will be taxed. Where he previously would have been required to pay income tax on a $35,000 gain, he now can avoid the tax completely.

💡**PLANNING POINTERS:** Since the portion of any gain attributable to depreciation deducted after May 6, 1997, must be currently taxed when you sell your principal residence, the key to minimizing any tax due is proper record keeping.

Be careful to keep records distinguishing depreciation deducted before May 7, 1997, and after May 6, 1997. The amount of depreciation deducted before May 7, 1997, still reduces your overall tax basis for the purpose of calculating your total gain on the sale of the house—but, as long as this total gain does not exceed the $500,000/$250,000 limits, any gain related to pre–May 7, 1997, business use will avoid tax. Only the amount of any depreciation deducted after May 6, 1997, will be currently taxed when you sell your residence.

☑ **CHECKLIST:**
- Keep all purchase documents for your principal residence. If the tax basis in your principal residence is a reduced basis due to a previous rollover, keep all records that indicate this reduced basis.
- Keep records showing depreciation deducted prior to May 7, 1997.
- Keep records showing depreciation deducted after May 6, 1997.
- Continue to keep records of improvements you have made to your principal residence. The cost of any improvements reduces the total gain on the sale of the residence. This is especially important for taxpayers who expect to own their home for many years. If the value of your home increases over the years so that it exceeds the exclusion amount of $500,000 for married taxpayers filing jointly ($250,000 for single taxpayers), the amount of any improvements will reduce the taxable gain in excess of the exclusion.

19 Rent a Portion of Your Principal Residence to Your Corporation and Exclude the Business Gain from Tax When You Sell Your House

$ This loophole is for shareholder-employees of a regular C corporation.

$ Rent a portion of your principal residence to your corporation and use it for corporate business purposes.

$ The rent you charge is a tax-smart way to take cash out of your corporation.

$ When you sell your principal residence, exclude the entire gain on the sale from income tax—even the gain allocable to the rental portion.

Traditionally, taxpayers who used their principal residence for both business and personal purposes and then sold their principal residence could save income tax only on the sale of the personal-use portion of their residence. For the purposes of both the rollover of gain on the sale of a principal residence and the lifetime exclusion of gain on the sale of a principal residence, taxpayers were required to pay tax (when they sold their residence) on the portion of the gain related to business or rental use of the residence.

The Taxpayer Relief Act of 1997 has repealed the so-called rollover rules and has replaced the lifetime exclusion rules. For principal residences sold after May 6, 1997, taxpayers who file a joint income tax return may now exclude up to $500,000 of gain on the sale of a principal residence ($250,000 if filing as a single taxpayer). This tax-saving exclusion is no longer limited to once in a lifetime but can be used every two years.

In addition, the rules requiring separate treatment for personal and business use of a principal residence have been replaced by a new rule requiring taxable recognition of gain for any depreciation taken or allowed to be taken after May 6, 1997. This change will allow individuals who rent a portion of their principal residence to their corporation for business purposes to avoid any tax on the gain from the sale of their principal residence (up to the $500,000/$250,000 limits).

How is this possible? Since 1987, individuals who rent a portion of their principal residence to their business corporation have been prohibited from taking a depreciation deduction for the rented portion of the residence. But now, when selling a principal residence after May 6, 1997, there is no depreciation to take into account. The entire gain (up to the $500,000/$250,000 limits) is eligible to be excluded from taxable gain.

☞ **EXAMPLE:** Ms. Smith is the sole shareholder of Smith Company. For some time, she has considered renting a portion of her principal residence to Smith Company for business use. A reasonable amount of rent paid to her by the corporation would be deductible for corporate income tax purposes. Although Ms. Smith would have to pay personal income tax on the rent income, the corporation saves the payroll taxes it would have to pay if the payments were characterized as a salary payment. More important, the payments would avoid characterization as corporate dividend payments (nondeductible by the corporation and taxable to Ms. Smith personally). In short, characterizing payments as rent would be a relatively tax-inexpensive way for Ms. Smith to take cash out of the corporation.

The problem is that Ms. Smith does not want to pay income tax on the business-use portion of her residence when she sells it.

Let's say the value of Ms. Smith's principal residence has increased by $60,000 since she purchased it. If Ms. Smith rents 25% of the space in her house to her corporation, under the old rules she would have had to pay tax on 25% of the gain when she sells the house. Thus, she would have owed a current income tax on $15,000 ($60,000 times 25%) of taxable gain. But under the new rules, Ms. Smith is only required to recognize taxable gain to the extent of any depreciation allowed or allowable. Since Ms. Smith is prohibited from taking a depreciation deduction for the rental of principal residence space to her business corporation, she can sell her principal residence without recognizing any taxable gain. The entire $60,000 gain is tax free.

♀ PLANNING POINTERS: This new tax treatment applies to principal residences sold after May 6, 1997. Individuals who have previously rented principal residence space—as well as individuals who begin renting space to their corporations after May 6, 1997— benefit from the new rule. As long as you do not take depreciation after May 6, 1997, you can exclude the entire gain on the sale of your principal residence up to the $500,000/$250,000 limits.

Here is a bonus: If you rented a portion of your principal residence to your business corporation prior to 1987 and took depreciation deductions, the amount of these deductions is not required to be treated as taxable gain if you sell your principal residence after May 6, 1997.

☑ CHECKLIST:

- If you are a shareholder-employee in a business corporation, rent a portion of your principal residence to your corporation for business-use purposes.
- Charge your corporation a reasonable rent (fair market rent).
- When declaring the rental income on your personal income tax return, be careful not to take a related deduction for depreciation.
- If you sell your principal residence after May 6, 1997, the entire gain up to the $500,000/$250,000 limits (including any gain allocable to the portion of your residence rented to your corporation) is excluded from income tax.

20 Use a "Wraparound" When You Sell Your Home or Other Real Estate Property

$ **Use this loophole when selling a home or other real estate property and taking back a mortgage from the buyer.**

$ **The wraparound method allows a longer period of tax deferral on the profits from the sale than with a traditional installment sale.**

$ **It can also involve profits on the point spread between the original mortgage and the wraparound.**

When selling your home or any other real estate on an installment basis, don't overlook the "wraparound" installment method. This method will stretch out your capital gains tax further than a traditional installment sale. This arrangement can be an effective sales inducement to potential buyers who might have problems arranging more traditional forms of financing, such as bank loans. If their credit histories are less than perfect or if they lack the down payment banks require, they may be unwelcome at banks—even though they may be creditworthy customers. In any case, by helping one such buyer with financing, it may be easier for you to sell the property at the price you are asking. Furthermore, by taking back a mortgage, you can defer the receipt of the profit from the sale and thereby defer the tax on that profit.

Using the traditional installment method, the profit portion of the sale is figured each year by first dividing the total profit for the sale by the total contract price and then multiplying the outcome of that calculation by the total amount of installments received in that year. By doing these two calculations, you can figure out what percentage of the profit you will have to pay taxes on each year you hold the mortgage.

Unfortunately, the IRS defines the total contract price used in the first calculation above as the selling price of the property less any mortgage assumed (or taken subject to) by the buyer. Thus, if the buyer takes over the mortgage you have on the property, the taxable amount of profit you must report on your tax return is accelerated into the earlier years of installment payments.

The best way to get around these accelerated profits and taxes is to use the wraparound installment method. With the wraparound method, the seller continues to pay the old mortgage, while the buyer gives the seller a new mortgage—a wraparound mortgage. The benefit of the wraparound strategy is that the selling price in the annual profit calculation is not reduced by the seller's old mortgage because the buyer has not taken it over. This means a smaller portion of the payments received by the seller will be treated as taxable profit.

☞**EXAMPLE 1:** Ms. Smith sells her home for $150,000 and makes a profit of $50,000. When she sells the house, she still has a $30,000 mortgage. Instead of allowing the buyer to assume her mortgage as part of the transaction, Ms. Smith stays liable for the mortgage and takes back a second mortgage from the buyer for the entire sales price. Ms. Smith knows she'll enjoy greater tax deferral with the wraparound method than with the traditional installment method. Since no mortgage has been assumed by the buyer, the selling price of $150,000 is not reduced and is, therefore, the total contract price used in the profit calculations.

Ms. Smith divides $50,000 by $150,000 (the total profit by the total contract price) for a "gross profit percentage" of 33.33%. During the first year, she receives $15,000 in payments (apart from interest received) and therefore must pay taxes on $5,000 ($15,000 times 33.33%). If Ms. Smith begins receiving payments after May 6, 1997, she is taxed at the new maximum capital gains tax rate of 20%, and this means an income tax of $1,000 ($5,000 times 20%).

Notice that Ms. Smith pays $250 less than Mr. Jones in Example 2 by using the wraparound method instead of the traditional installment method.

EXAMPLE 2: Mr. Jones sells his home according to the same terms as Ms. Smith in Example 1, except that Mr. Jones uses the traditional installment method instead of a wraparound. That is, instead of continuing to pay the existing mortgage of $30,000, Mr. Jones allows the buyer to assume it. With this arrangement, and after receipt of $15,000 in payments the first year (apart from interest received), Mr. Jones subtracts the $30,000 mortgage (which he no longer pays) from the selling price of $150,000 and arrives at a total contract price of $120,000. He then divides $50,000 by $120,000 (the total profit by the total contract price) for a "gross profit percentage" of 41.66%. Mr. Jones must pay taxes on a profit of $6,249 ($15,000 times 41.66%).

Using the new maximum capital gains tax rate of 20%, Mr. Jones owes an income tax of $1,250 ($6,249 times 20%). Mr. Jones pays $250, or 25% more in taxes than Ms. Smith, who used the wraparound method.

PLANNING POINTERS: Use of the wraparound method results in a longer period of tax deferral. But in times of rising interest rates, the wraparound method can also mean profits on an interest rate spread between the two mortgages. If you are paying 7% on the existing mortgage, and if a buyer pays yet a higher rate to you with the wraparound mortgage—say, 8.5%—then you are ahead a point and a half. You are making the money that the bank is missing, and you are also deferring tax on the profits from the sale for a longer period of time. However, even if the interest rates of the two mortgages are the same, you will still break even and enjoy the tax deferral on the profits from the sale. If you pay more in interest than the buyer pays you in interest, then this is the price of the tax deferral. In a case like this, make sure that getting the sales price you want—along with the extended tax deferral—is worth the price of the extra interest expense.

CHECKLIST:
- When taking back a mortgage on the sale of a home or other real estate property, calculate the taxes due on the installments using the traditional installment method and the wraparound method.

- If the tax deferral is worth the extra trouble (and there shouldn't be much trouble), set up the sale using the wraparound method.

21 Make Deductible Gifts to Your Children by Paying Their Mortgage

$ This tax break is for taxpayers who do not own a second residence.

$ This strategy allows you to make a tax-deductible gift to your child.

$ Instead of making nondeductible gifts to your child, treat your child's home as your second home and make mortgage payments on it.

$ The same strategy can be used to make deductible gifts to your elderly parents or certain other family members.

Ordinarily, gifts you make to your children are not tax deductible. You can deduct certain payments (e.g., medical payments) you make on their behalf, when, for income tax purposes, they are still young enough to be your dependents. But once they are grown, you can no longer deduct even these payments, much less gifts like a new car or a summer vacation.

You can get around these limitations, however, by making an indirect gift. Simply make their home mortgage payments for them, and then deduct the mortgage interest portion of the payments. This will free up the cash your children would otherwise have to use for mortgage payments. They can then use this cash to help pay for a new car, a summer vacation, or whatever they wish. That way, you're indirectly making a tax-deductible gift to your children.

EXAMPLE: Mr. Smith, a widower, owns his family home. He does not own a second home. When his son, John, and his son's wife, Mary, decided to buy their first home, Mr. Smith co-signed the home loan with them.

This year, Mr. Smith would like to do something special for his son and daughter-in-law. They have always wanted to visit Europe but have never been able to afford it. Instead of giving them the cash to take the trip, Mr. Smith takes over their mortgage payments for the year. He makes the mortgage payments directly to the mortgage company and takes the tax deduction for the mortgage interest portion of the payments. Since they don't have to pay the mortgage for the year, Mr. Smith's son and daughter-in-law can use the money to take their dream vacation.

PLANNING POINTERS: According to the tax code, you can deduct the mortgage interest you pay on your principal residence and one other residence you use during the year. The tax code defines "your use" to include use of the home by certain family members (spouse, brother or sister, ancestors or lineal descendants). So if you have only one residence, the home of a child can qualify as your second residence for the purpose of deducting mortgage interest.

Generally, to deduct interest, the interest must be part of a legally enforceable debt for which you are liable. Co-signing your child's loan makes the debt legally enforceable against you in the event your child does not make the payments.

Of course, it makes sense to make your children's mortgage payments only if they are in lower federal income tax brackets than you are. Assuming that you are in the higher tax bracket, you can save more in federal income tax by taking the deduction than they can lose by not taking the deduction.

The tax code also allows you to designate a different second residence from year to year. So if you have more than one child whom you wish to help with a tax-deductible gift, you can pay one child's mortgage one year and another child's mortgage the next year.

If you wish to make a smaller deductible gift, you aren't required to pay the mortgage for the entire year. You can pay it for any length of time you choose. What you cannot do is pay the mortgage on one child's house for part of the year and then switch and make mortgage payments on another child's house during the same year. You can have only one "second home" per year.

Finally, your children are not the only family members who qualify for these deductible indirect gifts. You can also give them to your parents, your grandparents, your grandchildren, or your brother or sister. For example, if your elderly parents purchase a smaller home for their retirement and you co-sign the home loan, you can make their mortgage payments and take the deduction. Again, this makes sense only if you are in a higher federal income tax bracket than your parents.

☑ **CHECKLIST:**

- If you do not own a second home, make the mortgage payments on your child's home and deduct the mortgage interest paid on your Form 1040 Schedule A.
- Your child can then use the money he or she would have used for mortgage payments for personal expenditures.
- You can do this for one "second home" each year. And you can change your deductible "second home" from year to year.

Withholding Strategies for Maximum Income—Without Underpayment Penalties

▼
▼
▼

22   Employees: Defer Withholding to Increase Interest Income and Avoid Underpayment Penalties

- $ This income tax withholding strategy benefits any employee.
- $ It defers income tax withholding into the later part of the year.
- $ It allows the employee to earn more interest income.
- $ The employee avoids underpayment penalties for failure to meet minimum withholding requirements.

Why pay the IRS more of your hard-earned cash than you actually owe? Millions of Americans unknowingly lose extra interest income because of the way the government withholds taxes. The convenience of letting the IRS withhold tax payments from your paychecks evenly throughout the year is paid for with the lost interest income that your money could be earning. So forget about convenience and increase your interest income.

Tax withholding—unlike estimated tax payments—is considered to be done evenly throughout the year no matter when the withholding is done. Underpayment penalties are assessed on a day-to-day basis when your tax withholding (or quarterly estimated tax payments) fail to meet the required minimum due during the year. Still, as long as you have withholding of 90% of this year's actual total tax due, or 100% of last year's total tax due before year-end, you will not be liable for underpayment penalties.

All employees who earn paychecks from which tax is withheld can use this tax break to their benefit. All they have to do is file a W-4 at the beginning of the year decreasing their withholding and increasing their net pay. Before year-end, they must file another W-4 increasing their tax withholding and decreasing their net pay—to make up for the lack of withholding throughout the year.

The upside of this strategy is that you will have more money available during the earlier part of the year; the downside is that you will have less money available during the later part of the year. The trick is to save the larger chunk of money you receive earlier in the year and earn interest on it. Later, when your paycheck has to be decreased to make up for the year's withholding, you can use the money you saved earlier in the year. The idea is for you to earn interest on the money during the year instead of the IRS earning it. What is best about this strategy is that it's perfectly allowable.

BUT TAKE CARE. If you spend the money you should be saving for the year's withholding, you may find yourself very cash short at year-end when your tax withholding has to be increased. If you have difficulty budgeting your expenses or saving money, this strategy is not for you. The decreased withholding is not a giveaway. It is a short-term method for increasing your interest income.

☞**EXAMPLE 1:** Last year, Ms. Smith's total federal tax due for the year on her Form 1040 was $10,000. Even though she will earn more this year and owe more in taxes, she is required to pay only $10,000 during the year. Any balance she owes above this she can pay by April 15 of next year, when she files her Form 1040 for this year. As long as she pays the $10,000, Ms. Smith will not be subject to underpayment penalties.

Ms. Smith is an employee. Consequently, this withholding option is available to her. It does not matter if she is a shareholder-employee or a rank-and-file employee. At the beginning of the year, she files a W-4 and decreases her withholding, thereby increasing her net pay. By October 1, she has received $7,500 more in net pay but has withheld only $2,500 for federal income tax. Planning ahead, Ms. Smith saves the $7,500 as she receives it, and because of her thrift she earns another $250 in interest income.

Before October 1, Ms. Smith files another W-4 to increase her withholding and decrease her net pay. This increase in withholding allows her to make up the $7,500 deficit in her tax withholding before the year-end. It also takes quite a bite out of her net pay. But since she

▾
▾
▾

has saved the earlier increase in net pay, she has enough to cover the shortfall in cash at the end of the year.

☞EXAMPLE 2: Mr. Jones is in the same situation as Ms. Smith in Example 1, except that Mr. Jones does not save the increased net pay generated earlier in the year. He does not budget his expenses but spends this "found money." At the end of the year, when he has to make up the shortfall in withholding or face underpayment penalties, he is hard pressed and has to borrow to pay all his bills.

♀PLANNING POINTERS: Before attempting this strategy, make an honest appraisal of your ability to save money. If you cannot keep to the discipline of the strategy—planning for the downside as well as enjoying the upside—this tax break is probably not for you.

If you expect to increase your taxable income significantly this year, you will probably benefit most by using 100% of last year's tax to figure the minimum amount of tax you have to pay during the year. (For 1997, taxpayers whose adjusted gross income for 1996 was more than $150,000 must use 110%, not 100%, of 1996's tax as a starting point.)

☑ CHECKLIST:
- Determine the minimum required tax that must be withheld during the year. Use 90% of this year's total tax or 100% of last year's total tax (110% for higher-income taxpayers).
- File a W-4, decreasing withholding and increasing your net pay.
- Save the increase in net pay, earning interest income on the increase.
- Before year-end—give yourself enough time—file another W-4, increasing withholding so that your minimum required tax withholding for the year will be met before year-end.
- To make up for any cash shortfall suffered at year-end due to the increased withholding, dig into what you saved earlier in the year.

23 Nonemployees: Use Your Spouse's Withholding to Avoid Underpayment Penalties

$ This is an estimated tax strategy for married couples filing jointly.
$ One spouse with earnings not subject to withholding can avoid making quarterly estimated tax payments.
$ One spouse must have earnings subject to withholding.
$ The couple earns interest income by not making estimated tax payments.
$ The couple avoids underpayment penalties when filing an income tax return for the year.

Marriage can be the penalty-free reason for skipping quarterly estimated income tax payments. A concern of the self-employed, the investor, of anyone not subject to the government's practice of wage withholding, estimated tax payments are distracting when remembered and costly if forgotten. Luckily, there is a way out if you are married and file a joint income tax return with your spouse.

Ordinarily, taxpayers whose incomes are not subject to withholding are required to pay quarterly estimated tax payments. Essentially, if you do not "annualize your income," you must pay 90% of the current year's tax, or 100% of the previous year's tax, in four equal installments (for 1997, 110% of 1996's total tax if 1996's adjusted gross income exceeded $150,000). For most taxpayers, these installments are due on April 15, June 15, September 15, and January 16, after the end of the calendar year. When these days fall on a weekend or holiday, the payments are due by the next business day.

Taxpayers who fail to make these estimates in a timely fashion must pay underpayment penalties when they file their income tax return for the year. IRS Form 2210 is used to calculate the penalties and is attached to Form 1040. Underpayment penalties are calculated on a day-to-day basis, so timely handling of your estimated tax payments usually saves you money.

You can skip the quarterly estimated payments without paying a single dime in underpayment penalties if your spouse has earnings subject to withholding and you file a joint income tax return.

If you have failed to make your quarterly estimated tax payments for the early quarters of the year, or if you have purposely not made these payments in order to earn interest on the money, you can avoid underpayment penalties by having sufficient taxes withheld from your spouse's pay before the end of the year. As long as you make up the shortfall in your estimated taxes in the withholding from your spouse's pay before year-end, you can avoid underpayment penalties completely and keep all the interest income you have earned in the meantime. This is because the IRS presumes that employers withhold income tax from wages—unlike quarterly estimated payments—evenly throughout the year, regardless of the actual time of withholding.

☞EXAMPLE: Mr. Smith is a self-employed individual whose income is not subject to withholding. His wife is a salaried employee who receives a weekly paycheck subject to income tax withholding. Mr. Smith did not make his quarterly estimated tax payments for April, June, and September but instead put the money into a savings account and earned interest income.

To avoid underpayment penalties when filing her and her spouse's joint income tax return for the year, Mrs. Smith changes her withholding for the last quarter of the year by filing a revised Form W-4 with her employer. Since they are basing their current year tax pay-ins on 100% of their previous year's tax, they can determine how much money must be withheld from Mrs. Smith's pay simply by looking at the total tax due on the previous year's Form 1040. The Smiths are able to avoid underpayment penalties by having the minimum required amount withheld from Mrs. Smith's pay, and at the same time they earn interest income they would have missed had Mr. Smith made timely quarterly estimate payments earlier in the year.

PLANNING POINTERS: Married taxpayers should attempt this strategy only if the spouse who is subject to withholding will have sufficient earnings at year-end to cover any estimated tax shortfalls earlier in the year. You must time the increased withholding so a sufficient amount can be withheld before year-end. Taxpayers who use this strategy should realize that the spouse subject to withholding will have less cash available to meet other needs during the increased withholding period. The year-end cash bite will have to be covered by the spouse not subject to the withholding.

CHECKLIST:
- Calculate the minimum amount of tax required to be paid in during the year in order to avoid underpayment penalties.
- Before year-end, determine how much has already been paid during the year through withholding.
- Subtract the amount of withholding that has already been paid in from the total amount that must be paid in before year-end, and adjust the withholding of the spouse who is subject to withholding so that a sufficient amount will be withheld before year-end to meet the total minimum requirement.
- Keep checking as you go along to make sure that the minimum required amount will be withheld before year-end.

24   Avoid Underpayment Penalties in the Year You Incorporate Your Self-Employed Business

$ Self-employed individuals avoid underpayment penalties on missed quarterly estimated payments.

$ Missed payments are made up in withholding from corporate paycheck once self-employed has incorporated.

$ Incur no underpayment penalties.

$ Money earns interest for you (not the IRS) during the year.

If you are self-employed, one of the benefits of incorporating your business (whether it is a regular C corporation or an S corporation) is that in the year you incorporate you can avoid underpayment penalties for failing to make estimated tax payments earlier in the year. Another benefit is that you earn interest income on money that you would have given to the government earlier in the year (rather than later).

If you are self-employed and do not have other earnings subject to withholding, you are required to make four estimated income tax payments in equal installments during the year—generally on April 15, June 15, September 15, and January 16 of the following year. Together, these four payments must equal either 90% of the current year's actual total tax or 100% of last year's total tax. If you fail to make these estimated payments in a timely fashion, you will be subject to underpayment penalties. These underpayment penalties are calculated on IRS Form 2210 on a day-to-day basis for late payments and then filed and paid along with your Form 1040 for the year.

However, the withholding rules are different for taxpayers who are employees. Tax withheld by an employer on any salary paid is considered to be withheld evenly throughout the year—no matter when the tax is actually withheld. When you incorporate, you become your own employer. Your earnings no longer come from self-employment funds but from the salary the corporation pays you, a salary that is subject to withholding. Consequently, you can skip the estimated payments early in the year, incorporate, and then withhold enough money from your salary to make up for the estimated payments you failed to make earlier in the year. Since withholding is considered to be done evenly throughout the year, no underpayment penalties will be due.

☞**EXAMPLE:** Ms. Smith is self-employed and as such is required to make quarterly estimated tax payments throughout the year. For various reasons, she has failed to make these payments for the first three-quarters of the year. She based her required estimates on 100%

of her previous year's tax of $16,000—so she should have been making quarterly estimated installments of $4,000 each.

Ordinarily, Ms. Smith would have to pay underpayment penalties on these missed payments. But this year she has decided to incorporate her self-employed business. She incorporates before year-end and pays herself a salary large enough to have sufficient withholding to cover her required estimated tax payments for the entire year. Out of this year-end corporate paycheck, $16,000 is withheld.

Even though the entire required annual tax payment is made a few days before year-end, the government still regards the withholding as having been done throughout the year, and Ms. Smith will not have to pay any underpayment penalties.

PLANNING POINTERS: If you are planning to incorporate your self-employed business later in the year, you may want to hold off on making any estimated tax payments in the meantime. Put the money you otherwise would have paid in estimated tax into an interest-bearing account.

CHECKLIST:

- Calculate your total minimum tax payments due during the year using either the 90% rule or the 100% rule.
- Before you incorporate, hold back on making estimated payments. Earn interest on the money instead.
- Once you incorporate and sometime before year-end, pay yourself a salary sufficiently large enough for the withholding to cover the year's minimum required tax payments. You don't have to do it all in one paycheck. It can be done with several smaller paychecks, just as long as the required minimum tax is withheld before year-end.

Your Investments and Taxes

25   Invest in the IRS for a Higher Rate of Return

$ Many taxpayers inadvertently overpay their
income taxes for years in which they can amend
their tax return for a refund.

$ Leaving the overpaid amount with the IRS
generates a better return on investment than
leaving it with a bank (say, in CDs or T-bills).

Most of the time, we want to keep our money out of the government's coffers and in our own pockets. But—believe it or not—sometimes it is to our advantage for the government to keep it for a while. A case in point: Suppose you discovered that you had overpaid your income taxes? Maybe you forgot to deduct the interest you paid on a home equity loan, or maybe you counted some self-employment receipts twice. Before you rush to file an amended return to get a refund of your overpaid taxes, think about it. You might do better by delaying the filing of the amended return and leaving your cash with the IRS for a while.

The IRS must pay interest on refund claims, and by law the rate of interest is always the federal short-term interest rate plus two percentage points. The rate is changed on a quarterly basis depending on the current federal short-term rate. As of this writing, it is 8% per year compounded on a daily basis. Compare this with six-month CDs held with a bank, which are currently only paying about $5^1/2$% per year. The rate of return paid on refunds of tax over-payments beats just about every other conservative short-term investment vehicle in the marketplace (e.g., CDs, money market accounts, T-bills).

However, there is a downside—the IRS does not pay interest for 30 days before issuing the refund check. This means you lose about a month's interest earnings—but even with this loss you are still well ahead.

And there are other benefits as well:

- If bank CD rates, for example, go up, the "refund rate" will also go up. This is because the refund rate is tied to the federal short-term rate. No matter what the average marketplace rate of return, you will always be ahead.
- Unlike many bank CDs and U.S. T-bills, there are no required minimum investments in order to enjoy the benefit of the refund rate. You receive the same interest rate on the refund you are due no matter what the refund amount.
- Investing in the IRS is flexible. With a bank CD, you commit your investment to a specific earnings period—three months, six months, etc. And if you cash out before the specified time period is up, you face early withdrawal fees that erode your earnings. On the other hand, you can file an amended tax return for your refund at any time within the allowable statutory period—generally, three years. If circumstances change and you need the money, you can file for a refund right away without an early withdrawal fee.
- With a "return on a refund," you can defer the tax on the interest earnings until you actually receive them. If you left the refund with the IRS for the allowable three-year period, you could defer paying the tax on any refund earnings for three years (or you can do it for a shorter period of time). The point is that you control the timing of the recognition of income for tax purposes. With a bank CD, you ordinarily recognize taxable earnings when the CD matures; once you invest in the CD, the bank (not you) controls the timing of the recognition of taxable income.

☞**EXAMPLE:** Mr. Smith reviewed his last year's 1040 and found that he had accidentally overstated the gross income from his consulting self-employment business. Making the corrections, he finds that he has overpaid his total federal taxes for the year by $2,500. Mr. Smith still has about 30 months before last year closes. If he wishes to have the overpaid taxes refunded, he must file an amended 1040X within that 30-month period.

Mr. Smith makes a few calculations and sees that if he were to invest that $2,500 in a six-month CD and then continue to roll it back into the CD for 30 months, at 5¹/₂% he would earn about $375 for the 30-month period. On the other hand, if he leaves it with the IRS for the same 30 months and the refund interest rate stays at 8%, he will earn 29 months' worth of interest (remember: the IRS keeps one month's earnings). At this rate for this time period he will earn approximately $525. This is $150, or about 40%, more than what he would have earned investing in the bank CD!

PLANNING POINTERS: Purposely overpaying your taxes on your original return so that you can amend it later and receive favorable refund interest rates could be considered a questionable practice. After all, when you sign your original 1040 you are affirming that it is correct to the best of your knowledge. Of course, it is all but impossible to determine whether someone has overpaid their taxes on purpose—or by mistake. In any event, care should be taken to use this strategy only when taxes have been mistakenly overpaid on your original return.

CHECKLIST:

- If you discover a tax overpayment, prepare the amended tax return right away—even if you want to hold off on filing it for a while to reap the larger refund rate of return.
- Be extra certain to remind yourself to file the amended return in a timely fashion—generally, three years from the due date for the original return. If you miss the amended return filing deadline, you lose the refund!
- Don't forget to file an amended state income tax return, if applicable.
- Use IRS Form 1040X to file an amended Form 1040.

26 Make the Best Use of Your Investment Interest Expense

> \$ This tip applies to taxpayers with long-term capital gain income and investment interest expense for 1993 and subsequent years.
> \$ The new 1997 tax act makes the election to convert long-term capital gain income into ordinary income less tax attractive.
> \$ Using the election in previous tax years may be beneficial. Amend previous years' income tax returns if you have overpaid.

Deducting investment interest expense used to be fairly straightforward. The 1993 tax law changed all that. Prior to 1993, you could include your net capital gains from the sale of investment assets in the calculation of your total net investment income. Net investment income is an important category, since your Schedule A deduction for investment interest expense (interest you pay on debt related to investment assets) is limited to the net investment income you earn for the same tax year. With the capital gains inclusion, you were able to increase other net investment income such as interest and dividend income and thereby increase your allowable deduction for investment interest expense. So, capital gains helped to increase your investment income, which in turn increased your allowable investment interest deduction.

With the 1993 tax law, those rules were gone. Now you cannot treat net capital gains as part of your investment income to increase your investment interest expense deduction unless you first elect to treat some or all of your net capital gains as ordinary income.

Prior to 1997, making the election to treat some or all of your net capital gains as ordinary income made sense under certain circumstances. The Taxpayer Relief Act of 1997 has all but killed this election. Most taxpayers will find that they will save more income tax in the long run if they carry over unused investment interest expense to future years rather than elect to treat net capital gains as ordinary income to deduct more investment interest expense in the current year.

☞**EXAMPLE:** In 1997, Mr. Smith, a single individual, has $5,000 in net long-term capital gains that he generated after May 6, 1997. He also paid $2,000 in investment interest expense, but his investment interest tax deduction is limited to $500 because that is all he has earned for the year in interest and dividend income.

Mr. Smith's first option is to deduct the $500 and carry the unused $1,500 investment interest expense to future years when he has sufficient investment income to allow him to deduct the unused investment interest expense. Using this option, Mr. Smith would retain the benefit of the new 20% maximum capital gains rate on the $5,000 in long-term capital gains. Assuming Mr. Smith has taxable ordinary income of $62,000 without the long-term capital gains, he is in the 31% federal income tax bracket and his total federal income tax will be $15,356 ($1,000 for the long-term capital gain plus $14,356 for his other ordinary taxable income).

Mr. Smith's second option is to elect to treat $1,500 of his long-term capital gain income as ordinary income and thus be able to deduct the otherwise unused $1,500 in investment interest expense. Using this option, the total tax would be $15,056 ($700 for the reduced long-term capital gain of $3,500 and $14,356 for his other ordinary taxable income). Using the second option, Mr. Smith has immediate tax savings of $300 ($15,356 first option total tax less $15,056 second option total tax). Because the extra $1,500 investment interest expense deduction offset the $1,500 in capital gains that was converted to ordinary income, there is no overall increase in ordinary income. At the same time, the capital gains of $5,000 has been reduced to $3,500, and this is where the extra tax savings come from.

Even though the election to convert part of Mr. Smith's capital gain income into ordinary income generates immediate tax savings of $300, this is probably not the option for him to use. If he carries the unused investment interest expense of $1,500 forward to a later tax year and uses it to offset ordinary income taxed at his 31% federal income tax rate, he will have future tax savings of $465 ($1,500 times 31%). It would make sense for Mr. Smith to make the special capital gain/ordinary income election (immediately saving the extra $300) if he knows he will not be able to deduct the carryforward of investment interest expense for several years. In this case, it would be better to save the lesser amount ($300) immediately.

♀ PLANNING POINTERS:
The 1993 tax law does not limit the time for making an election to convert some or all of your long-term capital gain to ordinary income. For most taxpayers, tax year 1994 will not close until April 1998. If you think you may not have used your investment interest deduction to your best advantage in 1994, 1995, and 1996, you still have time to go back, recrunch the numbers from year to year, and amend your returns for larger tax savings. Use IRS Form 1040X to amend a previous year's tax return, and mail it by certified mail.

☑ CHECKLIST:
- Calculate your total current-year income tax liability—without converting long-term capital gain income into ordinary income and assuming any unused investment interest expense will be carried forward to a future tax year.
- Calculate your total current-year income tax liability after converting long-term capital gain income into ordinary income, deducting more investment interest expense currently.
- Calculate approximately how much you would save in ordinary income tax by carrying forward unused investment interest expense.
- Choose the course of action offering the most in overall income tax savings.

27 Increase Your Investment Interest Deduction with a Charitable Deduction

$ This loophole is for taxpayers who borrow money and then loan the proceeds to a charity.

$ Turn nondeductible "personal interest expense" into deductible "investment interest expense."

$ "Imputed" interest income from the loan to the charity is completely tax sheltered because the same amount is an allowable charitable deduction.

$ Interest actually paid to borrow the money and then loan it to the charity is tax-deductible investment interest expense.

If you make contributions to a charity, the IRS has okayed a creative way for you to use a charitable deduction to deduct investment interest expense. Using this method, you can write off interest payments that otherwise would be characterized as nondeductible personal interest.

In a recent case, taxpayers borrowed money from a credit line and used the proceeds to make a loan to a charity. Because they didn't charge the charity any interest on the loan, the taxpayers had to "impute" the interest income they would have charged otherwise. This means that the taxpayers had to act as if they earned taxable interest income on the loan to the charity, even though they did not actually charge the charity any interest.

Imputing this interest did not create taxable income for the taxpayers because the imputed interest was also considered a charitable contribution. So, even though the taxpayers had to include the imputed interest in their taxable income, they were able to deduct the same amount of money as a charitable contribution (income in and then deduction out) with no change to their income tax.

The tax-saving benefit the taxpayers received was that they were able to deduct the interest they actually paid to their credit line as investment interest expense. This is true even though the taxpayers did not have a profit motive when they borrowed from the credit line. All that mattered was that the money the taxpayers borrowed from their credit line generated investment income—the imputed interest they had to take into income. Because of this imputed interest, they were able to deduct the interest they actually paid to the credit line as investment interest expense.

☞ **EXAMPLE:** Ms. Smith borrowed $7,500 from her credit line and loaned the proceeds to her church (the church roof was leaking and needed immediate repairs). The terms of the loan from Ms. Smith to the church were such that the church would repay the $7,500 to Ms. Smith after five years without interest.

Ms. Smith did not charge her church any interest for the use of the money, but her bank charged her interest at 10% per year. For the first year, Ms. Smith's interest expense paid to the credit line was $750.

Ordinarily, this interest expense to the credit line would have been characterized as nondeductible personal interest. However, since Ms. Smith was not charging interest for her loan to the church, she had to "impute" interest income. After she checked with the IRS for the imputed-interest rates in effect at the time she made the loan to the church, she found that the imputed interest she would have to take into taxable income was 8% of the loan proceeds—$600 for the first year.

She declared the $600 as taxable interest income for the year. But since she had not actually received the $600 from the church, it was considered a deductible charitable contribution to the church. The $600 she had to declare as interest income she also deducted as a charitable contribution.

Then came the tax-saving benefit. Since the proceeds from the credit line loan were used to earn interest income—even though it was "imputed" interest income—Ms. Smith was able to deduct the $750 she had to pay the credit line as investment interest expense.

Since Ms. Smith's interest and dividend earnings from all sources (the imputed interest income, interest income from her savings account, etc.) exceeded the amount of her investment interest expense for the year ($750), she was able to deduct the entire $750 as investment interest expense. As she was in the 28% federal income tax bracket, this meant a federal income tax savings of $210 for the first year.

Over five years, Ms. Smith will save about $1,000 in federal income tax because the interest expense to the credit line is deductible investment interest, not nondeductible personal interest.

♀PLANNING POINTERS: If you are planning to make a loan to a charity and are also contemplating purchasing a high-ticket personal item such as a car, do not borrow for the purchase of the car. Instead, pay for the car with cash, and use the proceeds of the loan for the loan to the charity. If you do it this way, you get a deduction for the interest paid. On the other hand, if you borrow to purchase the car and loan the charity cash from your pocket, the interest you pay on the auto loan is nondeductible personal interest.

To deduct investment interest expense for the year, you must have investment income such as interest and dividend income. The amount of investment interest expense allowed as a deduction is limited to the amount of the investment income you declare on your income tax return. If you have more investment interest expense than investment income for the year, you can carry the excess interest expense forward to a future year when you have sufficient investment income to "eat up" the unused investment interest expense.

The loan you make to the charity does not have to be a formal loan with a fixed repayment schedule, but you should have some documentation verifying that the loan exists, that no interest is being charged, and that you expect the loan to be repaid within a certain period of time.

☑ CHECKLIST:
- Determine the amount of imputed interest income you must include in your income. The interest rates change on a quarterly basis, so you must check with the IRS. The proper interest rate will be the one in effect for the date the loan was made to the charity.
- Include the imputed interest into taxable income on Form

1040 Schedule B and then deduct the same amount as a charitable contribution on Form 1040 Schedule A. If the charitable deduction amount is more than $250, you should ask the charity for a letter stating that the loan has been received from you and that no interest is being charged by you to the charity.

- Deduct any currently allowable investment expense (the interest you actually paid to borrow the money to lend to the charity) on Form 1040 Schedule A. You must also complete IRS Form 4952—the form for investment interest deducted—and attach it to your Form 1040.

28 Borrow from Your Retired Parents or Children and Use the Proceeds for Investment or Business Purposes

- $ This is a family tax-saving strategy.
- $ Use income shifting between high and low income tax bracket family members.
- $ Generates combined tax savings.
- $ Allows high tax bracket family member to borrow at interest rates that are lower than available third-party interest rates.
- $ Allows low tax bracket family member to earn interest income at rates that are higher than those available in the marketplace.

If you are in a higher federal income tax bracket than your children or your retired parents, you can save big on income taxes and maybe even self-employment taxes. You can do this by borrowing funds from your lower tax bracket family member and using the proceeds for investment or self-employment purposes.

Using this strategy, both you and your family member benefit, and the banks and the IRS lose. The benefits are twofold: First, you deduct the interest you pay and enjoy the tax deduction. Second, you pay your family member at a higher interest rate than what the marketplace is currently paying them, and they enjoy the benefit of a competitive rate of return on their interest income.

☞**EXAMPLE 1:** Mr. Smith is a self-employed individual in the 31% federal income tax bracket. His self-employment earnings have passed the Social Security cap for the year, but he must still pay the Medicare portion of the self-employment tax on those self-employment earnings that go beyond the cap. Since the Medicare tax rate for self-employeds is 2.9%, he can save 2.9% as well as 31% in federal income taxes—for a total of 33.9%—for any business deduction he takes from his self-employed income.

Mr. Smith wants to buy some new specialized computer and office equipment for his business. This equipment will cost him about $20,000. Checking with the banks, he finds that a business loan of this type for a 10-year period carries a 15% interest rate. Instead of borrowing from the bank, he borrows the money from his parents at a 12% annual interest rate. His parents are retired and are in the 15% federal income tax bracket. They are happy to make the loan because 8–9% is about the best they can earn investing conservatively for the same period of time.

The family loan strategy has its advantages:

First, Mr. Smith saves about three percentage points per year on the interest rate—compared with what he would have had to pay the bank. His parents also earn about three percentage points more per year than they would be able to earn in the marketplace.

Second, Mr. Smith can deduct the interest payments to his parents as a business expense. If the first year's interest expense is approximately $2,000, Mr. Smith will have a federal income tax and Medicare tax savings of $678 ($2,000 times 33.9%). Of course, Mr. Smith's parents will have to pay income tax on the $2,000 as earned interest income—but at their 15% tax rate, the tax will be only $300 ($2,000 times 15%).

Because of this "income shifting," Mr. Smith and his parents have a combined tax savings of $378 ($678 less $300). So the Smith family enjoys what the IRS will not receive.

☞EXAMPLE 2: Mr. Smith's daughter is a college freshman who recently inherited $40,000 when a great aunt passed away. She has a part-time job and will probably be in the 15% federal income tax bracket for at least the next six years. She will use half the $40,000 for college expenses and the other half she will loan to her father for a term of six years.

Mr. Smith agrees to pay her 8% per year on the loan, which is better than she could earn on a conservative investment in the marketplace. Mr. Smith then invests the borrowed money in blue chip shares of stock he hopes will generate a favorable return by the end of the six-year period.

Since the loan is used to make an investment, Mr. Smith can deduct the interest paid on the loan as investment interest on his Form 1040 Schedule A. If the first year's interest payment to his daughter is about $1,500, Mr. Smith will save $465 in federal income taxes. If his daughter pays income taxes at the 15% federal income tax rate, her federal income tax bill on the $1,500 in interest income she receives from her father will be $225. By shifting income, the Smiths have a combined tax savings of $240 for the first year. Over the six-year period, this income shifting will continue, and the Smiths will continue to save on their combined income taxes.

♀PLANNING POINTERS: Family members who are parties to a loan should set up the loan in a formal manner. Have a written loan agreement setting the terms of the loan. Use a reasonable rate of interest, and document why it is reasonable. The best way is to get loan rate quotes from unrelated third parties, so you can show the competitive available rates.

Avoid a gift-loanback transaction. This occurs when a low tax bracket family member does not have the funds to loan to the higher tax bracket family member. The high tax bracket family member gives the funds to the low tax bracket family member and the funds are loaned back to the high tax bracket family member. This type of transaction can easily be challenged by the IRS as a sham.

☑ CHECKLIST:

- Document interest rates charged by outside unrelated third parties for comparable loans.
- Based on third-party interest rates, determine a fair interest rate to be charged between family members.
- Determine the amount of combined tax savings—income tax and possibly self-employment tax—that will be generated by the interest deduction of the high tax bracket family member and the interest income of the low tax bracket family member.
- Share the combined tax savings with family members as you see fit.

29   A New Way to Justify Your Deduction for Bad-Debt Family Loans

$ This loophole allows family members to treat an undocumented loan to a family member as bona fide if previously undocumented loans to other family members have been repaid.

$ Bona fide loan treatment allows family member to take a bad debt deduction for an undocumented, unrepaid loan to a family member.

$ The taxpayer has seven years to amend a previous year's tax return and take the write-off.

If you make a bona fide loan to a family member and the loan goes unpaid, you are allowed to take a bad debt capital loss deduction on your income tax return. Unfortunately, the IRS is always ready to question whether a loan made between family members was bona fide. If the IRS isn't convinced the loan was bona fide, it will recharacterize the loan as a gift. When this happens, you lose the deduction for the bad debt. But the good news is that a Tax Court ruling has made it a little easier for you to prove your case.

As always, the best way to keep a family loan characterized as a loan is to document your "true intention to seek repayment." For this, the family member receiving the loan must be solvent, there must be a written loan agreement specifying a repayment period and an interest rate, and the family member must have repaid part of the loan in question or all of a previous loan.

While this is the best way to document the bona fide nature of a family loan, how many families do this? How many family members making loans to other family members—loans that they truly expect to be repaid—actually draw up a loan agreement with repayment terms and interest rate provisions? It is in the nature of most families to be informal, but surely this doesn't mean that one family member making an informal loan to another family member doesn't expect to be repaid.

The Tax Court has recently reasoned in a similar fashion and has established another indicator of a bona fide family loan where the loan is not formally documented. In the Tax Court case, a taxpayer had loaned his daughter money to start a business. The daughter was unable to repay the loan and the taxpayer wrote off the bad debt.

Even though the loan was undocumented, the court allowed the deduction because the taxpayer had made loans to his other children and had been repaid. The court reasoned that because previous loans had been repaid by other family members, loans were intended to be repaid in this family. The loan was bona fide and the bad debt was allowed.

If you have made an undocumented loan to a family member and can show that previous loans you made to other family members were repaid, then you can use the same justification to support your bad debt deduction.

☞**EXAMPLE:** Ms. Smith made a $10,000 loan to her son, who, because of various negative financial circumstances, is now unable to repay. Even though Ms. Smith did not document the loan with a formal agreement stating a repayment period and interest rate terms, she has made loans previously to another son that were repaid. Ms. Smith has made a bona fide loan and is able to take the bad debt deduction for the unrepaid loan.

PLANNING POINTERS: A personal (not business-related) bad debt is deducted as a short-term capital loss on Form 1040 Schedule D. It is subject to the general rules on the deductibility of capital losses: Capital losses for the year can be deducted to the extent of capital gains for the year. Capital losses in excess of capital gains for the year can be used as a deduction only against $3,000 of other income. Any remaining unused capital losses for the year must be carried forward to future tax years.

You cannot deduct a personal bad debt until after the debt becomes totally worthless. If in a particular year even the smallest part of the loan is repaid, the unpaid balance of the debt—the bad debt—cannot be deducted in that year. The earliest you can deduct a bad debt is the first year in which no repayment occurs.

If you have previously not taken a bad debt deduction for an unpaid family loan because the loan was undocumented, and you were concerned that it might be disallowed by the IRS (but you have previously made family loans that were repaid), you should consider filing an amended return for a refund for the year the bad debt became worthless. For most tax items, you can ordinarily file an amended return for only the previous three years. But with a bad debt, you can take up to seven years to file an amended return and still receive a tax refund. Use IRS Form 1040X. If the year you are amending is more than three years previous to the current year, note on Form 1040X that you are amending your return per IRC Section 6511(d)(1). Indicate that this code section allows a seven-year period for claiming a tax refund based on a bad debt deduction.

☑ CHECKLIST:

- To take a family bad debt deduction for the year, no partial repayments must have been received during the year.
- In taking a family bad debt deduction based on previously repaid family loans, document your deduction by asking the family members who repaid their loans to give you copies of the canceled checks with which they repaid their loans.
- Take the family bad debt deduction on Form 1040 Schedule D as a short-term capital loss.
- Review the previous seven years for undeducted family

bad debts and amend those years' tax returns with Form 1040X.

■ Remember to amend state income tax returns as well, if applicable.

30 Sell Profitable Long-Term Investments and Buy Them Right Back

$ This tax break is for those who own capital assets, are in the 15% federal income tax rate bracket this year, and expect to be in the 28% federal tax rate bracket next year.

$ The sale/buyback allows the taxpayer to recognize taxable gains at cheaper tax rates and protect his or her investment position.

$ In case the value of the capital assets should drop, the "stop loss" allows the taxpayer to walk away with the same position he or she was in before the sale/buyback.

If you are in the 15% tax bracket this year and expect your taxable income to increase next year, pushing you into the 28% tax bracket (or an even higher income tax bracket), you should consider selling profitable shares of long-term stock (stock or other capital assets held longer than one year). Then, turn around and buy the shares right back.

By making the sale when you are in the lower income tax bracket, you are paying taxes on the built-in gain at a lower tax rate. By purchasing the shares right back, you are protecting your investment position with an increased tax basis for the shares.

This strategy is best for shares of stock or other capital assets that you expect to grow in value. But even if the value of the shares drops and you ultimately take a loss, you may still be better off than if you had just held the shares.

Finally, this tax saver is tailor-made for the new lower capital gains tax rates established by the 1997 tax act.

☞ **EXAMPLE:** Mr. Smith is a single taxpayer who finished graduate school in June and obtained his first professional position in August. His annual salary is $45,000. Since he will work only five months this first year, his earnings for the year will be only about $19,000. With a standard deduction of $4,150 and a personal exemption of $2,650, he will have taxable income of $12,200 ($19,000 less $4,150 less $2650). All of his first year's income will be taxed at the 15% tax rate. For 1997, Mr. Smith can still earn another $12,450 and pay only 15% in taxes. After that, any further income would move him into the 28% tax bracket.

Next year, because he will work the entire year, Mr. Smith will earn more, surpass the 15% tax bracket, and pay taxes at the rate of 28% or higher on any income in excess of his salary.

A few years back, Mr. Smith's mother gave him 100 shares of stock in ABC Company. The 100 shares have a tax basis of $2,000 but have grown in value to $12,000. If Mr. Smith sells the shares, he will have a taxable gain of $10,000. The company has been doing well manufacturing school supplies. Since Mr. Smith expects continued growth, he would like to continue holding the shares, at least for a few more years.

Mr. Smith sells the shares this year and generates a taxable gain of $10,000. Since, under the new capital gains tax rates, the entire gain is taxed at 10%, he has a long-term capital gain income tax of $1,000. He will pay this tax out of his own pocket in April when he files his income tax return.

The same day he sells the shares of stock for $12,000, he takes the proceeds and buys the shares right back. Buying the shares back protects his investment position. He still has the same investment, except now he has increased his tax basis to $12,000. If he should sell the shares after holding them for another 18 months, when he is in the higher 28% tax bracket, he will pay only a 20% capital gains tax on anything he receives over his new $12,000 basis.

If he had just held the shares and sold them next year for the same $12,000, his tax on the same $10,000 gain would have been $2,000 ($10,000 times 20%). By selling and buying back the stock while in the lower 15% income tax bracket, he saves $1,000 ($2,000 less $1,000). Of course, any gain above the new $12,000 tax basis will be taxed at the new maximum capital gains rate (20%), but at least he has managed to keep the taxes down on his current built-in gain of $10,000.

But what if he makes these tax-saving moves this year and the shares of stock do not continue to grow but instead drop in value? Mr. Smith protects himself by determining how much he can afford to lose before he is back to where he started, and he places a "stop loss" order with his broker on the shares of stock. The stop loss is set at or slightly above the breakeven point.

Mr. Smith has $12,000 in stock, but it cost him $1,000 in federal income tax to have this $12,000. Therefore, the "real" value of his stock is $11,000 ($12,000 value less $1,000 tax cost). If the stock drops in value, as long as he can walk away with this $11,000 he won't be any worse off for having sold and bought back the stock.

He calculates that if the shares of stock drop from his new tax basis of $12,000 to $10,800 in value and he sells, he will still be a little better off than if he had not made the sale/buyback transaction when he was in the 15% ordinary income tax bracket. Why is this? Because the $1,200 capital loss will save him $240 in income taxes at the 20% tax rate ($1,200 times 20% equals $240). If the value drops to $10,800 and he sells, he will have $10,800 from the sale plus $240 in tax savings—for a total in his hand of $11,040. And this is a little bit more ($40 more) than the "real" value of his investment—$11,000.

In effect, because of the sale/buyback in the lower 15% ordinary income tax bracket, the taxman is insuring Mr. Smith against $1,200 in potential capital losses. Of course, the situation would be better if the stock continued to grow, but if it didn't, at least Mr. Smith can walk away no worse off than before the sale/buyback.

PLANNING POINTERS: This strategy works the same way for short-term capital gains (under the new rules, gains on capital assets held for less than 18 months), when the sale/buyback occurs in the 15% bracket and the taxpayer is in the 28% tax bracket the following year.

If you are in the 15% tax bracket this year, are holding either long- or short-term capital assets, and expect to be in the 28% tax bracket next year, consider selling and then buying back some or all these capital assets to increase your tax basis to a level that carries a cheaper tax cost.

☑ CHECKLIST:

- If you are in the 15% tax bracket this year and expect to be in the 28% tax bracket next year, determine how much more taxable income you can generate this year and still be taxed in the 15% ordinary income tax bracket. This is how much you can generate in long-term capital gains and still be taxed at the new lower 10% long-term capital gains tax rate.
- Sell capital gain assets, generating capital gain taxable income up to the limit of the 15% tax bracket. Don't generate taxable capital gain that exceeds this amount or you'll end up paying the new maximum 20% capital gains rate on the excess portion.
- Immediately buy back the shares of stock at the same price for which you sold them.
- Determine your breakeven point in case the capital assets begin to drop in value, and set a stop loss with your broker at that breakeven value.

31 Write Off Almost Worthless Stock

$ With this break, you can save income tax with capital assets that have dropped in value to almost nothing.

$ Take the tax loss while "keeping" the almost worthless asset.

$ Take the loss for the best current tax savings.

If you own stock (or some other capital asset) that has become totally worthless, you can take a capital loss deduction for the year it becomes totally worthless. But if the stock still has any value whatsoever, even the most negligible value, taking a write-off requires careful planning.

There are four basic strategies for writing off nearly worthless stock—two if you want to "keep" the stock and two if you want to get rid of the stock in a way that will save taxes sooner rather than later.

The two strategies for taking the write-off and keeping the stock are fairly straightforward:

- Sell the stock, take the capital loss (either long term or short term, depending on whether you have held the stock for more than 18 months), and then buy the stock back after 30 days. You have to wait the 30 days or you can't take the loss for tax purposes. If the price of the stock goes up in the meantime, you'll have to pay for the increase in value.

- Sell the stock to someone who for tax purposes is an unrelated party (an in-law, friend, etc.) and then take the capital loss. You may want him or her to keep the asset with its future potential for an increase in value; or, you can buy it back after 30 days at the price for which you sold it. Of course, if the value has increased during the 30 days and the party sells it to you for the lower price, the increased value comes to you as a gift. But this shouldn't be a problem if this party's cumulative gifts to you during the year do not exceed $10,000 ($20,000 if the party is married filing a joint return).

The other two write-off strategies assume that you do not want the stock back and that you want to save tax currently. These strategies depend on either already having other capital gains or creating other capital gains:

- When you have profited from the sale of other capital assets, the sale of the nearly worthless stock generates a capital loss that can shelter your capital gains from current taxes. There is an important limit to this strategy: The loss from the sale of the almost worthless stock can't exceed the capital gains from the sale of the other assets by more than $3,000 ($1,500 if you are married filing separately).

  Excess capital losses can be used only as a current deduction against $3,000 ($1,500 if you are married filing separately) of other income. If there are still unused capital losses after capital gains and $3,000 ($1,500 if you are married filing separately) of other income has been sheltered for the year, then these unused capital losses must be carried forward to future years.

- If you sell the almost worthless stock and generate a capital loss but do not have enough capital gains from the sales of other assets to use up the capital losses this year, you can do a sale/buyback with other capital assets.

  With a sale/buyback, you sell other capital assets to generate a capital gain, but then you turn around and immediately buy them back at the price for which you sold them. By doing this you will have effectively used your capital loss from the almost worthless stock to increase your tax basis in the other more profitable assets.

  When you finally sell these profitable capital gain assets, the tax you pay on the gain will be greatly reduced.

☞**EXAMPLE 1:** Ms. Smith purchased stock in ABC Company for $5,001. The stock now has a listed value of $1. Because the stock is not totally worthless, Ms. Smith cannot take a capital loss for tax purposes without making a taxable disposition of the stock. She wants the tax loss but also wants to keep the stock because there is a chance it may increase in value after a year or two. Ms. Smith sells the stock on the open market and takes the $5,000 capital loss ($5,001 tax basis less $1 sales proceeds).

After 30 days, she buys the stock back. Fortunately for Ms. Smith, the stock has not increased in value during the 30-day period—she is allowed the $5,000 tax loss and hasn't had to pay more to repurchase the stock than what she sold it for.

Ms. Smith uses the $5,000 loss to shelter $5,000 in capital gains from the sale of another asset and saves $1,000 in income tax ($5,000 times 20%, the new maximum capital gains rate) that she would have had to pay without the capital loss.

☞**EXAMPLE 2:** Ms. Smith is in the same situation as in Example 1, except that she does not want to sell the almost totally worthless stock on the open market. Instead, she sells it to her son-in-law for $1. Since her son-in-law is not considered a related party (for the purposes of taking a capital loss), Ms. Smith can take the $5,000 capital loss and save the same $1,000 in income tax as in Example 1.

Here, Ms. Smith's son-in-law can keep the stock for its potential increase in value or sell it back to Ms. Smith after 30 days. Either way, by means of the $1 he paid to his mother-in-law, he has saved her $1,000 in income tax.

☞**EXAMPLE 3:** Ms. Smith is in the same situation as in Example 1, except that she does not want to buy the nearly worthless stock back after she sells it and takes the loss. She sells the stock on the open market for $1, recognizes the $5,000 capital loss, and uses it to shelter capital gains she has recognized on the sale of other capital assets. She saves the same $1,000 in income tax.

☞**EXAMPLE 4:** Ms. Smith is in the same situation as in Example 1, except that she does not want to buy the almost worthless stock back after she sells it for the capital loss. Furthermore, she has not recognized any capital gains on the sale of other assets. Accordingly, she first sells the stock and recognizes the capital loss of $5,000.

Ms. Smith also owns 50 shares of XYZ Company, for which she originally paid $1,000 and which now has a market value of $3,000. She sells the shares in XYZ for $3,000 and immediately buys them back for $3,000. By selling them, she generates a capital gain of $2,000 ($3,000 sale proceeds less $1,000 tax basis). By immediately buying back the shares, she protects her investment position and increases her tax basis in the shares to $3,000.

She then uses her $5,000 capital loss to shelter her $2,000 capital gain from the sale of the XYZ stock and $3,000 of other ordinary income.

In this way, the $5,000 loss is used in the current year and Ms. Smith has increased her tax basis in XYZ to $3,000—without paying a dime in taxes on the $2,000 capital gain. When she ultimately sells this XYZ stock and doesn't buy it back, her tax basis for the sale will be

$3,000. She will pay income tax only on any sales proceeds above $3,000.

Ms. Smith also shelters $3,000 in current ordinary income. If she is in the 28% ordinary income tax bracket, this means a current income tax savings of $840 ($3,000 times 28%).

♀PLANNING POINTERS: Even though you can take a loss in the year a stock or other capital asset becomes totally worthless, it is often difficult to prove the total worthlessness of an asset. Similarly, it is difficult in many cases to determine when a capital asset became worthless. In cases like these, it is better to sell the "worthless" asset for a nominal amount and, in doing so, establish a fixed loss at a fixed time.

Capital losses generated by almost worthless stock are either long term, short term, or mid term, depending on how long you held the shares of almost worthless stock. Capital losses—long term, short term, and mid term—are deducted on Form 1040 Schedule D.

☑ CHECKLIST:

- Determine whether a worthless capital asset is completely worthless or has some negligible value.
- If it has a negligible value, determine the potential capital loss by subtracting its current value from your tax basis (usually your purchase price).
- If you wish to keep the stock and have the tax benefits of a loss, one option you have is to sell the stock on the open market and buy it back after 30 days. This will allow you to use the loss to save taxes.
- If you wish to keep the stock in the family and also have the tax benefits of a loss, another option is to sell the stock to an in-law. Whether or not you buy the shares of stock back after 30 days, selling to an in-law will allow you to use the loss to save taxes.
- If you wish to sell the shares of almost worthless stock and not repurchase them or keep them in the family, be certain to plan for an effective use of the capital losses generated. Plan to

use the losses to offset previously generated capital gains from the sale of other assets, or establish capital gains with a sale/buyback of other capital assets.

32   Use Them or Lose Them: A Deferred Payment Sale Can Swallow Up Unused Capital Losses

$ This loophole is for taxpayers (especially those who are elderly) who sustain excess capital losses and are concerned that they will not be able to use all the losses in carryforward years.

$ Unused capital losses are lost forever upon the death of the taxpayer who incurs them.

$ A deferred payment sale is made to avoid capital losses not being used.

Let's say that you've already sustained an economic loss, so you're hopeful that taking the loss on your tax return will give you tax relief without too much of a problem. But capital losses can be a problem, especially when you do not have much in the way of capital gains. There is, of course, a solution.

Generally, you can deduct capital losses only to the extent that you have capital gains. Once you have sheltered all your capital gains for the year with your capital losses, you can shelter only $3,000 in other income ($1,500 if you are married filing separately) with any excess capital losses you might have. After this, you must carry any unused capital losses forward to future years—years with the same sheltering limitations as the year in which the losses occurred.

This means that if you take down a capital loss and do not have any capital gains, you could watch several years pass before you see the tax-saving benefit of the entire capital loss. This is especially trouble-some for an older taxpayer who incurs an excessive capital loss without incurring capital gains. If the taxpayer dies before the unused capital loss is used, the loss cannot be used by his or her estate. Capital losses must be used up before death, or they are lost forever.

One way to get around this is to generate a capital gain by selling a profitable asset on an installment basis and then treating the gain as a "deferred payment sale." Generally, when you sell a capital asset on an installment basis, you report the capital gain as you receive it—usually over a number of years. Thus, using the installment method, you defer taxable gain into the future. The idea is exactly the opposite with a deferred payment sale. Instead of deferring the taxable gain, you count the entire capital gain as taxable income in the year of the sale. Then, in later years, when the capital gain is actually received, no taxes are due.

The idea is to match the capital gain accelerated into the sale year with any unused capital losses. In this way, the unused capital losses shelter the capital gain, and no tax is due. You make certain that the unused capital losses are used.

☞**EXAMPLE:** Mr. Smith is an elderly widower who owns mostly fixed-income investments—investments with little potential for capital appreciation. Several years ago he inherited some shares of stock from his father. Over the years the stock has decreased in value, although Mr. Smith continued to hold it, hoping it would rebound and climb in value. On the date of his father's death, the value of the stock was $67,000. Since then, it has dropped in value to $40,000. Mr. Smith can use the stepped-up value of $67,000—the fair market value of the stock as of the date of his father's death—as his tax basis.

Selling the stock for $40,000, he generates a $27,000 capital loss ($67,000 tax basis less $40,000 sales price). If he has no other capital gains, it could take him up to nine years ($3,000 per year for nine years equals $27,000) to use the capital losses against other income. If he should die in the meantime, no one will be able to take the benefit of the unused capital losses.

For some time, Mr. Smith has been considering selling a plot of raw land he purchased several years ago. He originally purchased the land for $25,000, and it is now worth $49,000. In the same year he sells the shares of stock and incurs the capital loss, he sells the plot of land and takes back a 20-year installment note on the sale. Because of the installment note, Mr. Smith could take the capital gain of $24,000 ($49,000 sales price less $25,000 original purchase price) into income over the life of the installment note, spreading the tax due on the capital gain over the 20-year life of the note.

Instead of doing this, he elects out of the installment method of reporting the capital gain and uses the deferred payment sale method. He shelters the entire taxable capital gain of $24,000 with his capital loss from the stock sale and still has $3,000 in capital losses to shelter other income for the current year. Then, in future years, as he receives payments against the house note, he does not have to pay taxes on the capital gain portion. He will pay tax only on any interest he receives as part of the note payments. He has used up his capital losses in the form of a deferred payment sale capital gain.

PLANNING POINTERS: There is no special election required to use the deferred payment sale method; you just include the total amount of the capital gain on your Form 1040 Schedule D for the year of sale. The election is considered to have been made in a timely manner if your tax return is filed by the due date for the return (including filing extensions). You should be careful to be timely in filing your income tax return for the year you elect the deferred payment method. You can make the election only on an amended return with IRS permission, and temporary IRS regulations make it clear that this permission will be granted only in rare circumstances.

✓ CHECKLIST:

- Once you have recognized an excessive capital loss, consider selling an asset that will provide a matching or near-matching capital gain.
- Sell the capital gain asset on the installment basis, but elect out of the installment method of figuring your capital gain by including the entire capital gain in your income for the year of sale.
- Shelter the capital gain for the current year with the capital loss.

- File your tax return for the year you elect the deferred payment sale method in a timely manner.
- Do not pay taxes on the capital gain portion of the installment proceeds as you receive them in future years.

33   Transfer Loss Assets to Joint Ownership with Your Spouse Before You Sell

$ This strategy ensures use of unused capital losses after the death of spouse.

$ Losses on capital assets owned separately by deceased spouse cannot be used by surviving spouse.

$ Transfer of loss assets to spousal joint tenancy before sale protects capital loss carryforward for surviving spouse.

If you are married and own assets separately from your spouse, be careful to arrange a joint tenancy ownership with your spouse for any capital assets that have declined in value. Do this just before you sell the assets. This is especially important for assets that will generate large capital losses. Given that unused capital losses are lost upon the death of the taxpayer who owned the assets that incurred the loss, a joint tenancy ownership of the loss assets ensures that your surviving spouse will be able to use the unused capital losses after your demise.

If you sell a capital asset at a loss, you are allowed to use the loss to offset any capital gain income for the year. If you have capital losses in excess of capital gains for the year, you are allowed to use these excess capital losses as a deduction against a maximum $3,000 of other income you earned during the year ($1,500 for married individuals filing separately).

And, if you still have unused capital losses after you shelter the $3,000 in other income, you can carry these unused losses to future years and deduct them each year, with the same limitation as the first year: against any capital gains first and then against $3,000 in other income.

There is one limit to this indefinite carryforward of unused capital losses. Unused capital losses are lost upon the death of the taxpayer who owned the capital loss assets. These unused losses cannot be used by the estate or the beneficiaries of the deceased.

The IRS applies this rule strictly to married couples. If you pass away with unused capital losses generated by an asset you owned separately from your spouse, your spouse is not allowed to use these losses after your final income tax return has been filed—even if the loss was originally taken on an income tax return filed jointly with your spouse!

☞**EXAMPLE 1:** Mrs. Smith inherited some shares of stock with a tax base of $15,000. Shortly after receiving her inheritance, the value of the stock quickly took a turn for the worse and dropped in value to $3,000. Before selling the stock, Mrs. Smith transferred the ownership of the stock to a joint tenancy with her husband. After the ownership transfer, she sold the stock and recognized a $12,000 capital loss ($15,000 tax basis less $3,000 proceeds from stock sale).

Mr. and Mrs. Smith file a joint income tax return, but they do not have—nor do they expect to have—any capital gain income for this year or future years. Thus, they can use only $3,000 of the unused capital loss each year as a deduction against other income. At this rate, it will take four years ($12,000 total capital losses divided by $3,000 allowed each year) to use up all the capital losses.

But because Mrs. Smith transferred ownership of the loss asset to a spousal joint tenancy before she sold the asset, if she should pass away before the unused capital losses have been completely used to shelter income from income tax, her husband will be able to continue using the capital losses until they are used up, or until he passes away.

If the Smiths' ordinary income tax bracket stays at 28% for the entire period, and all the losses are used over that period of time, the $12,000 in capital losses will save them $3,360 in federal income tax ($12,000 times 28%).

EXAMPLE 2: Mr. Jones was in a similar situation as Mrs. Smith was in Example 1, except that Mr. Jones did not transfer the ownership of the loss asset to a joint tenancy with his wife before he sold the loss asset. The year after the sale, Mr. Jones passed away. In the year of the sale, he deducted $3,000 of the loss on his and his wife's joint income tax return. His wife deducted another $3,000 on their final joint return for the year of his death.

After that, the unused capital losses were lost. Instead of being able to write off $12,000, Mrs. Jones was allowed to write off only $6,000. If Mrs. Jones was in the 28% federal ordinary income tax bracket, this meant that the lost $6,000 in capital loss deductions cost her $1,680 in unnecessary federal income taxes over the next two years.

PLANNING POINTERS: Because of the unlimited marital deduction for gifts between spouses, a transfer of separately owned property to joint tenancy ownership with a spouse is not subject to any gift taxes.

CHECKLIST:
- Before disposing of any capital loss assets, check to make certain that these are held in joint tenancy with your spouse.
- Keep the records of the ownership change. Make certain the transfer date is clearly indicated and that it precedes the sale of the loss asset.
- Keep all these related records as long as the capital loss has not been completely used. A surviving joint tenant spouse should keep these records to support the capital loss deductions for any years after the death of the first spouse.

34 Sell Capital Loss Assets to a Family Member in a Higher Tax Bracket

$ This loophole is for taxpayers with capital assets that have dropped in value.

$ Sell the capital asset at a loss to a family member in a higher federal income tax bracket, and then have the family member sell the asset to an unrelated third party.

$ Save more in federal income tax by making the sale in two transactions rather than one.

If you have a capital asset that is losing value, you can save tax money by keeping your loss in your family. When you sell a "loss asset" to a family member, you are prohibited from deducting the capital loss on your current income tax return. However, the higher bracket family member can use the loss more profitably when he or she sells the asset to an unrelated third party. As long as the family member is in a higher income tax bracket than you are, you will be ahead.

Once you sell the loss asset to a family member, one of three scenarios can occur:

- If the value of the asset rebounds and jumps up in value, the family member can sell the asset and use your loss to save more income tax than you could have saved using the same loss.

- If the value of the asset continues to drop, the family member can choose the right time and then sell the asset to an unrelated third party without losing a dime on the deal.

- If the value of the asset remains the same, the family member can sell the asset and use your loss to save more income tax than you could have saved using the same loss.

☞**EXAMPLE 1:** Mr. Smith is a retired widower with a taxable income of less than $24,650 for 1997. This means that he is in the 15% federal income tax bracket. For every dollar of long-term capital loss, he saves 10¢ in federal income tax. His son, on the other hand, earns enough in 1997 to put him in the 28% federal income tax bracket. For the son, every dollar of long-term capital loss results in 20¢ in federal income tax savings.

Mr. Smith owns 100 shares of stock that have dropped in value to $2,000 from the original purchase price of $5,000. If he sells the stock to an unrelated third party, he will be able to take a current capital loss of $3,000. Using the 10% long-term capital gain tax rate, the capital loss will save Mr. Smith $300 in federal income tax.

Instead, Mr. Smith sells the stock to his son for $2,000 and is prohibited from taking the $3,000 loss. His son holds the stock until it rebounds back up in value to $5,000. When his son sells the stock for $5,000 to an unrelated third party, he can use Mr. Smith's previously unused capital loss of $3,000. His tax basis for the sale is $5,000 ($2,000 purchase price from his father plus the $3,000 unused loss). Since his tax basis equals the sale price of $5,000, Mr. Smith's son has no taxable gain. The $3,000 profit goes into his pocket tax free.

Without the built-in loss, his tax on the $3,000 gain would have been $600 ($3,000 times 20%). If he makes his father a gift of $300 (what his father would have saved in federal income tax using the loss), he is still ahead $300 ($600 tax savings less $300 gift to his father). And, of course, if he so chooses, he can share any of the balance of the profit of $2,400 ($3,000 untaxed capital gains less $600 tax savings) with his father.

☞**EXAMPLE 2:** Assume that Mr. Smith makes the same transactions as in Example 1, except that instead of increasing in value, the stock continues to decrease in value.

In this situation, Mr. Smith's son calculates the maximum tax-saving benefit of the "built-in" capital loss and uses this information to define how much additional value the stock can lose before he must sell the stock.

Mr. Smith's son knows that the $3,000 built-in capital loss will save him $600 ($3,000 times 20%). So he uses this tax-savings to limit his losses. When the stock drops in value from $2,000 to $1,400

($1,400 equals $2,000 less $600 tax savings from built-in loss), Mr. Smith's son sells the stock to an unrelated third party.

By selling the stock when it is valued at $1,400, Mr. Smith's son is still a little ahead. This is because the further drop in value from $2,000 to $1,400 generates a further capital loss of $600. When he includes the built-in loss, Mr. Smith's son has total capital losses of $3,600 ($3,000 unused capital loss from his father plus $600 further capital loss). Since he uses the 20% long-term capital gains rate, this capital loss of $3,600 saves him $720 in federal income tax. Since Mr. Smith's son receives $1,400 in proceeds from the sale, his total "real" proceeds come to $2,120 ($1,400 proceeds from the sale plus $720 total federal income tax savings). Mr. Smith's son paid $2,000 for the stock but pockets $2,120 on the sale of the stock, even though it has dropped in value to $1,400.

☞**EXAMPLE 3:** Assume that Mr. Smith makes the same transactions as in Example 1, except that instead of increasing or decreasing in value, the value of the stock remains the same after Mr. Smith sells it to his son.

Mr. Smith's son sells the stock for $2,000—the same amount he paid for it—to an unrelated third party. By doing this, he can use the "built-in" $3,000 capital loss his father was not allowed to use.

There is no gain on the sale to the unrelated third party because the sales price of $2,000 equals the purchase price. As a result, there is no income tax due on the sale. At the same time, Mr. Smith's son uses the "built-in" loss as a deduction against $3,000 of long-term capital gain income. Doing so, he saves $600 in federal income tax.

If he makes a gift of $300 to his father (what his father would have saved in income tax by making the sale to an unrelated third party), Mr. Smith's son is still ahead $300 ($600 total federal income tax savings less $300 gift to his father). If he so chooses, he can make a gift to his father of all or part of this extra $300.

IMPORTANT NOTE: These examples assume that both the father and the son have other long-term capital gains incurred after May 6, 1997, that can be offset by the capital loss. If the son does not have other capital gains to offset, he can use the loss to shelter ordinary income of up to $3,000 for the year. As a result, the tax savings generated by the son would be even greater.

♀PLANNING POINTERS: Why waste capital losses in a lower income tax bracket when you can use a higher-taxed family member to get additional savings?

The Tax Relief Act of 1997 has reduced (and also complicated) the long-term capital gains tax rates. As a result, the strategy of selling capital loss assets to a family member in a higher tax bracket can be applied in a variety of new ways. The basic strategy, however, remains the same. Measure the tax savings you will receive using a capital loss, and then compare your savings with the tax savings that could be generated by a higher tax bracket family member using the same loss.

If you are in a lower federal income tax bracket, you can shift capital losses to a higher bracket brother or sister (whole or half blood) or to a higher bracket ancestor or lineal descendant (father, mother, son, daughter, etc). You can also shift capital losses to a higher bracket spouse, but this would make sense only if you file your income tax returns separately.

And if you want to keep the capital loss asset in the family (maybe you think it has good potential for long-term growth), first sell it to a family member in a higher bracket, and then have the higher bracket family member sell it to someone who is not considered a family member under the rules. For example, you could sell a capital loss asset to your higher bracket son. He could then sell it to his brother-in-law (your son-in-law). By doing this, your built-in capital loss is recognized by your higher income tax bracket son, but the asset stays in your family through your son-in-law.

☑ CHECKLIST:

- If you are in a lower federal income tax bracket, sell capital loss assets to higher bracket family members (without recognizing the capital loss for income tax purposes).
- The higher bracket family member can then sell the capital loss assets to an unrelated third party (taking down your capital losses in their higher income tax bracket).
- Once the higher bracket family member makes the loss sale, you can agree to split the extra tax savings any way you choose.

35 Take Your Capital Loss One Step Further, and Profit

$ This loophole benefits taxpayers who have
   suffered a capital loss and are also able to make
   deductible contributions to an IRA or other
   retirement plan.
$ It allows taxpayers to minimize economic loss
   with income tax savings.
$ In some cases, income tax savings can wipe out
   all economic loss.

If you sell a capital asset at a loss, you can use the loss—within certain limitations—to reduce your federal income tax. But if you take the process a step further, you can use the proceeds from the loss sale to reduce your taxes even more. You can do this by contributing all or part of the proceeds from the loss to a tax-deductible retirement account—an IRA account or, if you are self-employed, an SEP or Keogh account.

The idea is to use the tax-saving capabilities of the retirement plan to offset additional economic losses. Keeping the funds in your retirement account is the sacrifice you have to make for the tax savings. Still, while you won't be able to spend the sale proceeds currently, if you planned on reinvesting the proceeds anyway, reinvesting them through your retirement account will have the added benefit of deferring the income tax on any earnings until you begin making taxable withdrawals from the account.

☞EXAMPLE 1: Three years ago, Mr. Smith invested $5,100 in a mutual fund. Each year, the mutual fund has generated taxable earnings of $300 in dividends, and these dividends have been reinvested in the fund. Mr. Smith's tax basis in the fund for calculating gain or loss is $6,000 ($5,100 initial investment plus $900 [$300 times 3] in reinvested dividend income).

The fund has recently dropped in value, and Mr. Smith sells his shares for $4,000, generating a capital loss of $2,000 ($6,000 tax basis less $4,000 sales proceeds). Because Mr. Smith has no capital gains for the year, he can use his $2,000 capital loss as a deduction from his ordinary income (capital losses in excess of capital gains can be used to offset up to $3,000 each year on a jointly filed income tax return). Therefore, if Mr. Smith is in the 28% federal income tax bracket, the $2,000 capital loss will save him $560 in federal income tax.

Since neither Mr. Smith nor his wife are covered by a qualified retirement plan at work, Mr. Smith can contribute $2,000 to each of their IRA accounts. This combined $4,000 IRA contribution—made with the proceeds from the loss sale of the mutual fund shares—saves the Smiths another $1,120 ($4,000 times 28%) in federal income tax.

If Mr. Smith had not contributed the loss proceeds to the IRAs, his total tax savings generated by the loss would have been only $560. In effect, he would have been left with $4,560 from his investment ($4,000 sales proceeds plus $560 income tax savings). His economic loss would have been $1,440 ($6,000 basis less $4,560).

By contributing the loss proceeds to the IRAs, he is instead left with $5,680 ($4,000 sales proceeds contributed to the IRAs plus $560 income tax savings from the capital loss plus $1,120 income tax savings from the IRA contributions). His economic loss is now only $320 ($6,000 basis less $5,680).

☞EXAMPLE 2: Ms. Smith, a self-employed taxpayer, sells shares of stock for $10,000 that she originally purchased for $14,000, generating a $4,000 capital loss. During the year, Ms. Smith has no capital gain income and is therefore (per the capital loss limitation rules) limited to deducting only $3,000 of the capital loss in the current year. She can still carry forward the unused loss of $1,000 and use it to save income tax in the next year.

If Ms. Smith is in the 31% federal income tax bracket this year and plans to be in the 31% federal income tax bracket next year, the $4,000 capital loss will save her $1,240 ($4,000 times 31%) in federal income tax over the two-year period.

But Ms. Smith wants to cut her economic loss further by contributing all or a part of the proceeds from the stock sale to her deductible SEP profit-sharing plan. She knows that she will enjoy the tax-saving benefit generated by the capital loss and that this benefit effectively increases her proceeds from the sale to $11,240 ($10,000 sales proceeds plus $1,240 two-year tax savings). What she needs to know is how much to contribute to her SEP profit-sharing retirement plan.

Ms. Smith calculates that her remaining economic loss is $2,760 ($14,000 basis less $11,240). She divides the $2,760 by her 31% federal tax bracket and arrives at $8,904. If she contributes $8,904 of the $10,000 in sales proceeds to her SEP profit-sharing plan, she will enjoy further federal tax savings of $2,760 ($8,904 times 31%).

In effect, by contributing a large portion of the sales proceeds to her deductible SEP profit-sharing plan, Ms. Smith has completely wiped out any economic loss. Her sales proceeds of $10,000 plus the $1,240 federal income tax savings from the capital loss plus the $2,760 federal income tax savings from the deductible SEP contribution equal $14,000—what she originally paid for the stock. Though Ms. Smith hasn't made any money on the original investment, at least she hasn't lost any! And she still has $1,096 ($10,000 sales proceeds less $8,904 SEP contribution) to invest or otherwise do with as she pleases.

PLANNING POINTERS: Once you contribute capital loss sale proceeds to an IRA or other retirement plan, you may be tempted to use these retirement plan funds to reinvest in the same capital asset you have just sold at a loss. If you wish to do this, you should wait for more than 30 days before you have your retirement plan make the repurchase. Per the "wash sale" rules, if you sell a capital asset at a loss and then repurchase the loss asset within 30 days, you cannot deduct your capital loss.

There is some debate as to whether the "wash sale" rules would apply in this instance, but when in doubt it is best to be conservative. The debate in this case centers on the distinction that not you but a separate legal entity—your retirement plan—would be repurchasing the loss asset. And according to this logic, the "wash sale" rules would not apply. You could sell a capital asset at a tax-deductible loss and have your retirement plan repurchase the capital asset within 30 days. ▾

Unfortunately, a court has ruled that the "wash sale" rules do ▾

▾

apply in a case where a trust controlled by a taxpayer was used to repurchase loss assets within 30 days. Similarly, another court has ruled that the "wash sale" rules applied where a corporation wholly owned by a taxpayer was used to repurchase loss assets within 30 days. In both cases, the tax deductions for the capital losses were disallowed. Since a similar argument could be applied to an IRA or some other retirement plan, it is best to avoid this potential problem—just have your IRA or other retirement plan wait for more than 30 days before repurchasing the same loss assets.

☑ CHECKLIST:

- Determine the federal income tax savings generated by a capital loss.
- Determine the further federal income tax savings generated by contributing the proceeds from a capital loss to an IRA or self-employed retirement plan.
- Cut your economic loss by making a deductible contribution of all or a part of the loss proceeds to an IRA or self-employed retirement plan.
- Avoid any potential problems with the "wash sale" rules by keeping your IRA or other retirement plan from investing in the loss asset for at least 31 days.

36 Plan for Mutual Fund Earnings When Selling Mutual Fund Shares at a Loss

$ This loophole is for taxpayers who sell shares in a mutual fund at a loss.

$ To deduct the entire loss currently, earnings generated by the fund cannot be reinvested in the fund within 30 days before or after the loss sale.

$ Proper planning for mutual fund earnings can keep current tax savings from being lost.

When you have to sell mutual fund shares at a loss, you should try to use the loss to save as much income tax as possible. If you are not careful, you can limit the deductibility of your losses and end up paying more income tax than necessary. Find out whether the shares you are selling at a loss belong to a mutual fund that automatically reinvests dividends and other earnings in the purchase of more shares of the losing fund. The deductibility of your loss is limited by any earnings that have been reinvested in the fund within 30 days before or after the loss sale.

If you want to deduct the entire loss, hold off on the sale until at least 30 days have passed since the last reinvestment. At the same time, notify the fund that future earnings should be sent directly to you—not reinvested in the fund. You can always go back to reinvesting your fund earnings once enough time has passed, while your loss—or a portion of your loss—is no longer in danger of being currently disallowed.

☞ **EXAMPLE:** Mr. Smith owns shares in ABC mutual fund with a "tax basis" of $15,000 ($7,500 original purchase plus $7,500 several years' reinvested earnings). Recently, the fair market value of the fund dropped to $9,000, and Mr. Smith has decided to sell half his shares, take the loss for tax purposes, and reinvest the proceeds in another fund with better prospects.

He wishes to sell only half his shares because he hopes the fund will again increase in value and he will be able to recoup some of his loss.

By selling half his shares, he will generate a $3,000 capital loss (one-half of $15,000 total tax basis less $9,000 total fair market value, or, one-half of $6,000 drop in value).

Even without other capital gain income, under current law Mr. Smith is allowed to use up to $3,000 in capital losses to offset other ordinary income and reduce his income tax. If he is in the 31% federal income tax bracket, this means that the $3,000 capital loss could save him up to $930 in federal income tax.

Mr. Smith is also careful to plan for fund earnings so that no portion of his current capital loss is disallowed and no part of his current tax savings is threatened. Mr. Smith plans to sell his shares on

December 5. He looks at his mutual fund statements and sees that the fund last generated earnings and then reinvested them on October 31. This is more than 30 days before the sale of the shares, so Mr. Smith will not have to reduce his current tax loss by any part of the earnings reinvested on October 31.

Mr. Smith also notifies the fund to send future earnings directly to him instead of reinvesting them in more shares of the fund. By doing this, no portion of the earnings generated within 30 days after the sale of the loss shares can be used to reduce Mr. Smith's current capital loss and related tax savings. After the 30-day period has passed, Mr. Smith—if he so chooses—can notify the fund to begin reinvesting his earnings again. As long as the fund does not resume its reinvestment of earnings within 30 days of the loss sale, Mr. Smith's current capital loss and related tax savings will remain intact.

♀PLANNING POINTERS: Mutual fund capital loss planning is especially important at year-end, when mutual funds ordinarily distribute both capital gain earnings and dividend earnings. If you make a loss sale in December and do not notify the mutual fund to distribute all the year-end earnings directly to you, this combination of reinvested capital gains and reinvested dividends will cut even deeper into the loss you are allowed to deduct for the current year.

In addition to helping you deduct the entire loss currently, planning for mutual fund earnings also helps you avoid a record-keeping and tax-preparation nightmare.

If earnings are reinvested in the mutual fund within 30 days before or after the loss sale, a portion of the loss will be currently disallowed. But this does not mean the loss will be disallowed forever. First, you will have to determine how much of the loss is unusable for the current income tax. Then you will have to add this disallowed portion to the tax basis of the remaining shares you own. When you finally dispose of the remaining shares, you will then be able to use the previously disallowed portion of the loss. All this requires careful calculations, allocations, and additions to tax basis, all of which can be avoided by taking the entire loss currently.

- Before making a loss sale of mutual fund shares, determine the most recent date on which the mutual fund reinvested fund earnings.
- If the fund reinvested earnings within the last 30 days, wait until more than 30 days have passed since the fund reinvested earnings and then sell the fund shares at a loss. But be economically cautious: Do not wait to sell the shares if you believe they will drop even further in value while you wait.
- Once you have decided to sell the shares and take a deductible tax loss, notify the fund to distribute future earnings directly to you.
- If you so choose, 30 days after the loss sale, you can instruct the mutual fund to begin reinvesting earnings again.

37	Save by Keeping Accurate Mutual Fund Records

$ This is a tip for taxpayers who invest in mutual funds.

$ Use the "specific share" method to sell high-basis shares and save current income tax.

$ If you have capital losses from other sources, use the "specific share" method to sell low-basis shares and generate a larger current tax-sheltered capital gain.

When it comes to monitoring your mutual fund accounts, don't be lazy. If you keep good, accurate records and follow a few simple steps, you can minimize any current income tax due on the sale of mutual fund shares.

To reap these current income tax savings, all you have to do is sell high-basis shares in the fund and identify the sale of these shares in your records. When you make the sale, you must specify to the mutual fund which shares are to be sold. The mutual fund must then confirm to you in writing (within a reasonable period of time) the sale of the specific shares.

By selecting the highest-basis shares for sale, you are reducing your current taxable gain. Of course, the price for the current tax savings is that you are left holding lower-basis shares. In a later year, when you dispose of these lower-basis shares, you will then have to pay income tax on a larger gain. But if you have to choose between saving income tax sooner or later, it is always better to save sooner.

☞ **EXAMPLE:** Ms. Smith owns 205 shares in a mutual fund. She originally purchased 100 shares at $10 per share. The fund then paid her dividends of $60, which were automatically reinvested in the fund by purchasing 5 new shares at $12 per share. Later, Ms. Smith purchased another 100 shares at $14 per share.

The fund value has now increased to $16 per share, and Ms. Smith wants to sell 100 shares and take down a profit. But she wants to do so at the lowest possible current income tax cost.

To save current income tax, Ms. Smith decides to sell the 100 shares she purchased at $14 per share. These are her highest-basis shares. Selling the 100 shares, she generates sales proceeds of $1,600 (100 shares at $16 per share). Her basis for figuring taxable gain is $1,400 (100 shares at $14 per share). Her taxable capital gain is $200.

While making the sale, Ms. Smith notes in her records which shares are to be sold. She also specifies to the mutual fund which shares are to be sold and requests confirmation from the mutual fund in writing that (1) she specifically requested the sale of certain shares and (2) those shares were in fact sold.

If Ms. Smith had not used the "specific share" method, she would have been forced to use either the "FIFO" (first-in, first-out) method or one of the "basis averaging" methods. If she used any of these latter methods, her current capital gain and related income tax would have been higher because the basis of the shares sold would have been lower.

For example, using the "FIFO" method, Ms. Smith would have been required to use the value of the first shares purchased as her basis, which would have been $1,000 (100 shares at $10 per share). Her taxable gain would have been $600 ($1,600 sales price less $1,000 basis).

By using the "specific share" method and not the "FIFO" method, Ms. Smith saves current income tax on $400 of taxable gain ($200 in taxable gain versus $600 in taxable gain).

♀ PLANNING POINTERS: If you have previously used one of the "basis averaging" methods (where the cost of all your shares is lumped together to figure an average basis), you must continue to use that method for all the accounts you have in that particular mutual fund. However, if you open an account with a different mutual fund or move funds from the "average basis" mutual fund to a different mutual fund (even if it is in the same family of funds), you can use the "specific share" method when selling shares from the new mutual fund.

If you have previously limited yourself to using the "FIFO" method, either because you failed to use the "specific share" method or because you did not wish to use one of the "basis averaging" methods, you can switch to the "specific share" method at any time.

One final important note: With the "specific share" method, you do not necessarily have to choose the highest-basis shares for the sale. If you have already generated capital losses elsewhere, so that shelter is available for any capital gains you generate, you may want to use the "specific share" method to choose low-basis shares to sell, reap a larger capital gain now, and shelter that larger capital gain with the available capital losses. By doing this, you save your high-basis shares for future tax savings.

☑ CHECKLIST:

- Keep good records on the basis of any mutual fund shares purchased by you directly (or indirectly with reinvested earnings).
- If you have not previously used a "basis averaging" method for a particular mutual fund, use the "specific share" method to determine the basis of any shares sold.
- Specify to the mutual fund which shares are to be sold, and

request a confirmation in writing from the mutual fund stating that (1) you specifically requested that those shares be sold and (2) those shares were in fact sold.

- Keep good records of the shares specifically sold.
- Use the "specific share" method to choose low-basis shares to sell if it suits your overall tax savings plan.

38   Minimize Taxes—and Headaches—by Limiting Mutual Fund Check Transactions

$ This loophole is for taxpayers who invest in mutual funds with check-writing privileges.

$ The cost in hours or dollars spent preparing year-end taxes far outweighs any increase in current earnings.

$ Instead, use the mutual fund as a savings account, making only a few transfers to your checkbook each year.

Many mutual funds offer investors the convenience of writing checks out of their mutual fund account. But this check-writing privilege should be used only in an emergency—not on a regular basis.

At first glance, using a mutual fund like a checkbook may seem advantageous. By keeping cash in the mutual fund instead of a bank checking account, you can earn dividend income at a much more competitive rate than the interest income you earn with an interest-bearing checking account. But there are at least three tax disadvantages to using your mutual fund as a checkbook, and these easily outweigh the advantage of a higher current income.

- Every check written from the mutual fund triggers a separate taxable transaction. Writing a check is considered a sale of a capital asset.

  For each transaction, a separate tax basis must be calculated and then subtracted from the "sale proceeds" (amount of the check) to determine the taxable capital gain or loss.

So even if you write only 25 checks out of your mutual fund over the course of the year—no matter how small the dollar amount—you will have 25 different capital gain transactions to account for when preparing your tax return at year-end.

- Even with a tax-exempt mutual fund, every check written from the fund triggers a separate taxable transaction. Tax-exempt funds generate only tax-exempt dividend income. When you dispose of a tax-exempt mutual fund asset—in this case, when you write a check—you still trigger a capital gain or loss transaction.

  For each transaction, as with a taxable mutual fund, a separate tax basis must be calculated and then subtracted from the "sale proceeds" (the amount of the check) to determine the taxable capital gain or loss.

- Further tax complications may arise when you make "deposits" to the mutual fund account or when the dividend income generated by the mutual fund is reinvested in shares of the fund. If you generated capital losses by writing checks, and you deposit or reinvest money in the fund within 30 days before or after a capital loss occurs, you will not be able to deduct all or a portion of the capital loss on your current tax return.

  At year-end you (or your tax preparer) will have to crunch out complicated loss allocations. Some of the losses will be currently deductible, and some will not. The losses that will not be currently deductible will have to be added to the tax basis of the remaining shares in your mutual fund account. In short, these multiple small transactions can result in a tax-preparation nightmare, and this means more expensive tax-preparation fees.

☞**EXAMPLE:** Mr. Smith has shares in a mutual fund that offers check-writing privileges. The mutual fund is generating about a 7% dividend income rate per year, while his interest-bearing checking account is generating a 3% interest income rate per year.

At first glance, Mr. Smith concludes that by using his mutual fund as a checkbook he will come out ahead. He does not ordinarily keep more than $2,500 in his checkbook at a time. If he were to keep this balance in his mutual fund constantly over a year (instead of in the checking account), he would be ahead $100 ($2,500 times 4% earnings difference between the mutual fund and the checking account). If Mr. Smith is in the 31% federal income tax bracket, he will pay $31 in federal income tax on this increase in earnings, and he will keep $69.

At second glance, Mr. Smith realizes that using the mutual fund as a checkbook may not be such a good idea. To put an extra $69 in his pocket, he will have to spend countless hours tracking and calculating the capital gains and losses generated by each check he writes. Either he will have to time his deposits to the mutual fund so that they do not occur within 30 days before or after a check is written, or he will have to calculate what portion of any capital losses can be taken currently versus what portion cannot be taken currently. At year-end, he will have to organize and document all these transactions to properly complete his income tax return.

If he does not want to spend the time doing this, he will have to pay someone else to do it, and the cost for this service will far surpass the $69 he will have put in his pocket.

♀ PLANNING POINTERS: Using your mutual fund as a checkbook is an option only if you ordinarily keep considerable sums in your checkbook. The increase in earnings generated by using a mutual fund instead of a checking account must exceed the cost—including the value of your time—of using the mutual fund as a checkbook.

But even if you ordinarily keep considerable sums in your checkbook, it is wiser to use your mutual fund as a savings account only—making larger transfers to your checking account a few times each year instead of using the mutual fund to write checks for every expense that comes up during the year.

By doing this, you still generate more in current dividend income than you would by just leaving the funds in the checking account, and you do so with only a few capital gain transactions. The time (or money) spent tracking and "controlling" capital gain and loss transactions is considerably less just because there are fewer transactions.

☑ CHECKLIST:

- Before using a mutual fund as a checking account, compare the earnings rates of the mutual fund and the checking account and calculate approximately what your increase in current earnings (after income tax) will be if you use the mutual fund as a checking account.
- Compare your increased earnings with the cost of tracking the capital gain/loss transactions in the mutual fund. This cost will be either in the hours you will have to spend to do it yourself or the dollars you will have to spend to have someone else do it. If you pay a tax preparer to prepare your income tax returns, ask him or her what it will cost for the increased tax-preparation time that results from the multiple capital gain/loss transactions.
- Rather than using your mutual fund as a checking account, consider using it as a savings account. Do not write checks for all your separate expenses. Instead, use the mutual fund to accumulate excess cash during the year. Then make transfers to your checking account at a few scheduled times during the year. With fewer capital gain/loss transactions, you will spend less time (or less money) tracking the transactions. Planning for the tax consequences of the transactions will also be quite a bit less complicated.

Get the Most
from Your
Retirement Plan

▼
▼
▼

Roth IRAs Are Custom-Made for Older, Upper-Middle-Income Taxpayers

$ This loophole involves IRAs that are especially beneficial for older working taxpayers.

$ Contributions can be made after you reach age 70½.

$ Qualified distributions made after a five-year holding period are completely tax free.

$ Tax-free distributions are not taken into account to determine the taxability of Social Security benefits.

$ The ability to make contributions to a Roth IRA is phased out at a much higher level of income than with a deductible IRA.

Traditionally, taxpayers over the age of 70½ were prohibited from making a contribution to an IRA. This prohibition applied to deductible and nondeductible IRAs. Beginning in 1998, taxpayers of all ages can establish a new Roth IRA and contribute up to $2,000 per year.

Contributions to a Roth IRA are not deductible. However, when qualified distributions (including accumulated untaxed earnings on the contributions) are made from a Roth IRA, there is no tax due. This is different from a traditional nondeductible IRA, for which the distribution of contributions is not taxed but the distribution of earnings on the contributions is taxed. Unlike a traditional nondeductible IRA, the entire qualified distribution from a Roth IRA—contributions and earnings—is tax free.

The Roth IRA has one more important benefit. For the entire distribution from a Roth IRA to be tax free, it must satisfy a five-year holding period. A qualified distribution may not be made from a Roth

IRA before the end of five tax years after the first tax year you make a contribution to a Roth IRA. But what if you need to make a withdrawal before the end of the five-year period? Per the new rules, you can withdraw your nondeductible contributions prior to the end of the five-year period and avoid tax. That is, withdrawals are considered to be made first from your nondeductible contributions and then from the earnings on those contributions. As long as you leave your earnings in the Roth IRA account for the required five-year holding period, you will avoid income tax.

Only when you withdraw the earnings in the account prior to the end of the five-year period does a taxable event occur. If you are forced to withdraw the earnings before the end of the five-year period, you will have to pay tax on the withdrawn earnings. If you make an early withdrawal of the earnings and are under age $59^1/2$, you will also be liable for the 10% early withdrawal penalty tax (subject to the same exceptions as traditional IRAs).

EXAMPLE: In 1998, at age $70^1/2$, Ms. Smith establishes a Roth IRA. For five years, she contributes $2,000 per year. At the end of the five-year period, the account balance is $14,000 ($10,000 from annual nondeductible contributions and $4,000 from earnings on the account). Since five years have passed, Ms. Smith can make a qualified distribution from the Roth IRA. The entire $14,000 is distributed tax free.

Here is a bonus: Since the entire distribution is tax free, it is not included in Ms. Smith's adjusted gross income for the purpose of determining how much of her Social Security benefits are taxable. Distributions from a taxable IRA (and distributions from a traditional nondeductible IRA representing taxable earnings) would be included in Ms. Smith's adjusted gross income for the purpose of determining the taxability of Social Security benefits.

PLANNING POINTERS: The Roth IRA is ideal for upper-middle-income taxpayers because it is phased out at a much higher level of income than a traditional deductible IRA. For married taxpayers filing jointly, the maximum annual contribution of $2,000 is phased out for adjusted gross incomes between $150,000 and

$160,000, with no contribution allowed for an adjusted gross income in excess of $160,000. For single taxpayers, the maximum annual contribution of $2,000 is phased out for adjusted gross incomes between $95,000 and $110,000, with no contribution allowed for a single taxpayer with an adjusted gross income in excess of $110,000.

If you expect your adjusted gross income to exceed these phaseout levels within the next few years, you should consider establishing a Roth IRA and contributing to it until your annual level of income prohibits you from doing so. By doing this, you can withdraw the funds tax free after five years or you can leave the funds in the account to continue to accumulate tax free.

To contribute to a Roth IRA, you must have earned income during the year or you must establish the account as a spousal Roth IRA. Contributions can be made to a Roth IRA up to the due date for filing your income tax return for the year (but not including extensions).

☑ CHECKLIST:

- Beginning in 1998, establish and contribute to a Roth IRA.
- To ensure the tax-free status of a distribution from your Roth IRA, be certain to leave the funds in the Roth IRA account for at least five years.
- If you have to make a withdrawal from your Roth IRA before the five-year period has passed, be certain to limit the withdrawal to the amount of your nondeductible contributions to the account. In this way, you will avoid being taxed on an early withdrawal of the earnings in the account.

40 | Take an Extra Two Months to Fund Your IRA

$ This is a tip for taxpayers who can make
deductible IRA contributions.

$ It extends by two months the deadline for making
a deductible IRA contribution.

$ Use your previously funded IRA to fund the
current year's deductible contribution.

$ Replace funds distributed from your IRA account
within 60 days.

If you don't have enough cash to make a deductible contribution to your IRA by April 15, here is how you can still take the tax deduction and have until June 12 to make the full $2,000 contribution. To get the extra time, all you need is an IRA funded in previous years.

On April 15 have $2,500 distributed to you from your IRA. Since your bank is now required to withhold 20% (for income tax withholding) of any IRA distribution, you should receive $2,000. As soon as you receive the $2,000, immediately deposit it back into your IRA. As long as you do this by April 15, this "deposit" is your deductible contribution for the year.

Now you have 59 days to "make up" the withdrawal—or to be taxed. All you have to do is deposit $2,500 in the same IRA account by June 12. By making this "rollback" deposit, you avoid the tax on the original distribution made to you.

In effect, you are taking a short-term loan from your IRA to make this year's deductible IRA contribution by the April 15 due date. But to avoid being taxed, you have to pay back the short-term loan within 60 days by redepositing the total distribution back into your IRA account.

☞**EXAMPLE:** Ms. Smith is single. Although she earned $50,000 for the year, she was not covered by an employer retirement plan at any time during the year and therefore has an option of making a full $2,000 contribution to her IRA. To deduct the full $2,000 IRA contribution on her tax return that year, she must contribute the $2,000 to her IRA by April 15 of the following year.

Unfortunately, on April 15 Ms. Smith is a little short of cash, but she will have the required cash by June 12. With this in mind, on April 15 Ms. Smith takes a $2,500 distribution from her IRA—from which the bank withholds $500 for income tax withholding—leaving Ms. Smith with $2,000 in hand. She immediately deposits the $2,000 into her IRA and deducts this deposit as her IRA contribution for the year on her income tax return.

Ms. Smith then remembers to fund her IRA account with $2,500 by June 12. This way, she avoids being taxed on the original $2,500 distribution.

💡**PLANNING POINTERS:** Banks and other IRA institutions are now required to withhold 20% from any IRA distributions. However, many banks do not seem to be aware of the requirement and still distribute the full amounts requested. If this happens to you, use the amount in excess of your April 15 deposit to help fund your June 12 contribution.

If you do have 20% of the IRA distribution withheld—as you are supposed to—you can either recoup this amount as a refund at year-end when you file your income tax return or reduce accordingly your current withholding at work or your next estimated tax payment (if you make estimated tax payments).

It is important that the entire original distribution—including any withholding by the bank from that distribution—be deposited back into your IRA account by June 12. So if you take a $2,500 distribution (from which $500 is withheld and $2,000 is deposited as this year's contribution), you must deposit the entire $2,500 by June 12.

Rollbacks of this type can be made only once a year from each IRA account. You should not use this strategy if you plan to make a distribution to yourself for another purpose during the year.

Even if you cannot make a current deductible contribution to an IRA—maybe you are covered by an employer plan and your adjusted gross income exceeds $35,000 if you are single ($50,000 if you are married filing jointly)—your teenage or young adult children may be able to benefit from this IRA funding strategy. If you are giving them the money with which to fund their IRAs, this gives you an extra two months before you have to part with the cash.

☑ CHECKLIST:

- On April 15 take a $2,500 distribution from your previously funded IRA. Of this $2,500, $500 (20%) should be withheld for income taxes by the bank.
- Immediately deposit the net distribution of $2,000 to your IRA.
- Take the deduction on your income tax return for the previous year (due to be filed that day—April 15).
- Fund your IRA with $2,500 on or before June 12.

41 In a Pinch, Use Penalty-Free Distributions from Your IRA

$ Take distributions from your IRA without paying the 10% early withdrawal penalty.

$ This tip is ideal for taxpayers above age 50 who need to withdraw limited funds from their IRA but do not wish to withdraw the entire amount.

$ Once begun, as long as you make withdrawals for five years, annual IRA withdrawals are required only until you reach age 59½.

$ Take some of your IRA now, but leave the bulk of the IRA for retirement.

$ Doing this avoids "bracket creep"—it can save on income tax.

The best bet is to keep your retirement savings until you retire. After all, your retirement savings are your nest egg for when you stop working. But sometimes, expenses come up (e.g., providing for an elderly parent, helping pay for a child's college education) that force you to tap into your IRA account sooner than you had planned.

No matter how old you are, if you take a distribution from your IRA, you must pay income tax. Fortunately, there is a way to take IRA distributions without having to pay the 10% early withdrawal penalty. Just take the distributions in the form of an IRA annuity. If you can avoid the 10% early withdrawal penalty, over a period of time you can save a bundle.

With an IRA annuity, you make annual IRA withdrawals based on life expectancy tables provided by the IRS. If you set up an IRA annuity withdrawal schedule, you must make withdrawals until you are 59¹/₂. You must also have made withdrawals for at least five years. Once you have met the requirements, you can either continue to make withdrawals or wait until you reach age 70¹/₂, when you're required to make withdrawals anyway.

These kind of withdrawal restrictions make the IRA annuity approach a good idea for people in their 50s who have extraordinary expenses to meet but do not want to be forced to withdraw everything from their IRA account before they retire.

☞EXAMPLE: Mr. Smith is 56 years old and has two children in college. He has managed to cover one child's college expenses without too much trouble, but now with his younger child attending college classes, meeting the expenses has become a problem. Mr. Smith has an IRA account into which he rolled over his retirement plan from a previous employer when he changed jobs. This IRA account is currently worth $100,000.

To meet some of these college expenses a little more comfortably, Mr. Smith begins taking distributions in the form of an IRA annuity. He checks the IRS life expectancy tables at the back of IRS Publication 590 and finds that at age 56 his life expectancy "divisor" is 27.7. He divides the $100,000 in the IRA account by 27.7 and arrives at an annual withdrawal amount of $3,610.

Mr. Smith withdraws $3,610 for five years, pays the income tax, and uses what is left after the income tax has been paid to help with his children's college expenses. Since he is in the 28% federal and 5% state income tax brackets, the combined income tax he must pay each year is $1,191 ($3,610 annual IRA distribution times 33% combined federal/state income tax rate). This leaves him $2,419 each year to help with his children's college expenses.

Although Mr. Smith must pay income taxes due on the annual IRA distributions, he does not have to pay the 10% early withdrawal penalty. Using the IRA annuity saves him $361 each year in penalties. After five years, he has saved $1,805. Once Mr. Smith has taken at least five annual distributions and has reached age $59^{1}/_{2}$, he can stop taking the annual distributions until he reaches age $70^{1}/_{2}$.

If Mr. Smith were age 50 when he began taking the IRA annuity distributions, he would have to take the distributions for 10 years— until he reached age $59^{1}/_{2}$. If Mr. Smith were age 58 when he began taking the IRA annuity distributions, he would have to take the distributions for at least five years—even though he had reached age $59^{1}/_{2}$ within two years.

If Mr. Smith stops taking distributions after five years, he will have taken $18,050 in IRA distributions ($3,610 times 5 years). This still leaves $81,950 ($100,000 less $18,050) in his IRA—and he is not required to take any more distributions until he reaches age $70^{1}/_{2}$.

☿PLANNING POINTERS: Taking IRA distributions in an annuity form may also save you income tax as well as the early withdrawal penalties. If you are considering taking a big lump sum distribution from an IRA in one year—and you haven't reached age $59^{1}/_{2}$—you will pay the 10% early withdrawal amount on the entire distribution. But you will also pay more in income tax if the lump sum distribution is large enough to push your total taxable income into a higher tax bracket.

For example, if you're in the 28% federal income tax bracket, a large enough lump sum distribution might push you into either the 31% or 36% federal tax brackets. This means you'll be paying three to eight cents more on the dollar in federal income tax for the portion of your lump sum distribution that falls into the higher income tax brackets. On the other hand, level annuity payments over a period of years usually prevent this "bracket creep."

- Use the life expectancy tables at the back of IRS Publication 590 to determine how much you can withdraw annually from your IRA without paying early withdrawal penalties. You can pick up IRS Publication 590 free of charge at any IRS forms location.
- When you file your IRS Form 1040 for each year, take IRA annuity withdrawals, attach IRS Form 5329, indicating that you are not liable for the 10% early withdrawal penalty due to the IRA annuity withdrawal method.

42 Should You Defer Your First Required IRA Distribution?

$ This tip involves choosing whether you should defer your first IRA distribution.

$ Deferring your required first-year IRA distribution may save more tax the first year, but it might end up costing you more in the long run.

$ Bunching IRA distributions into the second year can increase taxable Social Security benefits and push you into a higher income tax bracket.

You already know that you have to begin taking taxable distributions from your IRA in the year you reach age $70^1/2$. You can begin sooner, but you must begin by $70^1/2$. When you reach $70^1/2$, you can either take the required distribution before year-end or defer taking the first required distribution until April 1 of the following year.

CAUTION: Although this one-year deferral of IRA income is inviting, it could be a mistake. There is no option to defer the second-year required IRA distribution into the third year. By deferring the first-year distribution into the second year, you are bunching two years' taxable distributions into one taxable year. Depending on the level of your other taxable income, this could force you to pay income tax on Social Security benefits you receive.

Before electing to defer your first-year required IRA distribution, make two tax projections for the two-year period. In the first projection, assume no deferral, and include the first-year IRA distribution in the first year's income and the second-year IRA distribution in the second year's income. In the second projection, include both years' IRA distributions in the second year's income.

Then choose the two-year option with the lowest total tax.

☞ **EXAMPLE:** Ms. Smith is a single taxpayer who turned 70$^{1}/_{2}$ in 1997. Her total income for that year without an IRA distribution was $22,000. This included Social Security benefits of $7,000. Ms. Smith expects her income level to be the same for 1998. She also has an IRA with approximately $100,000 in it, rolled over from a company pension plan a few years back.

Using the life expectancy tables in IRS Publication 590, Ms. Smith calculates that she will have to make a first-year IRA distribution of $6,250 and a second-year IRA distribution of $6,454. Should Ms. Smith defer the first-year distribution into the second year?

If Ms. Smith defers the first-year IRA distribution into the second year, her total federal income tax due for 1997 (assuming she takes the standard deduction) will be approximately $1,080 and her total federal income tax due for 1998 will be approximately $3,451 (using 1997 tax rates to approximate). The two-year total is $4,531.

If Ms. Smith does not defer the first-year IRA distribution but takes one distribution each year, her total federal income tax due for 1997 (assuming she takes the standard deduction) will be approximately $2,018 and her total federal income tax due for 1998 will be approximately $2,048 (using 1998 tax rates to approximate). The two-year total is $4,066.

It is easy to see why Ms. Smith might be tempted to defer the first year's required IRA distribution. If she defers, she'll have to pay only $1,080 for the first year, compared with $2,018 if she does not defer.

But when you total the tax for the two-year period, Ms. Smith saves $465 ($4,531 less $4,066) more over the two-year period when she does not defer receipt of the first-year IRA distribution. It is important to note here that this is not because of a difference in income tax rates. All the examples use the 15% federal income tax bracket. Ms. Smith pays more income tax by deferring the first-year IRA distribution because the deferral causes her to have to take Social Security benefits into taxable income.

♀**PLANNING POINTERS:** Testing whether it is better to defer receipt of your required first IRA distribution is even more important if you enjoy a higher level of income. Beginning in 1993, up to 85% of your Social Security benefits could be included in your taxable income. If this higher level of income pushes you into a higher income tax bracket—as well as forcing you to count a larger amount of your Social Security benefits as taxable income—you could be looking at a really expensive one-year deferral. The first year will be fine, but the second year will be painful. And after two years, you will have paid more.

☑ **CHECKLIST:**
- Calculate your federal income tax for the first two years you are required to take IRA distributions, using two sets of calculations.
- The first calculation should tell you how much you will pay in income tax if you defer receipt of the first year's distribution into the second year, bunching it with the second year's required distribution. Calculate the income tax due for both years.
- The second calculation should tell you how much you will pay in income tax if you do not defer the first year's distribution. Calculate the income tax due for both years.
- Use the option that will save you more income tax overall for the two-year period, not necessarily the option that will save you more the first year.

43 Fund Your Retirement Account Sooner and Your Employees' Retirement Accounts Later

$ This loophole is for employers who have a Keogh or SEP defined contribution retirement plan.

$ Accelerate the retirement contributions made on your behalf and enjoy greater "inside buildup" of earnings in your own retirement account.

$ Defer making retirement contributions on your employees' behalf until the last possible minute, and use the funds in the meantime.

If you have a defined contribution Keogh or SEP (a retirement plan in which annual contributions are determined on a percentage of an employee's compensation or of a self-employed person's net self-employment income), then you are required to make retirement contributions on behalf of your employees as well as yourself. Fortunately, you are not required to make these contributions at the same time. Instead, you can make contributions to your own account as early in the year as possible, and you can defer contributions to your employees' accounts until the last possible allowable minute.

Using this strategy, your retirement account starts earning tax-deferred income right away. And because each year these compounded earnings are saved from the erosion of current taxation, when you stop working your retirement savings will be all the greater for it. Your account earns income from the beginning of each year instead of the end of each year.

Of course, the opposite will be true for your employees—the inside buildup of their retirement accounts will be less, because their accounts will have been funded at the last possible moment each year. You'll be able to use the money for a longer period of time before you have to deposit it into their retirement accounts.

☞**EXAMPLE:** Mr. Smith is a self-employed construction contractor with two employees. He will have net self-employment income for 1997 of approximately $60,000—after paying two employees $20,000 each. Mr. Smith has an SEP retirement plan for his business.

Based on his projected income for 1997, he determines that he will be able to make a maximum annual SEP contribution to his own account for $7,225. But this also means he will have to make contributions of $3,000 each on behalf of his two employees.

On January 1, 1997, Mr. Smith contributes the $7,225 to his own account, and it begins earning tax-deferred income right away. He does not do the same for his two employees. Instead, he waits until the very last required minute to make contributions on their behalf.

Since he is not required to make retirement plan contributions until he files his tax return for the year (including extensions) he files an automatic extension on April 15, 1998, giving himself another four months to file his final income tax return for the year and to finish making required contributions to the SEP retirement plan.

On August 15, 1998, 17 and a half months after he made a contribution to the SEP on his own behalf, he makes the required contributions on behalf of his employees. By deferring making these contributions ($3,000 for each employee), Mr. Smith has had the use of the funds for the entire time. Even if he keeps the funds in a money market account earning 4% per year, after 17 months he is approximately $350 ahead.

💡**PLANNING POINTERS:** Even though you defer the time for contributing to the defined contribution retirement accounts of your employees, you should be careful to determine well ahead of time what the contributions you make on their behalf will be. Earmark the funds and set them aside to earn interest for you in the meantime. If you use the cash instead, you may come up short when the last minute for making the contributions finally arrives.

☑ **CHECKLIST:**

- Determine your allowable retirement contribution for the tax year as early as possible and make the contribution to your account.

- Determine the retirement contributions that you will have to make on behalf of your employees, and set the funds aside so they will be available when the time comes to contribute on their behalf—but earning interest for you in the meantime.
- File an automatic extension to extend the time for filing your income tax return for the year so that you can defer even longer the required time for making retirement contributions on behalf of your employees.

44 Increase Retirement Contributions for Your Family Business

$ Family members who work in your business are allowed increased retirement plan contributions.

$ Making larger family retirement contributions results in reduced income taxes and a larger family retirement nest egg.

$ Measure the effect on cash flow and estimated income tax payments.

Beginning in 1997, you may be able to increase your contributions to the retirement accounts belonging to you and the members of your family employed in your business. This is due to the 1996 tax law's repeal of the so-called family aggregation rules. Under these old rules, contributions to your business retirement plan were limited by the amount of the contributions made on behalf of family members employed in your business, including your spouse and children under age 19.

Under the new rules, the compensation of your spouse and children under age 19 will not be aggregated with your compensation when calculating the allowable deductible contributions to your company retirement plan. This means that the deductible retirement plan contributions that you'll make on behalf of your family can be larger than they were in the past.

EXAMPLE: Mrs. Smith is the sole shareholder of Smith Company. She is also employed by the corporation. She pays herself a salary of $70,000 per year. Her husband also works for the company, earning $40,000 per year, and her four children—ages 14 to 18—also work for the company, each earning $10,000 per year. All together, the Smith family's annual salaries total $150,000.

The Smith Company has a defined contribution retirement plan that generally allows a contribution on each employee's behalf of up to 25% of each employee's annual compensation—up to a maximum contribution of $30,000 per employee per year.

Under the pre-1997 family aggregation rules, however, the combined contribution for the Smith family was limited to one $30,000 cap. No more than $30,000 could be contributed to the combined retirement accounts of the Smith family each year.

Under the new rules, the $30,000 cap applies to each family member. At 25% of compensation, an annual retirement contribution of $17,500 can be made on behalf of Mrs. Smith, an annual retirement contribution of $10,000 can be made on behalf of Mr. Smith, and annual retirement contributions of $2,500 can be made on behalf of each of their children.

All together, Smith Company will be able to make $37,500 in annual retirement contributions on behalf of the Smith family members—$7,500 more than before the repeal of the family aggregation rules.

If Smith Company is in the 25% corporate federal income tax bracket, the $7,500 in increased tax-deductible retirement contributions will mean an annual corporate federal income tax savings of $1,875—not to mention state income tax savings and the increased retirement savings for the family members.

PLANNING POINTERS: Review this year's projected salaries for family members who work in your business. Calculate any increase that their retirement plan contributions for the year and the effects of these increases will have on the cash flow of your business. Also calculate the tax savings generated by the increased contributions.

If your business does not currently have a retirement plan and you employ several family members, you may want to consider setting up a defined contribution plan that offers you the ability to make the maximum possible annual deductible retirement contributions—a combined money purchase/profit-sharing plan. In contrast to other types of defined contribution retirement plans, a combined money purchase/profit-sharing plan generates larger annual retirement plan contributions. And this means larger current income tax savings.

☑ CHECKLIST:

- Determine the increase in retirement plan contributions on behalf of family members due to the repeal of the family aggregation rules.
- Determine the increased cash flow requirements for funding the higher available retirement plan contributions.
- Determine the resulting income tax savings from the increased retirement plan contributions and adjust any estimated income tax payments accordingly.

45 An Almost-Too-Good-to-Be-True Retirement Plan Benefit for Self-Employed People

$ This benefit is for self-employed individuals—including self-employed partners—who own more than one business.

$ Establish a retirement plan for one business without establishing retirement plans for other businesses.

$ Contribute to a retirement plan on your own behalf without contributing on behalf of your employees.

If you are self-employed and involved in multiple businesses, even if you have partners, the new tax act has made a change allowing you to contribute to a self-employed retirement plan on your own behalf without requiring you to make contributions on behalf of your employees. The new act has repealed the so-called aggregation rules that previously applied to self-employed retirement plans.

Under the old aggregation rules, if a self-employed person owned or was part owner of more than one business, and a retirement plan was provided for the employees in one business, the law required that a retirement plan be provided for the employees of the other businesses.

Beginning in 1997, the new tax law removes this requirement. If you own two businesses, the law allows you the option of establishing a retirement plan for only the business with the fewest employees, even if you work by yourself in that business.

There is only one drawback under the new tax law, a condition that might limit the amount you can contribute on your own behalf. According to the new tax law, the amount of money a self-employed person can contribute to a retirement plan is based on the self-employment earnings generated by the business with the retirement plan. If your business without employees has smaller net earnings than your business with employees, the amount you can contribute to a retirement plan will be based on the smaller net earnings. While the rule change means that you can avoid contributing to a retirement plan for your employees, it also means that you could be limited to making the smallest (rather than the largest) potential contributions to your personal retirement account.

☞ **EXAMPLE:** Mr. Smith is a self-employed accountant with three employees. His annual net income from his accounting business (reduced by his income tax deduction for one half of self-employment tax) is $75,000. A profit-sharing-type retirement plan established for this business would allow him to contribute up to $9,780 ($75,000 times 13.04%) each year on his own behalf. But he would also have to contribute on behalf of his three employees. If their total combined annual salaries equal $75,000, Mr. Smith will have to contribute $11,250 ($75,000 times 15%) on their combined behalf each year he makes a full contribution to his own account.

Mr. Smith is also self-employed as a writer and does not have any employees in his writing business. His net income for his writing business is approximately $25,000 per year (after being reduced by his income tax deduction for one half of self-employment tax paid). If he establishes a profit-sharing-type retirement plan for his writing business, he will be limited to annual contributions on his own behalf of $3,260 ($25,000 times 13.04%). But since he will not have to contribute on behalf of any employees, he will save an annual $11,250 that he would have otherwise had to contribute.

Under the new tax law, Mr. Smith can contribute $9,780 on his own behalf as an accountant and $11,250 on behalf of his employees, or he can contribute $3,260 on his own behalf as a writer and nothing on behalf of his employees.

♀ PLANNING POINTERS: If you are an owner in more than one self-employed business and are considering establishing a self-employed retirement plan, determine which business offers the most favorable retirement plan scenario. Obviously, this new tax break is ideal if you have one business that generates larger net profits and has fewer employees than your other businesses.

One creative response to this change in the rules may be to divide up a business into different businesses. The IRS will undoubtedly restrict artificial business divisions established to avoid contributions to retirement plans on behalf of employees. Until the IRS makes such restrictions, you should be careful to actually separate the businesses as much as possible. One business should not be identified with the other. Keep separate sets of books, and open separate bank accounts. Use separate business locations if possible. File separate Schedule Cs when you file your IRS Form 1040 for the year.

☑ CHECKLIST:
- For each self-employed business you own (including partnership interests), determine the amount you can contribute to a retirement plan on behalf of yourself and then the amount you must also contribute on behalf of your employees.
- If possible, choose to establish a retirement plan for the business that allows you to contribute as much as possible on your ▾

own behalf while contributing as little as possible on behalf of
your employees.

- Be careful to keep your different self-employed businesses as
separate as possible.

46 Take a Lump Sum Retirement Plan Distribution Before the Year 2000 and Beat the Repeal of Five-Year Averaging

$ This break is for the qualifying taxpayer who can
withdraw money from his or her retirement plan in
a lump sum before the year 2000.

$ This break is especially important for taxpayers
who reached age 50 after December 31, 1985.

$ There is still time to save income tax before the
repeal of the five-year forward-averaging method
is effective.

If you reached age 50 after 1985, the so-called five-year forward-
averaging method may be your only hope for reducing the income tax
on a lump sum distribution from your retirement plan. Unfortunately,
because of a recent repeal, this method of income averaging will no
longer be allowable for lump sum retirement plan distributions made
after December 31, 1999. Time is of the essence! If you are nearing
retirement, before the repeal becomes effective you should calculate
the benefits of a lump sum distribution (using five-year forward averaging).

The five-year forward-averaging method is especially important
for taxpayers who did not reach age 50 prior to January 1, 1986, since
they are denied the advantage of the ten-year forward-averaging
method, a method available to taxpayers who reached age 50 before
January 1, 1986.

When the repeal of five-year forward averaging becomes effective, your age will be the main factor in determining whether you can trim the income tax on a lump sum retirement plan distribution:

- If you reached age 50 before January 1, 1986, you will not be able to use five-year forward averaging, but you will still have the option of using the ten-year forward-averaging method.
- If you reached age 50 on or after January 1, 1986, you will not be able to use either the five- or the ten-year forward-averaging methods. You will either have to pay the income tax on the entire lump sum distribution at ordinary income tax rates or roll over the lump sum distribution into an IRA, deferring the income tax (at ordinary income tax rates) until you begin making withdrawals from the IRA.

☞**EXAMPLE:** In 1996, at age 60, Ms. Smith made a $75,000 lump sum withdrawal from a qualified retirement plan. Since she had not reached age 50 before January 1, 1986, she was unable to use the ten-year forward-averaging method to reduce the income tax on this distribution. She was, however, able to take advantage of the five-year forward-averaging method.

Ms. Smith, a single taxpayer, had taxable income of $35,222 before including the lump sum distribution into income. If Ms. Smith had taken the entire lump sum distribution into income and had not used the five-year forward-averaging method, her total federal income tax due for the year would have been $29,382.

Instead, using the five-year forward-averaging method with her lump sum retirement plan distribution, her total federal income tax due for the year was $17,995—a federal income tax savings of $11,387!

Simply by using five-year forward averaging, Ms. Smith was able to keep an extra 15% ($11,387 divided by $75,000) of her total lump sum distribution out of the hands of the IRS and in her own pocket.

💡**PLANNING POINTERS:** To be able to use the five-year forward-averaging method, you must have completed five years of participation in the retirement plan and you must not receive the lump sum distribution until after you reach age 59¹/₂.

Be careful if you have reached 59¹/₂ and have completed five years of participation in two retirement plans. You must use five-year averaging for all qualifying lump sum distributions you receive in a given year. It is all or nothing. You cannot use five-year averaging for a distribution from one plan and then in the same year roll over the proceeds from another plan into an IRA. Instead, the lump distributions from the two qualifying plans should be made in two separate years. Take the lump sum distribution from one plan in one year and use five-year forward averaging to reduce your income tax on the distribution. Then take the lump sum distribution from the second plan in a later year and roll over the proceeds from the second plan into an IRA.

Unless the lump sum distribution is especially large, five-year forward averaging usually generates a lower income tax. This is another reason why it may be best to take lump sum distributions from different retirement plans in different years. If you take distributions from two plans in the same year, the combined total of the two lump sum distributions may be so high that the benefit of five-year averaging is lost or greatly reduced.

In any case, before taking lump sum distributions from more than one retirement plan in one year, determine what the income tax would be with and without the benefit of the five-year forward-averaging method. In most cases, taking the separate lump sum distributions in separate years increases the benefit of five-year forward averaging and saves more income tax overall.

☑ CHECKLIST:

- Determine whether you can take a qualifying lump sum retirement plan distribution before the year 2000. To do this, you must be at least 59¹/₂ and you must have completed at least five years of participation in the retirement plan.
- If you reached age 50 on or after January 1, 1986, you must take a lump sum distribution in 1997, 1998, or 1999 to benefit from the five-year forward-averaging method. Lump sum distributions taken after 1999 will be taxed at ordinary income

tax rates without the benefit of the five-year forward-averaging method.

- To project your tax liability with and without the five-year forward-averaging method, use IRS Form 4972 and the related instructions. This is a relatively straightforward tax form with a checklist at the beginning to see whether you qualify to use either five-year or ten-year forward averaging. The instructions include step-by-step directions, tax tables, and the required calculations for both averaging methods.

47 Choose the Right Funding Strategy for Your Keogh Account

$ This tip is for self-employed individuals and self-employed partners who want to establish a Keogh retirement plan.

$ There are three ways to fund a Keogh, and there are advantages and disadvantages to each way.

$ Fund more and have less flexibility in future years, or fund less and have more flexibility in future years.

Self-employed individuals and partners who are setting up Keogh accounts for the first time need to plan carefully and consider both the short term and the long term. The most common type of Keogh is a "defined contribution" plan. Central to a defined contribution Keogh is the idea that annual contributions to the plan are based on a percentage of an employee's compensation or a self-employed's net self-employment income. If you are setting up such an account, there are three ways to fund your plan: a money purchase plan, a profit-sharing plan, or a combined money purchase/profit-sharing plan. The three Keogh funding methods differ in the extent to which they trade up-front tax savings for long-term flexibility. How you decide to fund your Keogh the first year it is in existence will be the way you continue to fund it in years to come. Each of the three funding strategies has its advantages and disadvantages.

- *Money purchase plan.* This type of Keogh allows for maximum yearly funding—25% of employees' compensation and 20% of a self-employed's "adjusted" net income from self-employment up to $30,000 per year. Since this plan allows for larger yearly contributions than the other plans, it follows that it also allows for larger tax write-offs. However, the problem with a money purchase plan is that it lacks flexibility. Once you set up the plan and establish the percentage of compensation you will contribute each year, you have to stick with it. At present, you may want the larger write-offs afforded by the larger contributions, but 10 years from now you may have other needs (like sending your kids to college), and the required annual retirement plan contributions could be a burden.
- *Profit-sharing plan.* With this type of Keogh, the maximum amount of annual contributions is less than that made in a money purchase plan, but it does have the advantage of year-to-year flexibility. You can contribute up to 15% of an employees' compensation and 13.04% of a self-employed's "adjusted" net income from self-employment up to $30,000 per year. What is significant about the plan is that you can adjust your contributions year to year, from the maximum allowable percentage to a lesser percentage or even nothing at all. With this plan, funding does not have to be a burden in years when you have other needs for your cash.
- *Combined money purchase/profit-sharing plan.* This third type of Keogh offers the best of both worlds—maximum allowable contributions with limited flexibility. If you wish to have a plan that allows for maximum contributions this year but still allows for smaller contributions in future years, then you should set up a combined plan. For this year, if you were self-employed you would contribute 6.96% to the money purchase portion and 13.04% to the profit-sharing portion of the combined plan (for a total combined contribution of 20%—up to a $30,000 total contribution).

In later years, you would have to fund only the money purchase side of the plan. Your contribution to the profit-sharing side of the plan would be optional from year to year. And if you don't need the maximum funding for the first year, you can establish a smaller required percentage for the money purchase side of the plan—say, 3%. At 3%, your self-employed first year's combined contribution would be 16.04% (3% for the money purchase plan plus 13.04% for the profit-sharing plan). By doing this, your required year-to-year pay-in to the money purchase part of the combined plan will be only the 3% established in the first year.

☞**EXAMPLE:** Ms. Smith is a self-employed individual with no employees. She wants to set up a Keogh and contribute as much as possible this year but does not know how much she will be able to afford to contribute in future years. She does not even know whether she will be able to make a nominal contribution to a money purchase plan from year to year.

Ms. Smith decides to set up a profit-sharing plan. She will be able to deduct only up to 13.04% of her adjusted self-employment income for the year—not the maximum 20% she could have deducted with a money purchase plan or a combined money purchase/profit-sharing plan. But she will have flexibility in future years—if she does not want to, she will not be required to make contributions.

Ms. Smith opens her profit-sharing Keogh plan prior to year-end but does not immediately fund it. After year-end, she calculates that her net income from self-employment is $60,000. From this, she must subtract one-half of the self-employment tax she owes; then she can calculate her Keogh contribution percentage. Her total self-employment tax equals $9,180, so she must reduce, or "adjust," her net self-employment income of $60,000 by $4,590 (one-half of $9,180). This gives her an adjusted net income of $55,410 ($60,000 less $4,590). She applies her maximum allowable profit-sharing plan percentage of 13.04% to $55,410 and arrives at an allowable Keogh contribution for the year of $7,225 (note that this dollar amount cannot be more than $30,000 each year).

As long as Ms. Smith contributes this amount to her Keogh account before she files her final income tax return for the year (including extensions), she can deduct the contribution on her income tax return, even though she makes it after year-end.

If Ms. Smith is in the 28% federal income tax bracket, this means a federal income tax savings of $2,023 ($7,225 times 28%). If she had contributed 20% to the plan, she would have saved federal income tax of $3,103. The difference of $1,080 ($3,103 less $2,023) that she does not save this year is the price of her long-term flexibility.

♀PLANNING POINTERS:

Because a combined money purchase/profit-sharing plan can offer the same maximum funding that a regular money purchase plan offers and at the same time offer more year-to-year flexibility than a regular money purchase plan, there is no good reason to establish a regular money purchase plan with its fixed maximum contribution percentage. Don't restrict your flexibility for future years—select either a profit-sharing plan or a combined money purchase/profit-sharing plan.

To take a tax deduction for a Keogh for the current year, the plan must have been established before year-end. You can wait to fund it until after year-end, but the plan must be in existence before year-end.

☑ CHECKLIST:

- Determine the type of Keogh you want, measuring current tax savings against long-term flexibility.
- Establish the Keogh plan before year-end.
- Fund the Keogh plan once you have determined your "adjusted" net self-employment income for the year. You can wait to fund your Keogh until you file your income tax return for the year (including extensions).
- You must also file an IRS Form 5500 before the last day of the seventh month following the close of your retirement plan year. For most calendar-year taxpayers, their retirement plan year is also the calendar year. This means that IRS Form 5500 must be filed before July 31. If you are self-employed and have no employees, use the simplified IRS Form 5500EZ.

48 Open an SEP Retirement Plan for a Very-Last-Minute Tax Shelter

$ For self-employed individuals, an SEP can mean a big tax deduction after the tax year has ended.
$ An SEP reduces income tax for the previous year. It can also reduce the current year's quarterly estimated tax payments.
$ File an automatic extension and wait until August 15 to fund the SEP.

If you are self-employed and the tax year has ended, you can still open an SEP retirement account. With an SEP, you save income taxes for the year just past and at the same time cut your required estimated income tax payments for the current year. You can do all this without having to fund the SEP until the middle of August. That's leveraged tax savings—take the write-off now, and part with the cash later.

An SEP is a profit-sharing type of defined contribution retirement plan. If you are self-employed, each year you are allowed to contribute up to 13.04% of your "adjusted" net income from self-employment earnings. "Adjusted" means you have to subtract from your net self-employment earnings your income tax deduction equal to one-half of the self-employment tax you owe (i.e., Social Security and Medicare tax) (see example). Once you make this adjustment, you simply multiply the adjusted net income amount by 13.04% to determine the maximum amount of money you can contribute to your SEP account for that year.

With an SEP, you don't have to contribute the maximum allowable amount—you can contribute less than the maximum or none at all. And you can change the contribution amount from year to year. You can use it for a tax shelter when you can afford to make contributions or ignore it when you cannot.

☞**EXAMPLE:** Mr. Smith is a single taxpayer and self-employed. His net income from self-employment earnings for 1997 is $50,000. He has no other earnings for the year.

In early January 1998, Mr. Smith calculates his income tax liabilities for 1997. First, he owes a self-employment tax of $7,650 ($50,000 times 15.3%). He is allowed an income tax deduction for one-half of this amount, $3,825, but since he does not itemize personal deductions, his only other reductions in taxable income for federal income tax purposes are his personal exemption of $2,650 and his standard deduction of $4,150. For federal income tax purposes, his taxable income is therefore $39,375 ($50,000 less $3,825 less $2,650 less $4,150) and generates a total federal income tax due of $7,821.

Mr. Smith's total federal tax liability for 1997 is $15,471 (self-employment tax of $7,650 plus federal income tax of $7,821). He also has a total state income tax due of $1,981.

During the year, Mr. Smith has made estimated federal tax payments of $12,000 and estimated state tax payments of $1,500. If Mr. Smith cannot find another deduction, by April 15, 1998, he will have to make a final 1997 federal tax payment of $3,471 ($15,471 total federal liability less $12,000 previous estimated payments). He will also have to make a final 1997 state income tax payment of $481 ($1,981 total state liability less $1,500 previous estimated payments).

In short, he still owes $3,952 for 1997.

Instead of settling for this tax scenario, Mr. Smith calculates the benefit of contributing to an SEP for 1997. Even though the year has ended, he can still open an SEP account, fund it, and take a tax deduction for 1997.

From his net self-employment earnings, Mr. Smith subtracts a tax deduction equal to one-half of the self-employment tax he owes. By means of this calculation, he arrives at his adjusted net income of $46,175 ($50,000 less $3,825). He then multiplies this $46,175 by 13.04%, his maximum SEP contribution rate, and finds that he can contribute a maximum of $6,021 to an SEP account for 1997. If he makes this tax-deductible contribution to his retirement plan, he will save $1,686 in federal income tax and $301 in state income tax—a total tax savings of $1,987. Then, instead of owing $3,952 for 1997, he will owe only $1,965 ($3,952 tax balance due less $1,987 tax savings).

Mr. Smith will also be able to reduce his required estimated income tax payments for 1998. Since he will base his quarterly payments for 1998 on 100% of his tax liability for 1997, his reduced 1997 tax liability will also lessen the minimum size of the quarterly payments he will have to make in 1998.

♀PLANNING POINTERS: While you can wait until August 15 of the following year to fund the SEP, orchestrate this with care. You cannot file the final income tax return for the preceding year until after you have made the contribution to your SEP. Because of this, if you want to extend the time for funding your SEP, you must also extend the time for filing your final income tax return. On April 15, do not file your final return. Instead, file an automatic extension, IRS Form 4868, and pay all the tax you still owe after taking the deduction for the SEP. Remember to file an automatic extension for your state income tax return as well.

If you have already completed your final income tax returns for the year (including the calculation of the SEP deduction) and could file them by April 15, stop and think. If you file them by April 15, then you must also fund the SEP by April 15. If you are not ready to make the contribution, file federal and state automatic extensions and wait to file the final income tax returns for the previous year until after you have funded your SEP. This gives you until August 15—almost eight months after the close of the year—to fund your SEP.

If you cannot afford to fund the maximum SEP contribution for the year, run the numbers with half the allowable SEP amount, or a quarter of the allowable SEP amount—whatever you can afford. If you can contribute anything, you will save income tax.

☑ CHECKLIST:
- Calculate your federal and state taxes for the year without an SEP.
- Calculate your federal and state taxes for the year with an SEP deduction—the maximum allowable SEP deduction if you can afford it, or a smaller contribution if you cannot afford the maximum.
- Once you have arrived at the SEP amount you want to contribute, deduct the amount on your income tax return for the previous year.

- Do not file the return on April 15. Instead, file federal and state automatic extensions.
- On or before August 15, fund your SEP account—you can open one at most banks—and then file your final income tax returns for the preceding year.
- When you file the automatic extensions on April 15, you must pay any income tax liabilities still due—an extension to file is not an extension to pay.
- When you have decided on the amount of your SEP contribution, make a "cash-out calendar" for the year. List any income tax liabilities for the previous year that are due on April 15, list the quarterly estimated payments for the current year and the dates they are due, and then list the SEP contribution that must be made by August 15. By viewing your overall tax-cash requirements for the year, you will have a better idea of whether you can afford to fund the maximum SEP contribution.

49	**Older Taxpayers: Combine Two Strategies to Shelter Required SEP Retirement Plan Distributions**

$ This loophole is for older self-employed taxpayers and shareholder-employees who own 5% or more of their employer corporation.

$ It is best for taxpayers who do not need maximum annual distributions and wish to leave a larger tax-deferred nest egg for their spouse or children.

$ Continue to make maximum deductible SEP retirement plan contributions after you begin taking required annual distributions.

$ Use the annual recalculation method for SEP distributions.

$ This allows for larger tax-deferred earnings,

smaller taxable distributions, and a continued buildup in your SEP account.

If you are self-employed or employed by a corporation in which you own an interest of 5% or more, you are required to begin taking distributions from your SEP retirement account by April 1 of the year following the year you reach age 70^1/$_2$. This can mean quite a tax bite, especially if you are still working in the business and have self-employment or salary income. But you can sharply reduce this tax bite (and at the same time build up your SEP account) by recalculating your SEP distributions annually and continuing to make your SEP contributions as long as you work.

When you "annually recalculate" your life expectancy using IRS-provided tables, the number of distribution years is extended beyond the number of years the IRS ordinarily allows for distributions. This extension of years means that less money in your account has to be distributed from year to year. And because you have a larger balance left in your account, you can increase your account's tax-deferred earnings. Your account grows larger because the required distributions are smaller.

At the same time you are taking required distributions, you should continue to contribute the maximum allowable amount to your SEP. Just because you have to start taking distributions does not mean you cannot continue to make contributions. If you are self-employed, you can reduce your personal income tax by contributing up to 13.04% of your net self-employment earnings to your SEP (up to $20,864). If you are a shareholder-employee of a corporation, your corporation can reduce its taxable income by contributing up to 15% of your employee salary to your SEP account (up to $24,000).

☞ **EXAMPLE:** Mr. Smith, a widower, is a self-employed antique refinisher, a craftsman with no desire to stop working. As his needs are met by his current earnings, he wishes to continue to build up his SEP retirement account so that he can leave as large a nest egg as possible for his children. He also wishes to reduce his own current income tax liability as much as possible.

At the end of 1996, he has a balance of $100,000 in his SEP

retirement account. In 1997 he reaches age 70½. He sees that he will have to begin taking distributions from his SEP by April 1, 1998.

First, Mr. Smith determines that he can continue to contribute $5,000 each year to his SEP account. If he makes $5,000 contributions to the SEP in each of the 16 years allowed for in the IRS life expectancy tables, he will have contributed, and deducted, $80,000.

Second, assume Mr. Smith has a 5% annual earnings rate and a beginning distribution balance of $100,000 (the balance in the account at the end of the year prior to reaching age 70½). If Mr. Smith uses the "ordinary" distribution tables and does not recalculate the required distribution annually, the account will generate further earnings of approximately $77,164 over the 16-year period. There will be required taxable distributions to Mr. Smith of approximately $257,164, and at the end of the 16 years the SEP account will be empty.

So, with the "ordinary" distribution tables, Mr. Smith will be able to deduct $80,000 but will also have to include $257,164 into taxable income. In effect, his annual SEP contributions will shelter 31% ($80,000 divided by $257,164) of his required annual distributions. The SEP account will generate a further $77,164 in earnings over the distribution period, but the account will be empty at the end of the period.

If, instead, Mr. Smith uses the "annual recalculation" method of distribution, the account will generate further earnings of $89,146 over the same 16-year period, there will be required taxable distributions to Mr. Smith of only approximately $171,161, and at the end of the 16 years there will still be approximately $97,986 left in the SEP account.

By recalculating his required distributions annually, Mr. Smith will still be able to deduct the cumulative $80,000 in contributions but will have to include only $171,161 into taxable income. In effect, his annual SEP contributions will shelter 46% ($80,000 divided by $171,161) of his required annual distributions. The SEP account will generate $11,982 more in tax-deferred earnings by recalculating the distributions annually, rather than using the ordinary distribution tables, and the SEP account balance will still be almost as much as it was when Mr. Smith began taking the required distributions.

♡PLANNING POINTERS: The Small Business Job Protection Act of 1996 established an extension of the time at which required SEP distributions must begin—but only for rank-and-file employees. For rank-and-file employees, distributions can begin the later of either April 1 of the calendar year following the year the employee reaches age 70$^{1}/_{2}$ or April 1 of the calendar year following the year the employee retires.

This possible extension of distributions to the year after retirement does not apply to self-employed persons and employees who own 5% or more of their employer corporation.

In the example above, the taxpayer is a widower, but if you are married and have elected to receive distributions over both your life expectancy and that of your spouse, you can recalculate both life expectancies annually.

Even if you do not survive for the entire IRS life expectancy period and you use the annual recalculation method, each year that you do survive, your required annual taxable distribution will be smaller, your SEP account will generate more in tax-deferred earnings, and your ending SEP account balance will be larger than if you use the ordinary distribution method.

☑ CHECKLIST:

- Before electing the method of distribution from your SEP retirement account, consider your current living requirements and your long-term plans for the funds in the account.
- If you do not need maximum annual distributions from the account and wish to continue generating the maximum amount of tax-deferred earnings with the account, use the annual recalculation method for determining annual required distributions.
- As long as you work, continue to make maximum deductible contributions to your SEP.

You Don't Have to Be Wealthy to Save on Estate Taxes

▼

▼

▼

$ This income tax–saving benefit is for the beneficiary of a small estate with unused estate administration expenses.

$ It is applicable when the estate has administration expenses that exceed estate income.

$ The estate beneficiary is allowed to deduct excess estate administration expenses on his or her personal return in the year the estate closes.

A small estate can generate a personal income tax deduction for the estate beneficiaries. Estate beneficiaries are allowed to deduct excess estate administration expenses (administration expenses in excess of estate income) for the year the estate closes. So be careful not to miss out on this often overlooked tax break.

Most estates incur some administration expenses. This is true whether the estate is large or small. Even with the smallest of estates, there can be executor commissions, attorney's fees, appraisal fees, accounting and tax-preparation expenses, court costs, estate asset storage costs, and other related miscellaneous expenses. Larger estates will ordinarily deduct these expenses on the estate's federal estate tax return. This is because an estate tax deduction will generally save the estate more than an income tax deduction. But what about smaller estates that are not required to file a federal estate tax return?

Since the smaller estates do not have to worry about paying federal estate taxes, executors should be careful to take the expenses as income tax deductions on an estate income tax return (Form 1041). Even if the small estate does not directly benefit from these income tax deductions (for example, it may already have insufficient income to be liable for an income tax), the beneficiaries of the estate can benefit from the unused estate administration expenses. Any unused administration expenses can be carried over to, and deducted on, the personal income tax returns of the beneficiaries in the year the estate closes.

☞EXAMPLE: Mr. Smith's uncle passed away, leaving a small real estate property, personal assets, and cash holdings in savings accounts. Mr. Smith was the sole beneficiary of the estate. Even though the estate was small, various expenses were incurred in the administration, closure, and proper distribution of its assets. Court costs, appraisal fees, attorney's fees, and estate asset storage fees were incurred and paid in the process. The administration fees totaled $5,000 and were paid out of the cash assets of the estate.

For the short period the estate was open, it generated $500 in interest income from its cash assets. After the estate closed, Mr. Smith filed IRS Form 1041 (estate income tax return) for the estate. He declared the $500 in estate income and deducted it from the $5,000 cost of estate administration. This left $4,500 ($5,000 less $500) in unused administration expenses. He listed these unused expenses on IRS Form K-1 and attached it to Form 1041.

Mr. Smith then deducted these unused expenses on his own Form 1040 Schedule A as a miscellaneous itemized deduction for the year in which the estate closed. That year, Mr. Smith had $2,000 in other miscellaneous expenses. These, added with the unused estate administration expenses, gave him a miscellaneous deductions total of $6,500. After disallowing $1,000 of these miscellaneous expenses based on the "2% of adjusted gross income rule," Mr. Smith, whose adjusted gross icome was $50,000, had an allowable miscellaneous itemized deduction of $5,500.

If Mr. Smith is in the 28% federal income tax bracket, this means that the deduction for the unused administration expenses ultimately saved him—after all the tax ins and outs—$1,260 in federal income tax.

♀PLANNING POINTERS: Beneficiaries can benefit from unused estate administrative expenses only if they itemize deductions on their personal income tax return. Since unused estate administrative expenses are treated as miscellaneous itemized deductions on the beneficiary's Schedule A, they are subject to the "2% of adjusted gross income rule." A beneficiary who itemizes deductions but ordinarily does not get to deduct miscellaneous expenses because of the 2% limitation should "bunch" his or her other miscellaneous deductions into the year he or she will have the benefit of the unused estate administration expenses. For example, prepay tax-preparation fees or investment advisory fees. In this way, the beneficiary will have a deduction in the current year that would be prevented the next year by the 2% limitation.

If you are the beneficiary of a small estate that incurred excess estate administrative expenses and closed within the last three years, and you have previously not taken advantage of these unused administration expenses on your personal income tax return, you can correct your return for the year the estate closed. File IRS Form 1040X for the tax refund due to you.

☑ CHECKLIST:

- File IRS Form 1041 (estate income tax return) with attached K-1 showing estate income, administrative expenses, and unused administrative expenses flowing through to estate beneficiary (or beneficiaries) in the year the estate closes.

- The beneficiary who itemizes deductions on Form 1040 Schedule A deducts the unused administration expenses as a miscellaneous itemized deduction subject to the 2% limitation in the year the estate closes.

- If you are an estate beneficiary who has failed to take this benefit within the last three years, amend your personal income tax return for the year in question, take the missed deduction, and file for a refund. Use Form 1040X. Make sure a related estate income tax return Form 1041 with attached Form K-1 is also filed for the year in question.

51 Unmarried Joint Tenants: Keeping Records Is the Key to Saving Taxes— Sometimes

$ This is a planning consideration for unmarried individuals who own assets as joint tenants.

$ It is applicable to parents and children, brothers and sisters, friends.

$ Whether taxes can be saved on joint tenancy assets often depends on whether records have been kept to show which of the joint tenants contributed to the acquisition or improvement of the assets in question.

$ Depending on the particular circumstance, taxes can be saved with or without records.

$ Most middle-income taxpayers will save more tax without records.

If you plan to co-own an asset with another person, a joint tenancy lasting until one of you dies, the key to minimizing your taxes (federal estate taxes or federal income taxes) lies in keeping or not keeping good records of ownership. To determine which record-keeping strategy will benefit you most, you must consider the possible future tax scenarios.

For federal estate tax purposes, and ultimately for federal income tax purposes, the general rule governing joint tenancy between unmarried individuals is straightforward: The full value of the jointly owned asset must be included in the estate of the first tenant to die. The full value is the fair market value of the entire asset at the time of the deceased tenant's death.

There are two exceptions to this general joint tenancy rule:

First, the rule does not apply when all or part of the asset belonged to the surviving tenant before the joint tenancy was created or when the joint tenants originally acquired the asset as a gift or inheritance.

Second, this rule does not apply when it can be demonstrated—with appropriate records—that the surviving tenant contributed "something" to the acquisition or improvement of the asset.

The second exception is the most common and can make all the difference. If "good" records were not kept, such that it is unclear who contributed what, the full fair market value of the entire asset is included in the estate of the deceased joint tenant and the surviving joint tenant enjoys the benefit of a full "stepped-up" basis for income tax purposes. With a stepped-up basis, the surviving tenant takes ownership of the entire asset as valued at the time of the death of the deceased joint tenant. This stepped-up basis translates into income tax savings when the asset is sold. The trade-off for this benefit is that, for federal estate tax purposes, the stepped-up value must be included in the estate of the tenant who died.

The trick is to determine whether it is better for the estate of the deceased tenant to save federal estate taxes or for the surviving tenant to save federal income taxes when the asset is sold. If the deceased tenant's estate is not large enough to incur federal estate tax, then the surviving tenant should act to minimize the income tax that comes with the asset's sale.

For most middle-income taxpayers, the federal estate tax will not be applicable, so including the full fair market value of the jointly owned asset in the estate of the deceased joint tenant will not result in a federal estate tax liability. At the same time, the surviving joint tenant can use the stepped-up basis to save income tax when the asset is sold. To maximize this benefit, there should be no appropriate records of contributions to ownership of the asset by the surviving joint tenant.

☞ **EXAMPLE:** Ms. Smith and her uncle owned rental real estate as joint tenants. The original purchase price was $50,000, and the fair market value of the property as of the date of death of Ms. Smith's uncle was $200,000. Although both contributed to the purchase of the property, no records were kept, and it is unclear exactly how much each contributed to the purchase. Because the allocation of the purchase price cannot be clearly shown, the entire fair market value of the property, $200,000, has to be included in the estate of Ms. Smith's uncle. And Ms. Smith receives a stepped-up basis for federal income tax purposes.

Fortunately, apart from his share of the rental real estate property, Ms. Smith's uncle has few other assets—certainly not enough to make his estate liable for payment of federal estate taxes (generally, an individual must have a taxable estate of $600,000 [the 1997 tax act increases this amount to $1,000,000 by the year 2006] before the federal estate tax is applicable). So even though the entire value of the rental real estate property is included in her uncle's estate, there are no federal estate taxes due as a result.

Shortly after the death of her uncle, Ms. Smith sells the property for $200,000. Because of the stepped-up basis, Ms. Smith has no taxable gain and owes no federal income tax on the sale. She pockets the $200,000, and the IRS doesn't get a dime.

💡 **PLANNING POINTERS:** Determine as carefully as possible the potential federal estate and income tax consequences of joint tenancy before keeping careful records of the joint tenants' individual contributions to ownership. There is no requirement that careful records must be kept. The IRS only defines what will happen if there are records and if there are no records.

As most middle-income taxpayers are not subject to the federal estate tax, it is better for the surviving joint tenant to save as much income tax as possible. The surviving joint tenant can do this by not keeping records of his or her contribution to ownership. Without records, the entire fair market value of the asset is included in the estate of the deceased tenant, and the surviving joint tenant receives a stepped-up basis. No federal estate taxes are generated because the deceased joint tenant's estate is still not large enough to generate the federal estate tax, and the surviving joint tenant has reduced his or her income tax when the asset is sold.

- Calculate any potential federal estate tax and/or income tax liabilities for both joint tenants—with and without records of contribution to ownership.
- For the best overall tax savings, decide whether to keep records.

52 Surviving Spouses: Save Income Tax on Certain Jointly Owned Assets

$ This income tax benefit is for the surviving spouse who sells an asset jointly acquired prior to 1977 with a since-deceased spouse.

$ The asset can be a family home, rental property, stocks and bonds—any asset that has increased in value since it was acquired (prior to 1977).

$ It does not matter whether the deceased spouse's estate was required to file a federal estate tax return.

$ Surviving spouses who have overpaid their income tax within the last three years can amend for a refund.

If you purchased assets prior to 1977 with your since-deceased spouse, you can enjoy large income tax savings when you sell them. Qualifying assets include your principal residence, a rental real estate property, stocks and bonds, whatever. This opportunity is all due to a Court of Appeals case limiting the IRS's power to retroactively apply a more recent tax law.

Here's the gist of it. The current general rule governing the ownership of property held jointly by spouses—either as joint tenants or as tenants by the entirety—does not apply to assets acquired prior to 1977. Instead, the old rules apply. The current rule says that no matter which spouse originally acquired the asset (purchased it with their own funds, inherited it, received it as a gift, etc.), only one-half of the value of the asset is included in the estate of the first spouse to die. In other words, each spouse is considered to own one-half of the asset for federal estate tax purposes. In contrast, the old rule says that the full value of the asset is included in the estate of the first spouse to die—unless it can be shown that the surviving spouse contributed to the acquisition of the asset.

As far as federal estate taxes go, this distinction between old and new rules is not important because of the unlimited marital deduction in the federal estate tax calculation. The spouse who dies first can pass his or her share of the jointly owned property to the surviving spouse without paying a dime in federal estate tax. This is true whether one-half of the value or even the entire value of the asset is included in the estate of the first spouse to die. On the other hand, the distinction is important for income tax purposes—and this means all taxpayers can benefit, even those whose estates are too small to be slapped with a federal estate tax.

Where does the benefit come from? It comes from a "stepped-up" basis. When the surviving spouse sells the asset, the tax is assessed according to the stepped-up basis—the larger the stepped-up basis, the larger the income tax savings. Under the old rule, the surviving spouse can potentially receive a stepped-up basis for the entire asset. Under the new rule, the surviving spouse receives a stepped-up basis for only one-half the value of the asset. As a result, you can save big on income taxes if you can calculate your tax according to the old rule and "step up" the entire basis.

☞**EXAMPLE 1:** In 1974 Mr. and Mrs. Smith purchased a raw land property as joint tenants. Both were working at the time, and it is uncertain who contributed what to the purchase price. The original purchase was $50,000. Last year Mr. Smith passed away, and the property was appraised as of the date of his death at $200,000. Mr. Smith left his share of the property to his wife. Whether or not Mr. Smith's estate is large enough to be subject to the federal estate tax is not important here—no federal estate tax would be due on the property because of the unlimited marital deduction.

This year Mrs. Smith sold the property for $210,000. Because of the court ruling, she calculates her income tax in this way: Since the full value of the property is included in the estate of the first spouse to die under the old rule, Mrs. Smith receives a stepped-up basis of the full value. Her taxable gain is $10,000 ($210,000 sales price less $200,000 stepped-up basis). If she sells the property after May 6, 1997, and pays capital gains tax at the new maximum capital gains tax rate of 20%, she will have an income tax liability of $2,000 ($10,000 times 20%).

If the IRS had its way, the tax bite would be a lot bigger. Only one-half of the value of the asset would receive a stepped-up basis— one-half would keep its original basis. Mrs. Smith's tax basis would be $125,000 ($100,000 one-half stepped-up basis plus $25,000 one-half of original cost). Her taxable gain would be $85,000 ($210,000 sales price less $125,000 half-and-half tax basis). On this taxable gain of $85,000—at the same new capital gains rate of 20%—her capital gains tax would be $17,000!

By figuring her tax using the court-approved pre-1977 rule, Mrs. Smith saves $15,000 ($17,000 less $2,000).

☞**EXAMPLE 2:** Mr. and Mrs. Jones are in the exact same situation as Mr. and Mrs. Smith in Example 1—except that records were kept indicating that Mrs. Jones originally contributed 75% of the purchase price of the property and Mr. Jones contributed 25%. Unfortunately, with this scenario the court ruling works in favor of the IRS. Since it can be shown who contributed what, only that percentage of the stepped-up basis is included in the estate of the first spouse to die.

Since Mr. Jones passed away first, only 25% of the stepped-basis is included in his estate. If the value of the property is $200,000 on the date of his death, then $50,000 is included in his estate. If his wife later sells the property for $210,000, her taxable gain will be a whopping $122,500, generating a whopping capital gains tax of $24,500 (using the same new capital gains tax rate of 20%). This is because Mrs. Jones's tax basis is only $87,500 ($50,000 stepped-up basis from her husband plus 75% of original $50,000 basis).

▾ ♀**PLANNING POINTERS:** This is one of those rare times
▾ where keeping exact records can hurt instead of help. As you can see
▾

from the second example, keeping careful purchase records generates a tax of $24,500, while the lack of records means a tax of only $2,000 on the same sales proceeds. It is extremely important to note that taxpayers are not required to keep records showing which spouse contributed what to the acquisition cost. Only when such records are available must the surviving spouse suffer a larger tax bite.

You should amend a previous year's income tax return if you have sold assets acquired prior to 1977, if you purchased the assets in conjunction with a spouse who has since died, and if you did not take advantage of this favorable court ruling in figuring your taxable gain. You can do this if the asset was sold within the last three years. Use IRS Form 1040X and send it by certified mail.

If you and your spouse are both still living but you wish to plan ahead, you should do the following. Identify jointly held assets acquired prior to 1977 and plan for the full value (or whatever contributory value) to be included in the estate of the first to die. That way, the surviving spouse will have the largest stepped-up basis possible.

☑ CHECKLIST:

- If you are a surviving spouse, review your assets to see whether any were acquired prior to 1977 in conjunction with a since-deceased spouse. Correct the tax basis of each asset to reflect the full stepped-up basis (or contributory basis) of each as of the date of death of the spouse. You could be eligible to use a fully stepped-up basis to reduce the tax bite that comes with selling the asset.
- If you are a surviving spouse and have sold an asset within the last three years, and if that asset was acquired prior to 1977 jointly with a since-deceased spouse (and if no records are available to show contributory basis), recalculate your tax basis to include a fully stepped-up basis and file an amended 1040X for a refund from the IRS.
- If both you and your spouse are still living and you jointly own assets acquired prior to 1977, plan for the best future income tax benefit for the surviving spouse. Don't let the IRS take more than what the law allows.

53 Defer Capital Gains Taxes on Property Sold to Children

$ This break is for taxpayers who have taken back an installment note, deferring capital gains income tax.

$ Forgiving the installment note in your will triggers immediate income tax on the entire deferred capital gain.

$ Instead of forgiving the installment note, leave the installment note to another beneficiary and continue the tax deferral.

It often happens that a parent sells a property to a child and takes back a note on the sale. If you are involved in such a transaction, you should think twice before including a provision in your will that forgives any balance due on the note at the time of your death.

If you forgive the note, the remaining balance of any deferred, untaxed capital gain will have to be included in full on your final income tax return. And this could mean that a large amount of your estate's available cash will have to be used to pay the income tax due on what was a previously untaxed capital gain. Instead, consider leaving the note to another beneficiary so that the deferral of the tax on the capital gain can continue.

☞**EXAMPLE:** Mr. Smith is a widower with two sons, John and Robert. Five years ago Mr. Smith sold a number of acres of undeveloped raw land to his son John for $75,000. Mr. Smith had bought the land several years before for $25,000, and although he would have liked to gift the land outright to his son, his limited income made it impossible for him to do so.

Although his income was limited, Mr. Smith did not need full payment at the time of the sale. Instead, he was able to offer cash terms favorable enough that his son could buy the property without having to make a down payment. The life of the note was set at 20 years with a 7.5% interest rate.

Per these terms, Mr. Smith was to receive a $604 payment (consisting partly of interest and partly of principal) each month from his son for 20 years.

The tax breakdown of each payment is as follows. The interest portion of the note payments is currently taxable to Mr. Smith. The principal portion of the note payment consists of two parts—the return of Mr. Smith's initial investment in the property (his tax basis), which is tax free, and the capital gain portion (his profit), which is taxed as he receives it.

What portion of the principal payment is capital gain to Mr. Smith? His profit from the sale was $50,000 ($75,000 sales price less $25,000 purchase price). So for every dollar of principal he receives as part of the note payment, two-thirds of the payment ($50,000 divided by $75,000) is taxable capital gain. The other one-third of the principal portion of the payment ($25,000 divided by $75,000) is a nontaxable return of his original investment in the property.

Let's say Mr. Smith receives payments for five years before he passes away. For the five-year period, the principal portion of the payments comes to $9,824. Of this, the taxable capital gain portion is $6,549. This means that as of Mr. Smith's date of death, there is still $43,451 ($50,000 less $6,549) in untaxed capital gains.

If Mr. Smith provides in his will for the forgiveness of the note, the entire remaining capital gain balance of $43,451 must be included on his final income tax return and taxed in full. Even with the favorable new maximum capital gains tax rate of 20%, this would mean an immediate income tax due of $8,690 ($43,451 times 20%).

On the other hand, if Mr. Smith leaves the note to another beneficiary—say, his other son, Robert—the remaining capital gain would continue to be tax deferred. Robert would pay capital gains as he receives the note payments from his brother, John, over the remaining 15 years of the life of the note. Under the new capital gains tax rates, Robert would also enjoy a maximum 20% rate, but he would have the further benefit of spreading the payment of the tax over a 15-year period.

Instead of forgiving the note, Mr. Smith could leave cash or other assets, which John could use to pay the note. Ultimately, the results are the same. Robert will receive the cash and John will have the property free and clear after the note is paid off with the cash he has been left by his father. The difference is that the tax on the $43,451 in capital gains is paid over 15 years instead of at the time of Mr. Smith's final income tax return.

♀ PLANNING POINTERS: This income tax deferral strategy is not limited to use by family members only. If your will provides for the forgiveness of any debt with a previously untaxed capital gain, you should consider amending your will and leaving the balance of the unsatisfied note to another beneficiary.

If you do leave the note to another beneficiary, that beneficiary should be aware that he or she is subject to the same rules that applied to you. If all or even a portion of the debt is forgiven, the taxable gain on the forgiven debt is immediately triggered and the beneficiary will owe any income tax that is due. To preserve the tax deferral, your beneficiary will have to continue to collect on the note per the terms of the note.

☑ CHECKLIST:
- To continue the capital gains tax deferral built in to note payments due to you, do not provide for the forgiveness of the note in your will.
- Leave the note to another beneficiary. Instruct the other beneficiary that the tax deferral can continue over the life of the note as long as the beneficiary does not forgive all or a portion of the debt.

Business
Tax Angles for
Any Business

▼
▼
▼

54 Amend Business Auto Use for Hindsight Tax Savings

> $ This loophole is for employees and self-employed individuals who use a car for business.
> $ To benefit, you must have placed the car in business service in the last three years.
> $ Switch from actual method with accelerated depreciation to standard mileage rate method.
> $ Use hindsight to take bigger auto deductions.

A little-known strategy for reducing your tax burden involves changing your method for writing off the business use of your car. It doesn't matter whether you are an employee or self-employed. While you can generally choose between two methods—the standard method using Modified Accelerated Cost Recovery System (MACRS) accelerated depreciation or the "standard mileage rate method"—that choice need not be final. If you have previously used MACRS but have not depreciated your car using MACRS more than three years prior to the current tax year, you can switch to the standard mileage method. If you have used your car for business purposes for less than four years, this change of method could root out hidden tax savings.

Here's how it's done. If you have used the actual auto deduction method for less than four years, you should compare your original tax savings with what you could have saved by using the standard mileage rate instead. The standard mileage rate method involves multiplying the number of business miles you drive by an IRS mileage rate (which changes from year to year). For 1997, the standard mileage rate for business miles driven is 31.5¢ per mile.

If hindsight proves valuable for you, and you find that a larger business-use deduction is available with the standard mileage rate, you can amend the previous years' tax returns and recalculate auto use mileage by means of the standard rate method rather than the actual auto use method. By filing the required amended forms, you can then use the standard mileage rate method for the current and future tax years.

BE CAREFUL. Sometimes, use of the standard mileage rate for previous years generates a tax liability—not a refund. Even so, it might still result in a higher tax savings for the current and future tax years. Here, you must measure whether more will be saved overall in the current and future years by switching to the standard mileage rate method. Saving money through such a tactic would mean that you would have to amend the applicable previous years' returns and pay any tax liability due, plus interest. You can't have it both ways. To use the standard mileage rate method for some years, you must use it for all years.

Watch the clock! If you used MACRS depreciation as part of your auto deduction for a "closed year" (i.e., a year that cannot be amended because too much time has passed), you will not be able to make the switch from the actual mileage method to the standard mileage rate for any years. If you still have time to make the switch, you should keep an eye on the clock so that any amended returns for previous years can be filed on time.

☞**EXAMPLE 1:** Ms. Smith began using her car for business purposes in 1995. She deducted car expenses of $5,000 for 1995 and $5,000 for 1996 using the actual method with accelerated depreciation. In 1997 her auto business use doubled, and she expects this increased business use to continue for as long as she owns her present car. Using the actual method, she would be able to deduct only approximately $7,000 per year for 1997 and future years. But with the standard mileage rate, she would be able to deduct $9,000 per year for 1997 and future years.

To take advantage of the increased write-offs for 1997 and future years, Ms. Smith will have to amend her tax returns for 1995 and 1996 and replace the original actual method deductions with standard mileage rate deductions. Since 1995 is an "open" year, she is able to do this.

Unfortunately, Ms. Smith's standard mileage rate deductions for

1995 and 1996 amount to $4,000 for each year. She must pay the extra tax, plus interest on the lost $1,000 auto deduction ($5,000 less $4,000) for 1995 and 1996. This is the price for reaping $2,000 more in auto deductions ($9,000 less $7,000) in 1997 and future years.

☞**EXAMPLE 2:** Mr. Jones began using his car for business purposes in 1992, using the actual method with accelerated depreciation. Since 1992 is a "closed" year, he is unable to amend all the years for which he has used accelerated depreciation. He may not switch to the standard mileage rate method for any of the previous, current, or future tax years.

💡**PLANNING POINTERS:** When you are comparing the actual use method with the standard mileage rate method, you combine all auto-related costs such as gas, insurance, repairs, and so on with the MACRS depreciation taken and then compare the total with the standard mileage rate total. Any first-year equipment expense deduction taken under IRS Section 179 must also be included in determining the actual method tax deduction for the year.

When you are using the standard mileage rate method, be careful to use the proper standard mileage rate for the tax year in question. Tolls and parking costs can also be deducted separately, and self-employed individuals can deduct the business-use portion of any auto interest paid when using the standard mileage rate method. The standard mileage rates for 1994 through 1997 are, respectively, 29¢ per mile, 30¢ per mile, 31¢ per mile, and 31.5¢ per mile.

☑ **CHECKLIST:**
- Verify that you have not taken a MACRS depreciation deduction or a first-year business equipment expense deduction for the car you are now driving in a "closed" tax year.
- If all applicable tax years are still "open," calculate the auto-use deduction using the standard mileage rate.
- If you benefit by using the standard mileage rate instead of the

actual method, amend the previous years' tax returns with IRS Form 1040X and begin to use the standard mileage rate method currently.

55 Minimize or Avoid Tax Liability When Selling a Business-Use Car

$ This tip is for taxpayers who use one car at least partly for business purposes and have another car that is used only for personal purposes.

$ It involves a method for avoiding current tax on the sale of an old business-use car.

$ You can avoid reduced depreciation on a new business-use car.

$ Don't "rotate" or trade in your old business-use car if there is a tax loss.

If you use your car for both deductible business purposes and personal use, selling the car or trading it in for another car can have expensive tax consequences. If your family is a two-car family, the best bet is to establish a car rotation schedule. By doing this, you can minimize or avoid the potential negatives of selling a business car.

Following a car rotation schedule, when you are ready to buy another business-use car, you convert your old business-use car to personal use and keep it as your second family car. Do this rather than selling it or trading it in on the new car.

Why avoid selling or trading in your old business-use car? If you sell a car previously used for business purposes, to figure your taxable gain you must reduce your tax basis in the car by any allowable depreciation or depreciation actually taken. Because depreciation must be "recaptured" in this fashion, even though your old business-use car has dropped in value, you may still have a gain. This could mean a surprise tax liability.

On the other hand, if you trade in a business-use car for a car that will also be used for business, you must reduce the tax basis in your new car by any gain on the old car. Unlike selling your old car, a trade-in avoids any current tax; however, it reduces your depreciation basis on the new car.

Using the standard mileage rate method doesn't help either. Part of the allowable annual standard mileage rate is considered to be depreciation. So when you sell or trade in a car on which you have used the standard mileage rate, a portion of the standard mileage rate deduction, taken while you owned the car, reduces your tax basis for determining your gain. This is true whether the gain is currently taxed in a sale or "rolled over" with a trade-in. By rotating the use of your car, you can avoid the current taxes on its sale and can also avoid the reduction of its depreciation basis that results from its trade-in.

EXAMPLE: The Smith family owns two cars. Mrs. Smith uses one of the cars part-time for business purposes in her self-employed business. The other car is used strictly for personal purposes.

The business-use car was originally purchased for $14,000, but, because of heavy business use, it has been depreciated $12,000. Consequently, the car has a $2,000 tax basis for determining gain.

If Mrs. Smith sells the car outright for $6,000 and then uses the proceeds to purchase another vehicle, she will have a currently taxable gain of $4,000 ($6,000 sale proceeds less $2,000 tax basis).

On the other hand, if she trades the car in for another car and is allowed the same $6,000 on the trade-in, she will not have a currently taxable gain, but she will have to roll over the gain into the depreciable basis of her new car. If her new car costs $18,000, the $4,000 rolled over gain will reduce the depreciable basis on the new car to $14,000. Because of the rolled-over gain, she will be forced to limit the depreciation of the new car to $14,000.

So instead of selling or trading in the old business-use car, Mrs. Smith rotates the car (converts it to 100% personal use). She trades in the old 100% personal-use car for a new car that she will then use as her business car. She then lets her family take the old business-use car as their new personal-use car. By doing this, the trade-in value of the old personal-use car will not reduce the depreciable basis of the new business-use car. This is because no depreciation was taken on the old personal-use car.

By rotating the old business-use car and trading in the old personal-use car, Mrs. Smith will be able to depreciate the full $18,000 cost of the new business-use vehicle.

♀ PLANNING POINTERS: Rotating your business-use car (converting it to 100% personal use instead of disposing of it) is a good idea when the tax basis of the business-use car has been reduced by depreciation to the point where a taxable gain will be generated upon the car's disposition.

On the other hand, if selling a business-use car will generate a tax loss, then you should neither trade in nor rotate it. In a situation where a tax loss will occur, sell the business-use car, recognize the tax loss, and then use the proceeds from the sale to help pay for a new business-use car.

☑ CHECKLIST:

- If you are considering disposing of a car used for business purposes, determine whether a gain or loss will occur on the disposition. Remember to reduce your tax basis for any depreciation taken.
- If a gain will occur, avoid selling or trading in the old car. Instead, rotate the car (convert it to 100% personal use and continue to use it for personal purposes). Sell or trade in your family's other car (one used for personal purposes that will not generate a taxable gain upon disposition) to help with the purchase price of the new business-use car.
- If a loss will occur, don't rotate or trade in the old business-use car. Instead, sell it, recognize a tax loss, and use the sales proceeds to help with the purchase price of the new business-use car.

56 Escape Restrictive "Luxury Vehicle" Depreciation Deduction Limitations

> $ Sports utility vehicles that weigh more than 6,000 pounds are not subject to the restrictive "luxury vehicle" depreciation deduction limitations.
>
> $ With a qualifying sports utility vehicle, you can take bigger up-front depreciation deductions for bigger tax savings.
>
> $ This can make a sports utility vehicle used for business purposes more cash affordable.

Is a sports utility vehicle out of your price range? If you use your car for business purposes, a sports utility vehicle may be a lot less expensive than you think. Since the accelerated depreciation available for a sports utility vehicle is not available for other smaller vehicles, the extra money you save in taxes could more than offset the big-ticket expense of a sports utility vehicle.

The so-called luxury vehicle rules that severely limit depreciation deductions for most automobiles do not apply to sports utility vehicles that weigh more than 6,000 pounds. If 100% of your use of the vehicle is for business, you can write off its entire cost within six years. And even if you use the vehicle less than 100% for business purposes, you can still get much bigger write-offs than you can with a lighter "luxury" vehicle.

☞**EXAMPLE:** Mr. Smith has wanted to purchase a sports utility vehicle (weighing more than 6,000 pounds), but the price tag of $40,000 is just too much. It looks like he may have to settle for a sedan costing $25,000.

But Mr. Smith is also aware that the sports utility vehicle can be written off much more quickly than the sedan (which is subject to the "luxury vehicle" rules). So he does the math to see what the difference in depreciation will save.

About 65% of his use of the vehicle is for business, and he expects to continue using it that way for some years to come. He is in the 31% federal income tax bracket and 5% state income tax bracket, so every dollar of depreciation will save him 36¢ on the dollar.

With the sedan, using the 1997 luxury vehicle depreciation tables and assuming 65% business usage, he will have depreciation deductions of $2,054 (year 1), $3,250 (year 2), $1,983 (year 3), and $1,154 (years 4–6). His total depreciation deductions for the first six years will total $10,749. So his income tax savings generated by the depreciation deductions for the first six years will be approximately $3,870 ($10,749 times 36%). He doesn't plan to own the vehicle longer than six years, so this is approximately the total tax savings he will receive. In effect, the real cost of the sedan is $21,130 (the $25,000 price less $3,870 income tax savings).

On the other hand, he can depreciate the sports utility vehicle much more quickly and thereby receive a larger tax savings. For the same six-year period, using the five-year MACRS depreciation tables and assuming the same 65% business usage, he would have depreciation deductions of $5,200 (year 1), $8,320 (year 2), $4,992 (year 3), $2,995 (year 4), $2,995 (year 5), and $1,498 (year 6). His total depreciation deductions for the same six-year period would be $26,000. And his income tax savings generated by the depreciation deductions for the six-year period would be $9,360 ($26,000 times 36%). So the real cost of the sports utility vehicle would be $30,640 ($40,000 price less $9,360 income tax savings).

Now the after-depreciation cost of the sports utility vehicle at $30,640 is still quite a bit more than the after-depreciation cost of the sedan at $21,130, but the difference in price has been narrowed quite a bit. The cost of the sports utility vehicle at $30,640 is a lot more affordable than $40,000. And since the "reduced" price is quite a bit closer to Mr. Smith's price range, he decides to purchase the sports utility vehicle. Besides, he can always use the vehicle more than 65% for business and increase his tax savings even more.

♀**PLANNING POINTERS:** Sports utility vehicles that fall into the appropriate weight category (more than 6,000 pounds) include the

GMC Yukon, the Toyota Land Cruiser, the Chevrolet Suburban, and the Mitsubishi Montero.

The weight distinction is critical for taking the accelerated depreciation deductions, so be certain to double-check the weight specifications before making the purchase.

☑ CHECKLIST:

- Project the tax savings generated with the accelerated depreciation available to sports utility vehicles of more than 6,000 pounds. Use the five-year MACRS depreciation tables (accelerated depreciation tables) applied to the business-use portion of the cost of the vehicle.
- Compare this with savings that would be generated purchasing a vehicle subject to the "luxury vehicle" rules. Use the "luxury vehicle" depreciation limitations for the year the vehicle would be placed in service, and project the available depreciation deductions and tax savings. These luxury vehicle depreciation limitations are provided on a year-to-year basis by the IRS.
- If you are self-employed, don't forget to include any self-employment tax savings (Social Security and Medicare tax) in your projections. These tax savings would also result from increased depreciation deductions.

57 Time Your Business Equipment Purchases for the Largest First-Year Depreciation Deduction

$ Large first-year depreciation deductions require proper timing.

$ Use rules of thumb for timing equipment purchases.

$ Large first-year depreciation deductions mean larger first-year tax savings.

Timing is everything when it comes to buying equipment for your business. If you plan the timing of an equipment purchase properly, you can increase the depreciation write-off in the first year and reduce your taxes right away. If possible, you should purchase business equipment and put it into service with the following priorities:

- If your total business equipment purchases for 1997 will be less than $18,000, it does not really matter what time of the year you place it in service. As long as the equipment you place in service does not cost more than $200,000, you will be able to deduct the entire cost under the equipment expensing rules.

- If your total business equipment purchases for 1997 will be more than $18,000, the largest depreciation deduction for the year will be generated if you place 59% of the business equipment in service during the first two quarters of the year and 41% of the business equipment in service in the fourth quarter of the year.

  Obviously, it will be difficult to place equipment in service in exactly this 59/41 ratio. But the closer you can get to it, the larger the deduction will be. More than 40% of the equipment must be placed in service in the fourth quarter. To generate the ideal depreciation deduction, you must place the first 59% of the equipment in service as soon as possible during the first two quarters of the year, preferably during the first quarter of the year.

- If your total business equipment purchases for 1997 will be more than $18,000, the second-largest depreciation deduction will be generated for the year if you place more than 60% of the business equipment in service during the first three quarters of the year.

- If your total business equipment purchases for 1997 will be more than $18,000, the smallest depreciation deduction will be generated for the year if you place up to 59% of the business equipment in service during the third quarter of the year and more than 40% of the business equipment in service in the fourth quarter of the year. The more equipment placed in service in the fourth quarter, the smaller the depreciation deduction will be.

☞EXAMPLE 1: Smith Company places $30,000 of seven-year business equipment into service during the year. Of this $30,000, $17,500 (58%) is placed in service during the first quarter and $12,500 (42%) is placed in service during the fourth quarter.

Smith Company elects to expense the $12,500 placed in service in the fourth quarter and $5,500 of the equipment placed in service in the first quarter. This gives the company its allowable $18,000 ($12,500 plus $5,500) equipment expense deduction for 1997. The balance of the equipment placed in service during the first quarter, $12,000, is depreciated at 25% for a seven-year MACRS depreciation deduction of $3,000.

Of the $30,000 placed in service, Smith Company has a first-year tax deduction of $21,000 ($18,000 equipment expense plus $3,000 MACRS depreciation deduction).

☞EXAMPLE 2: Smith Company places $30,000 of seven-year business equipment into service during the year. Of this $30,000, $19,500 (65%) is placed in service at various times during the first three quarters of the year and $10,500 (35%) is placed in service during the fourth quarter.

Smith Company elects to expense $18,000 under the equipment expensing rules (expensing the $10,500 in equipment placed in service in the fourth quarter and $7,500 of the equipment placed in service during the first three quarters of the year). The balance of the equipment placed in service during the first three quarters of the year, $12,000, is depreciated at 14.29% for a seven-year MACRS depreciation deduction of $1,715.

Of the $30,000 placed in service, Smith Company has a first-year tax deduction of $19,715 ($18,000 equipment expense plus $1,715 MACRS depreciation deduction).

☞EXAMPLE 3: Smith Company places $30,000 of seven-year business equipment into service during the year. All the equipment is placed in service in the fourth quarter (more than 40% in the fourth quarter).

Smith Company elects to expense $18,000 under the equipment expensing rules. The balance of the equipment placed in service during the year, $12,000, is depreciated at 3.57% for a seven-year MACRS depreciation deduction of $428.

Of the $30,000 placed in service, Smith Company has a first-year tax deduction of $18,428 ($18,000 equipment expense plus $428 MACRS depreciation deduction).

Depending on when Smith Company places into service the same $30,000 of business equipment, it could have a first-year depreciation deduction for 1997 of $21,000, $19,715, or $18,428. Between the best first-year depreciation deduction and the worst, there is a $2,572 difference ($21,000 less $18,428). If Smith Company is in the 25% corporate federal income tax bracket, this difference in depreciation equals $643 in federal income tax either saved or spent.

💡 **PLANNING POINTERS:** From the examples, it is clear that the timing of placing business equipment in service is crucial. When too much equipment is placed in service in the fourth quarter of the year, depreciation deductions will not be as large as possible.

When electing which equipment to expense under the equipment expensing rules, elect fourth-quarter purchases first. This will allow for larger MACRS depreciation deductions for the equipment placed in service earlier in the year.

Under the 1996 tax law, you can expense up to $18,000 in business equipment for 1997, $18,500 for 1998, $19,000 for 1999, $20,000 for 2000, $24,000 for 2001 and 2002, and $25,000 for the year 2003 and following years.

☑ **CHECKLIST:**

- Plan the timing of equipment purchases as far ahead of the purchase as possible.
- Before the end of the third quarter, determine the total equipment purchases to date. If it looks like more than 40% of the total equipment purchases for the year will be made in the fourth quarter, accelerate enough of these fourth-quarter equipment purchases into the third quarter and avoid the "more than 40%" rule.

58 Catch Up on All Your Lost Depreciation Without Amending Previous Years' Tax Returns

$ A new IRS method allows you to catch up on depreciation deductions that you have not previously taken.

$ The procedure allows you to take the entire deduction in the current year; no need to file amended tax returns.

$ The method must be elected in the first half of the tax year in which the catch-up deduction will be taken.

$ This method benefits anyone who is allowed to take depreciation deductions.

The IRS has recently okayed a depreciation tax deduction that is easy to take advantage of and provides tax savings that were not previously available. With this new procedure, you can deduct depreciation in a current tax year that you failed to deduct in past years—even "closed" tax years (usually, tax years more than three years prior that you can no longer amend for a corrected tax refund).

Prior to this recent change, if you failed to take an allowable depreciation deduction, you could go back and amend your tax returns only for the three previous years. So if you failed to take a depreciation deduction in each of the last five years, you were out of luck—the tax deduction for the fourth and fifth year back were lost.

Actually, by not taking depreciation you lose more than a deduction. This is because depreciation is treated differently for tax purposes than other deductions. After you take a depreciation deduction, you don't just forget about it and move on. When you sell a depreciable asset, you must reduce your tax basis in the asset by any depreciation deducted (or that could have been deducted) when you figure your taxable gain on the sale. So if you fail to take an allowable depreciation deduction, you are taxed twice! First, you have paid an unnecessary tax because you failed to take the original allowable depreciation deduction. And second, you have paid a larger tax on the gain from the sale of the asset because the gain is calculated as if you had taken the deduction.

Under the new IRS method, you can go back as many years as you want, add up all the depreciation you have failed to take on depreciable assets you own, and deduct them in the current year. You still have to reduce your tax basis for depreciation taken when you sell (or otherwise dispose of your assets in a taxable transaction), but at least you're getting the benefit of the deduction and avoiding double taxes.

☞**EXAMPLE:** Eight years ago, Ms. Smith purchased a warehouse and rented it out. She paid $100,000 for the property—$25,000 of the purchase price was for the land (not depreciable), and $75,000 of the purchase price was for the warehouse itself (depreciable). At the time, commercial property could be depreciated over a 31.5-year period using straight-line depreciation. Given this scenario, Ms. Smith could take an annual depreciation deduction of $2,381 ($75,000 divided by 31.5) on her Form 1040 Schedule E.

Unfortunately, Ms. Smith was under the mistaken impression that if she didn't take the depreciation deduction for the property she wouldn't have to "recapture" the depreciation when she sold the property (reduce her tax basis by the depreciation taken).

Under the old rules, once Ms. Smith realized her mistake, she would be limited to amending only the three previous years by filing a 1040X for each of the three years. She would then take a depreciation deduction for the current year and any future years she held the asset, but she would not be able to take the deduction for any of the "closed" years. In this case, she would lose the first four years' depreciation deductions, a total of $9,524 ($2,381 times 4). And even though she would not have the benefit of these deductions, she would still have to reduce her tax basis by the entire amount of that allowable depreciation to figure the taxable gain on the property's sale. Consequently, she would be paying taxes twice on the $9,524.

But with the new rules, Ms. Smith no longer loses the first four years' depreciation, and she no longer has to file a separate 1040X for each of the three previous open years. Instead, she takes a deduction in the current year for the entire eight-year period. She catches up to the current year with a $19,048 ($2,381 times 8) depreciation deduction. If she sells the warehouse next year, she will still have to reduce her basis by the depreciation taken to figure the taxable gain on the sale, but at least she will have a deduction for what she must later include in taxable income.

$\heartsuit$**PLANNING POINTERS:** To take advantage of this catch-up depreciation deduction, you must file IRS Form 3115 with the IRS on or before the 180th day after the beginning of the tax year in which the deduction will be taken. For taxpayers using the calendar year (most taxpayers), this means that it is too late to take the deduction for 1997. If you want to take the deduction for tax year 1998, file Form 3115 before June 30, 1998.

This is a deduction you have to plan for at the beginning of the year—it cannot be taken at year-end. A copy of the timely filed IRS Form 3115 must be attached to the income tax return for the year you are taking the deduction.

Don't be intimidated if Form 3115 seems a little complicated. You do not have to fill out the entire form. Only a few sections of the form need to be filled out to receive the deduction. For directions on how to fill out the form, contact the Freedom of Information Reading Room at IRS National Headquarters in Washington, D.C., and request a copy of IRS Revenue Procedure 96-31. The procedure is straightforward and tells you which lines on Form 3115 need to be completed.

The new method applies to most, but not all, types of depreciation. For example, you cannot use the new method to change from expensing the cost of business equipment to depreciating that equipment. There are only a few exceptions, and they do not apply to the more common depreciation situations. Still, you should double-check the short list of exceptions in Revenue Procedure 96-31 before filing with the IRS for the deduction.

IMPORTANT TAX SAVINGS STRATEGY: If you expect to be in a higher income tax bracket in future years, you may want to hold off on taking the catch-up deduction. This is because the deduction will save more in income taxes if you are in a higher tax bracket. If you are self-employed, when projecting which tax year is likely to give you the largest deductible benefit, do not forget to factor in any self-employment tax savings.

✓ CHECKLIST:

- During the first six months of your tax year, determine whether you have failed to take allowable depreciation deductions in any previous years on assets you own.
- Project the tax savings you could generate in the current tax year by deducting the previously undeducted depreciation. Compare this with possible tax savings in future years.
- If you can save more in the current year, or if you just want to take the catch-up deduction in the current year, timely file Form 3115 with the IRS. Use certified mail for proof of timely mailing.
- Take the catch-up deduction on your income tax return for the year. Attach a copy of Form 3115 to your return.

59 Negotiate Bigger Write-Offs with Your Landlord

$ Your landlord pays for leasehold improvements at your place of business.

$ You pay increased rent to cover the costs of the improvements.

$ Deduct accelerated rent expense instead of deducting the leasehold improvements over 39 years.

$ The landlord is "reimbursed" for the improvements in the form of rent payments and also enjoys an annual depreciation deduction.

Instead of paying for leasehold improvements at your place of business, ask your landlord to pay for them. In return, offer to pay your landlord more in rent over the term of the lease. By financing your leasehold improvements this way, both you and your landlord can save money in taxes.

Ordinarily, you must deduct the cost of leasehold improvements made to your place of business in an even fashion, straight-line, over a 39-year period. If in the year your lease term ends you move to another location, you can then deduct the portion of the improvement cost that you have not previously deducted. Unfortunately, this normal scenario won't save you tax in the earlier years of the lease.

However, if your landlord pays for the improvements, not only will you save tax early in the lease but your landlord will benefit as well. True, your landlord will have put up the initial cash for the improvements, but that is an expense that you'll cover through increased rent payments. At the same time, your landlord will gain depreciation deductions for the cost of the leasehold improvements. When you leave, your landlord will still have the improved property to offer to a new tenant.

EXAMPLE: Mr. Smith wants to break up a larger office space into smaller offices by putting up permanent walls. He rents the space with a lease that will run for nine more years. He has talked to a contractor who estimates the job will cost $7,500.

If Mr. Smith pays for the improvements, he can deduct $192 each year ($7,500 divided by 39). So for the nine years left on the lease, he will have total tax deductions of $1,728. If he leaves the space after the lease has ended (if he does not renew and moves), he can deduct, in the year he moves, the balance of the previously undeducted leasehold improvements, $5,772 ($7,500 less $1,728).

On the other hand, Mr. Smith could negotiate with his landlord. In this scenario, his landlord will pay the $7,500 for the improvements and Mr. Smith will pay an extra $2,500 per year in rent over the next three years. Mr. Smith will receive an accelerated deduction for the rent paid instead of deducting the cost over a longer period of time in the form of depreciation for the leasehold improvements.

Mr. Smith's landlord will have to spend the $7,500 up front but will recoup it within three years by means of the increased rent income. And since the landlord will have paid for the leasehold improvements, the landlord will be able to deduct the $7,500 over 39 years. Thus, a $192 annual tax deduction is extra "compensation" his landlord will receive for paying for the leasehold improvements.

𝒫PLANNING POINTERS: If you're the tenant, the disposition of the leasehold improvements at the end of the lease term will be the same no matter how you handle it. Since the improvements stay with the property either way, you will not lose anything if the landlord pays for the improvements.

If you are the landlord and you abandon the leasehold improvements at the end of the lease (maybe you tear the walls down for a new tenant), the new tax law provides you with beneficial tax treatment. If you abandon or dispose of improvements after June 12, 1996, you can deduct the cost of the improvements not previously deducted. You take this deduction in the year of abandonment or other disposition.

☑ CHECKLIST:

- If you are a tenant, do not pay for leasehold improvements.
- Have your landlord pay for the improvements and agree to pay an increased rent over a short period of time to reimburse the landlord for the expenditure.
- Take an increased deduction for rent paid while your landlord collects the increased rent and depreciates the cost of the improvements.

60 Buying a Business? Change Goodwill to Lease Value and Take Faster Tax Deductions

$ Accelerate the write-off period for a portion of the business purchase price.

$ Recharacterize a portion of "goodwill" as the "cost of acquiring a lease."

$ This tip is beneficial in areas where rents are increasing.

$ It is also beneficial when the remaining term of the lease is less than 15 years.

The game plan for using the tax write-offs that come with the purchase of a business changed in 1993. Now there are more tax deductions available, but the price is a longer, 15-year write-off period for the deductions that were previously available. But one item that still offers the potential for quicker deductibility is the value of a lease you acquire in purchasing a new business, when the lease period is less than 15 years.

Of course, depreciable assets, such as plant machinery and equipment, purchased as part of the transaction can still be depreciated more quickly. But you have to be careful not to overvalue these depreciable assets in an attempt to deduct a larger portion of the business purchase price in less than 15 years. The IRS is quick to disallow this type of overvaluation and is likely to reallocate it to the longer-life goodwill.

Under the new rules, the value allocated in the business purchase contract to goodwill, covenants not to compete, trade names, and other intangible items must now be amortized and deducted evenly over a 15-year period. The strategy is not to count the value of a lease as a part of goodwill. Although the rules have changed, lease value can still be deducted evenly over the term of the lease. If the term of the lease is less than 15 years, you'll be able to deduct its value in a shorter period of time than if you characterize it as goodwill.

The lease value you can deduct is the difference between the fair market rent value (for the use of the property over the term of the lease) and the value of the rent (reasonably expected to be paid for the use of the property for the term of the lease).

☞ **EXAMPLE:** Ms. Smith is purchasing a business. Part of the purchase agreement stipulates that Ms. Smith will become the new lessee of the building housing the business. The term of the lease already in place is five years, with an option to renew for another five years. Three years of the initial lease term have passed as of the business purchase date, leaving two years plus an option for five more.

Ms. Smith will pay a fixed rent of $900 per month for the remaining two years and can renew the lease for the optional five-year period with a monthly rent of $1,100. The amount of rent reasonably expected to be paid is therefore $87,600 ($900 per month for two years and $1,100 per month for five years).

Ms. Smith calls realty agents in the area and ascertains that the going rental rate for comparable properties is currently $1,200 per month. Thus, the fair market rent value for the property over the term of the lease is $100,800 ($1,200 per month for seven years).

The difference between the actual rent and the fair market value of the rent is $13,200 ($100,800 less $87,600). Ms. Smith can allocate this amount in the business purchase contract to the "cost of acquiring an interest as a lessee." It is just a matter of diminishing goodwill by this amount.

By doing this, Ms. Smith will be able to deduct $1,886 per year for seven years ($13,200 divided by 7) instead of treating the amount as goodwill and deducting $880 per year for 15 years ($13,200 divided by 15).

💡 **PLANNING POINTERS:** Be careful to document the fair market rental value of comparable properties or to get an objective fair market rental value appraisal from a third-party professional appraiser. This will give you a firm basis for the accelerated tax deductions in case of IRS scrutiny.

This strategy will be of benefit in situations where rents increase over a period of time. If the fair market value of rents in your area has dropped since the original lease was established, you will not receive any benefit.

Also, if the term of the lease is longer than 15 years, using this strategy would be disadvantageous. You would receive quicker write-offs leaving the lease cost amount characterized as goodwill.

☑ CHECKLIST:

- Determine the actual rent for the remaining term of the lease (including options).
- Determine the fair market value of the rent for the remaining term of the lease. Check the fair market rental value for comparable properties, or have a professional appraisal done. Carefully document your findings.
- If the remaining term of the lease is less than 15 years, recharacterize a portion of the goodwill in the business purchase contract as the "cost of acquiring a lease." This will allow for faster deductions for the recharacterized portion.
- Make certain the "cost of acquiring a lease" is written into the final business purchase contract.

61 Deduct Home Entertainment Expenses

$ Direct or associated home entertainment business expenses are 50% deductible.
$ No receipt is necessary for home entertainment that costs you less than $75.

You may not be able to treat clients to meals at expensive restaurants or to offer them tickets to the opera, but you can and should deduct expenses for entertaining clients at home.

There are basically two kinds of entertainment expenses: direct entertainment expenses and associated entertainment expenses. If you entertain at home for the purpose of business, and if business takes place during the entertainment, then the cost of entertaining at your home is deductible as a direct entertainment expense. On the other hand, if the home entertainment occurs immediately before or after a business meeting, the cost of entertaining at your home is deductible as an associated entertainment expense.

☞**EXAMPLE 1:** Mr. Smith, a construction contractor, invites a potential client over for dinner to discuss a bid he has made to renovate the potential client's home. Mr. Smith barbecues some steaks and opens a bottle of wine. Over dinner, Mr. Smith and the potential client discuss the details of the bid and potential changes that may have to be made. The cost of the steaks and the bottle of wine are deductible as a direct business entertainment expense.

☞**EXAMPLE 2:** Mr. Smith, a construction contractor, has a late afternoon appointment with a potential client during which changes to a job bid are discussed. After the meeting, Mr. Smith invites the potential client over for barbecued steaks and a bottle of wine. The cost of the steaks and the bottle of wine are deductible as an associated business entertainment expense.

♀**PLANNING POINTERS:** If the cost of entertaining clients at your home is less than $75 and this cost is paid in cash, it is not necessary to have a receipt to document it. An entry to your daybook or other business diary noting the date of the entertainment, the name of the clients who were entertained, their business relationship to you, and the cost of the entertainment is considered sufficient proof. To be on the safe side, you may also want to note whether the entertainment qualifies as a direct or associated entertainment expense.

Under current tax law, business meals and entertainment expenses are 50% deductible. Even so, a deduction for half your home entertaining is better than none.

☑ **CHECKLIST:**

- When you entertain at home and the cost of the entertainment is less than $75, make certain to note the cost of the deductible business meal and entertainment items. Include this cost in your daybook or other business diary.

- Retain these supporting diary entries to properly complete your income tax return for the year.

- Self-employed individuals can deduct 50% of their home entertainment expenses on their Form 1040 Schedule C.

- Employees who are not reimbursed for home entertainment expenses by their employer deduct 50% of these expenses on Form 1040 Schedule A as a miscellaneous itemized deduction, subject to the "2% miscellaneous deduction limitations."

- If your employer reimburses you for your home entertainment expenses, your employer can deduct 50% of these expenses without you or your employer being subject to the "2% miscellaneous deduction limitations."

62 Deduct $25 Holiday Gifts Without a Receipt

$ Holiday gifts made to business associates count as deductible business gifts.

$ For deductible business gifts up to $25, receipts for cash payments are not required.

$ Self-employed individuals can deduct the allowable limit in full.

$ Employees not reimbursed by their employer are subject to a 2% miscellaneous deduction limitation.

When you prepare your income tax return, don't overlook the deductible benefit of holiday gifts. Whether you are a rank-and-file employee, a self-employed individual, or a shareholder-employee in your own corporation, you can deduct as a business expense the cost of gifts made to clients or other business associates. This holds true no matter what time of year you give the gift, even the year-end holiday season.

Your annual deductible business-gift costs are limited to a $25 value for each gift recipient, but you do not have to keep receipts for gifts purchased with cash.

A few years ago, the Tax Court allowed an independent salesperson to deduct gifts to buyers, even though the buyers' employers prohibited the acceptance of such gifts. The Tax Court felt the gifts were not bribes but were a legitimate business expense. And because the gifts were small (less than $25 each but more than $2,000 in total), the taxpayer was not required to document the cash expenses with receipts. Entries in the salesperson's daybook were acceptable proof.

EXAMPLE: Mr. Smith is a self-employed bookkeeper. During the year-end holiday season, he makes small gifts to several of his clients. In his appointment book, he jots down a description of each gift, how much it costs, and to whom he gives it. A few of the gifts exceed $25, but most are less than the annual $25 cap—like a bouquet of Christmas flowers, a bottle of wine, special blend coffee, a cheese plate. For the gifts exceeding $25, Mr. Smith is limited to deducting only $25. For the gifts costing less than $25, Mr. Smith can deduct the entire amount.

Altogether, the holiday gifts total $400, but because of the $25 per recipient limitation, Mr. Smith can deduct only $300. Even so, if he considers that for each dollar deducted he will save 28¢ in federal income tax, 5¢ in state income tax, and 15.3¢ in self-employment tax, the $300 in allowable business gift deductions will still save him $145 in taxes for the year.

PLANNING POINTERS: Self-employed taxpayers can deduct the allowable business gift deduction in full on Form 1040 Schedule C.

Employees who are not reimbursed by their employers for the cost of the gifts must treat the expense as an unreimbursed employee business expense—deductible as a miscellaneous expense on Form 1040 Schedule A but subject to the "2% miscellaneous limitation rules."

To avoid this 2% limitation, shareholder-employees of their own corporations should account to the corporation for their deductible business gift expenses and receive a reimbursement for the expense prior to year-end. By doing this, the corporation can deduct the expense in full and the shareholder-employee can avoid the 2% limitation.

☑ CHECKLIST:

- If you do not keep your receipts for business gifts you paid for with cash, be certain to keep a record in your daybook or other business diary. Note the gift recipient, their business relationship to you, a short description of the gift, and the cost of the gift.

63 Take an Increased Home Office Deduction If You Operate a Home-Based Sales Business

$ Relaxed home office rules make larger tax deduction available for salespersons who store inventory and product samples at home.

$ The home must be the only location of the business.

$ Salespersons can take full deduction for regular use.

$ Space does not have to be used exclusively for business purposes.

$ This tax break is effective beginning with the 1996 tax year.

If you are in the business of selling products—either retail or wholesale—and your home is the only location of your business, changes resulting from the 1996 tax law may offer you a way to increase your home office business deduction. Ordinarily, you can take a deduction for home business space used only "regularly and exclusively" for business purposes. But now, if you are involved in sales and use space at home to store inventory or product samples, the "exclusively" part of this requirement does not apply to you. Even if the space is used for other nonbusiness purposes during the tax year, you can take a business deduction, if you use it "regularly" for business storage during the year.

☞EXAMPLE: Mr. Smith is a self-employed salesperson who sells stereos and other electronic equipment at discount prices. He uses his garage to store his inventory and product samples. His home is his only place of business. During peak periods, his inventory takes up the entire garage space, and he parks his car outside. At other times during the year, he carries less inventory and is able to use the garage to park his car and as a place to work on household fix-up projects.

Even though he does not use the space exclusively for business, he does use it regularly during the year. Under the new tax law, he can deduct the use of the entire space as a business deduction—beginning with tax year 1996.

♀PLANNING POINTERS: The IRS may come after this one. It has a long history of trying to shoot down home office deductions. So make sure to document regular usage. You may want to keep a log with entries showing use at peak periods as well as use during down times. This log should be enough to establish regular use.

You are entitled to take all home office deductions for the space for the entire tax year. Make sure you don't shortchange yourself on depreciation, utilities, property insurance, mortgage interest, property taxes, repairs and maintenance, and so on. For self-employed persons, this deduction can save self-employment taxes (Social Security and Medicare) as well as income taxes.

If you failed to take this allowable increased deduction for 1996, amend your 1996 income tax return for a tax refund. Use IRS Form 1040X.

- Retain documentation of regular use of home business storage space.
- Take the deductible benefit of all allowable home business use expenses.

64 **Make Your Home Computer Tax Deductible**

$ This tax loophole is for employees who purchase a home computer and use it for work-related purposes.

$ A security policy at your place of work can justify a tax deduction for some or all of the cost of your home computer.

$ Plan carefully to avoid the other stumbling blocks of a home computer tax deduction.

A recent Tax Court ruling may give you a tax deduction for your home computer. The ruling allowed an employee to deduct the cost of a home computer because she was required to complete work using a computer but was denied access to a computer at her employer's place of business after regular office hours. For security reasons, only high-level managers were allowed in the office after regular office hours. Because of this security policy, the Tax Court decided that the employee's purchase of a home computer was a bona fide condition of employment and was made for the convenience of her employer.

If you are an employee, the most difficult requirement to meet before you can deduct a home computer as an employee business expense is the requirement that the computer be used for the convenience of your employer and as a condition of your employment. But how do you establish that this requirement has been met? A statement from your employer saying the requirement has been satisfied is not enough by itself. You must also be able to show how the requirement has "in fact" been satisfied.

As a result of the Tax Court ruling, if your employer limits your access to a computer at work (for security reasons) but still requires that the work be completed, then you can deduct the portion of the cost of your home computer that is allocable to business use.

To use this deduction, however, you must plan carefully with regard to other related employee business expense requirements and limitations.

☞**EXAMPLE:** Mr. Smith is employed by the Jones Company. For security reasons, the company allows only managers access to the office after normal work hours. The Jones Company also requires employees to purchase home computers as a condition of employment.

In November 1997, Mr. Smith purchases a home computer, printer, and modem for $3,000. For the rest of 1997, Mr. Smith uses the computer equipment for business purposes 80% of the time.

Because Mr. Smith uses the computer for business purposes more than 50% of the time in 1997, he is able to take a first-year equipment expense deduction of $2,400 ($3,000 times 80%).

If Mr. Smith's adjusted gross income for 1997 is $45,000, he is not allowed to deduct $900 (2% of adjusted gross income) of his miscellaneous itemized deductions (of which employee business expenses are a part). If Mr. Smith has no other miscellaneous deductions besides the deduction for his home computer, he will be able to deduct $1,500 ($2,400 less the $900 disallowance). If Mr. Smith is in the 28% federal income tax bracket, this means a federal income tax savings of $420.

♀**PLANNING POINTERS:** As is obvious from the example, the requirement that a home computer be purchased by an employee for the convenience of the employer and as a condition of employment is not the only stumbling block to enjoying federal income tax savings.

First, you must establish that the purchase is for the convenience of your employer and is a condition of your employment. Documenting that security precautions exist at work is one way to show that this requirement has been satisfied. But after you establish this fact, you must also be careful not to waste your tax deduction.

Be certain to use the computer for business-related purposes more than 50% of the time during the first year the computer is in service. This will allow you to take a first-year equipment expense deduction for the business usage of the computer. For 1997, you can deduct up to $18,000 for business equipment placed in service during the year.

If you do not use the computer more than 50% of the time during the first year, you will not be able to take an equipment expense deduction, and you will have to deduct the cost of the computer "straight line" over a six-year period. Using straight-line depreciation greatly reduces your annual deduction. And because of the so-called 2% limitation (see example), you may not benefit from the deduction at all. Why no tax benefit? Using straight-line depreciation reduces the available deduction, and then the 2% limitation cuts into the reduced deduction even further.

☑ CHECKLIST:

- Determine whether a home computer purchase can be characterized as being made for the convenience of your employer and as a condition of employment. If it is, have your employer give you a written statement to that effect—but remember, a statement from your employer is not enough by itself.
- Once you have placed the computer in service, keep track of business usage. Keep the first-year usage above 50% to be able to take the first-year equipment expensing tax deduction.
- Project your adjusted gross income for the year to calculate what amount of your miscellaneous itemized deductions (which include your employee business expenses) will be disallowed as a result of the 2% limitation rule.

  After you have applied the 2% limitation, if you still have deductible miscellaneous expenses (such as a portion of your computer expenses), you should incur other miscellaneous itemized deductions before year-end (e.g., prepaid tax-preparation costs, other employee business expenses, job-related education costs). This strategy—known as "deduction bunching"—allows you to enjoy a greater tax-deductible benefit this year because your combined miscellaneous itemized deductions to date (including the deductible computer purchase) have already exceeded the 2% limitation.

If you don't bunch, and you wait until next year to incur the expenses, next year's 2% limitation may keep you from enjoying any tax-saving benefit for those miscellaneous deductions.

Three
Payroll Tax
Savers for a
Small Business
Employer

▼
▼
▼

Employers: Don't Overpay Your FUTA Tax—Even If the IRS Asks for More

$ This tip is for taxpayers who receive an IRS notice for additional FUTA tax due.

$ Double-check before you pay—the real amount due may be much less than you think.

If you receive a bill from the IRS showing an increase in your federal unemployment tax (FUTA) for a certain year because you did not pay your state unemployment tax (SUTA) on time, take a few minutes to double-check the IRS numbers. There is a good chance the IRS is asking you for more than you really have to pay. If you follow a few steps, you can cut the IRS bill down to a small percentage of what it is asking.

If you have employees, you are required to pay FUTA and SUTA tax on a portion of your employee wages. The timely filing and payment of the state unemployment tax ultimately determines how much federal unemployment tax you have to pay. If you file and pay the SUTA tax on time, you benefit from a large tax credit that reduces the FUTA tax. If you don't pay the SUTA tax on time, you lose some of that credit.

The problem is that once the IRS is notified by your state unemployment tax office that you did not pay the SUTA tax on time, it assumes that none of the FUTA credit is available to you and bills you for the entire amount of the credit. But if you have since paid the SUTA tax in full, you can still use 90% of the FUTA credit. Even with a small payroll, this 90% credit can make a big difference.

☞**EXAMPLE:** Last year, Smith Company employed five people, each of whom earned more than $7,000. The FUTA tax due was 6.2%

of the first $7,000 in wages of each employee, but this FUTA tax was then reduced by the FUTA tax credit of 5.4%. Because of this credit, Smith Company was required to pay a FUTA tax of only .8% of the first $7,000 in wages of each employee.

Put another way, on the basic FUTA tax of $2,170 ($7,000 times 5 employees times 6.2%), Smith Company had a credit of $1,890 ($7,000 times 5 employees times 5.4%) that reduced its FUTA tax to $280.

Last year, Smith Company also paid its SUTA tax late. The IRS has been notified by the state unemployment tax office and has sent Smith Company a bill for the entire amount of the disallowed FUTA tax credit—$1,890!

Instead of paying this $1,890, Mr. Smith, the president of Smith Company, contacts the state unemployment tax office and requests a copy of Form 940-C for the year in question. The 940-C shows that Smith Company has paid the entire SUTA tax—even though the tax was paid late.

Using the 940-C as supporting documentation, Smith Company can save 90% of the original credit, or 4.86% (5.4% original credit times 90%), of the FUTA tax. Thus, on the original FUTA tax of $2,170, Smith Company has a credit of $1,701 ($7,000 times 5 employees times 4.86%). This credit reduces the total FUTA tax due to $469. Since Smith Company paid $280 when it filed the original FUTA tax return, it owes the IRS only an additional $189 ($469 less $280).

Instead of having to pay the $1,890 the IRS has requested, Smith Company has to pay only an additional $189—that's a savings of $1,701.

💡**PLANNING POINTERS:** If you receive an increased FUTA tax notice from the IRS, the first step is to review the original FUTA tax return you filed for the year—Form 940. If the IRS has assessed you for the full amount of the FUTA credit originally taken on the tax return, immediately contact your state unemployment tax office and request Form 940-C for the year in question.

Once you receive Form 940-C, you can send a letter to the IRS making a claim for 90% of the original credit. Using this 90% credit, you will still owe the IRS additional FUTA tax, but the amount you owe will be greatly reduced. Include Form 940-C with your letter to the IRS, and also include a check for any FUTA tax due (the amount due reduced by the 90% credit).

If you have received a FUTA assessment within the past few years and paid the full amount without the benefit of the 90% credit, you may still have time to recoup your overpayment. Generally, you have two years after the date you overpay to apply for a refund.

Dig out the paperwork from your files, request a 940-C from your state unemployment tax office for the year in question, and send a letter to the IRS office where you made the overpayment. Include calculations in your letter showing what the additional FUTA tax should be after you subtract the 90% credit, and then request a refund for any overpaid amount.

☑ CHECKLIST:

- If you receive an additional FUTA tax assessment, determine whether it is a result of a late payment of your SUTA tax for the same year.
- Request Form 940-C from your state unemployment tax office.
- Recalculate the additional FUTA tax due with the benefit of the 90% credit.
- Send a letter to the IRS office with Form 940-C enclosed, outlining what the correct additional FUTA tax should be with the benefit of the 90% credit. Include a check for payment of the reduced additional FUTA tax as you have calculated it.
- Don't forget to take into account any payments you made when you filed the original FUTA tax form (Form 940).

66 Cut Your Payroll Tax Cost by Providing Benefits Instead of Wages to Employees

$ This tip is for business employers.

$ Save payroll taxes when you pay employees with benefits.

$ Employees cannot have the choice between cash wages or benefits.

Many employers provide benefits to their employees on top of the wages they pay. The employer deducts the cost of the benefit and saves income tax, and the employee enjoys a benefit free of personal income tax. But if your business cannot afford to provide benefits on top of wages, you should consider providing benefits *instead* of wages. As long as your employees do not have the choice of benefits or cash wages, you can avoid payroll taxes (Social Security and Medicare) on the amount of money it costs you to pay for the benefits.

☞**EXAMPLE:** Ms. Smith is starting a new business as a corporation and wants the corporation to make contributions to an SEP retirement plan on her own behalf as an employee. Her goal is for the company to contribute 10% of her annual salary to her SEP account. The problem is that Ms. Smith's new company will be hiring at least five employees within the first year. If the company contributes to an SEP plan on behalf of Ms. Smith, it will also have to contribute to the SEP plan on behalf of the other employees.

In the geographic area where Ms. Smith is starting her new company, employees earn $10 per hour for the type of labor that will be required by her company. If five employees each work 40-hour weeks for 50 weeks out of the year, Ms. Smith's gross payroll for one year will be $100,000 (5 employees times 40 hours times 50 weeks times $10 per hour). If the company has to contribute 10% of these wages to an SEP, this means the company will spend $10,000 annually to make SEP contributions of behalf of these five employees.

Instead of doing this, Ms. Smith hires the employees at a wage rate of $9.09 per hour. On top of this, for every hour worked, the company contributes 91¢ (10% of $9.09) to the SEP on behalf of the employee. The employee is not given a choice between receiving the 91¢ per hour as a cash wage or a retirement plan contribution. The lower wage plus the SEP contribution are the terms of employment.

To the employees who say they can get $10 elsewhere, Ms. Smith explains that the SEP benefit is income tax free. Employees also save the 7.65% FICA tax (Social Security and Medicare) they have to pay on taxable wages. In effect, the SEP becomes a "forced" savings account for a portion of the employees' wages.

By paying benefits instead of wages, the total wages plus employee SEP contributions come to $100,000 for the year. The company saves $10,000, and Ms. Smith can have the company contribute 10% of her salary to the SEP on her behalf. On top of this, the company saves its portion of the FICA tax (Social Security and Medicare) on the $9,100 contributed to the employees' SEP accounts. That is, instead of paying FICA on $100,000 in wages, the company is paying FICA on $90,900 in wages. The company will save an annual $696 ($9,100 times 7.65%) in company FICA taxes.

♀**PLANNING POINTERS:** The key to keeping benefits free of payroll tax is to not give employees a choice between benefits or cash wages. This is obviously easier to set up with new employees; however, employers with current employees can institute tax-free employee benefits and forgo cash pay raises for those employees. Again, the employer must decide this—employees cannot have a choice between enjoying a benefit or taking a cash pay raise. If the employees do have a choice, the benefits will not be payroll-tax free.

With most benefits, an employer cannot pick and choose which employees will enjoy the benefit. For example, if you set up a company SEP plan, you must contribute on behalf of all employees who qualify for coverage. To meet these requirements and keep costs down, you may have to forgo pay raises for current employees as well as hire new employees at reduced hourly rates.

An SEP retirement plan is not the only benefit that can save payroll taxes. The meals and lodging benefit, some types of pension plan contributions, child care assistance plans, some fringe benefits, and nontaxable payments made from "cafeteria" plans are all payroll tax-free benefits. With all these benefits, the rule is the same: For the benefit to be payroll-tax free, the employee cannot have a choice between cash wages or the benefit.

For a little more employee flexibility, you may want to consider a cafeteria plan. With this type of plan, employees can choose the particular benefits they want—but not instead of cash. With a cafeteria plan, you pay in benefits but the employee can choose which benefits to receive.

☑ CHECKLIST:

- Determine what tax-free benefits you wish to enjoy from your company and/or the tax-free benefits from which your employees could benefit.
- For new employees, offer a starting pay rate at less than the going rate, but supplement it with a tax-free benefit.
- For current employees, implement employee benefits and forgo cash pay raises.
- Under no circumstances can the employee have the choice between cash wages or the benefits.

67 Take a Hidden Tax Deduction That Favors a New Business

- $ This loophole is for business taxpayers who use the accrual method of accounting and have employees.
- $ This strategy works best if you begin using it during your first year of business.
- $ It allows you to deduct payroll taxes before they are actually paid.

If this is your first year in business and you use the accrual method of accounting, don't overlook a helpful year-end income tax deduction. You can deduct any "accrued" payroll taxes (FICA and FUTA), even though you haven't actually paid them yet. The tax benefit is fairly straightforward. Take the deduction this year instead of next year so you can save income tax sooner.

Unfortunately, you can't deduct accrued year-end payroll taxes if you use the cash method of accounting—you must use the accrual method. In an accrual method of accounting, you take amounts into income when sales are made and you deduct expenses when expenses are incurred—no matter when the cash comes in or goes out. This is the opposite of the cash method of accounting, whereby you recognize income only when a payment is received and you take deductions only when payments are actually made.

Whereas it formerly prohibited the practice, the IRS has recently reversed its position on deducting accrued payroll taxes and now says it's okay. Under the rule change, this deduction is allowable for all businesses that use the accrual accounting method. However, first-year businesses are in the best position to take advantage of the deduction, since first-year businesses can accrue and deduct year-end payroll taxes without any extraordinary paperwork.

If an older business has not previously accrued and deducted payroll taxes and then begins the practice, the IRS considers the change in the method of deduction to be a change in a method of accounting. For changes in methods of accounting, the IRS expects businesses to comply with tedious "change in accounting method" requirements, such as filing a timely application and paying for professional assistance. An older business has to consider the cost of making the change and should be certain that the potential accelerated tax savings justify the cost.

☞**EXAMPLE:** Mr. Smith started a restaurant and catering business this year. Since he carries an inventory as part of his business, he is required to use an accrual method of accounting. The business has grown quickly, and he now has 30 employees. He runs a payroll every two weeks. At the end of this year, he will have a payroll for the two-week period beginning December 22 and ending January 4.

Instead of waiting until next year to deduct the payroll taxes accrued for this year (the payroll taxes accrued for the period December 22 through December 31), Mr. Smith can deduct those accrued payroll taxes on this year's income tax return. He can do this even though he will not pay those taxes to the IRS until next year.

Assuming that the accrued payroll taxes (FICA and FUTA tax) come to $1,000, Mr. Smith can deduct this $1,000 currently. He doesn't have to wait until next year for the income tax savings.

💡**PLANNING POINTERS:** If you have a first-year business, your payroll may not be large enough yet to generate a substantial accrued payroll tax deduction at year-end. Even so, you should take the smaller deduction for this year and begin the process of deducting year-end accrued payroll taxes. If you begin doing this the first year you are in business, you can continue doing it each year as your business grows. Down the road, bigger tax deductions will mean bigger tax savings.

If you don't accrue and deduct the payroll taxes for your first year in business, then in a later year when you do want to take the accelerated deduction you will have to comply with the change in accounting method rules. So skip an unnecessary headache. Cement the strategy in place at the end of the first year.

The only serious limitation to deducting accrued payroll taxes—per the new IRS rules—is that the accrued amounts must be paid either before the date you file your income tax return for the year (including extensions) or before the fifteenth day of the ninth calendar month after the close of your taxable year, whichever comes first.

For example, if your business operates as a regular C corporation and has a calendar-year tax year, and you file its corporate income tax return on March 15, then the accrued payroll taxes must be paid before March 15. In a worst-case scenario, where you would be unable to actually pay the payroll taxes by March 15, you could still file an extension for the income tax return. The extension would give you until September 15 to actually pay the payroll taxes that you had accrued at the end of the previous calendar year.

Finally, a year-end accrual of payroll tax does not trigger an earlier payroll tax depository date (the day you are actually required to pay the payroll tax). The payroll tax depository date is a completely different animal, determined by the pay date and the amount of the payroll tax generated on that pay date. So, accruing payroll taxes at year-end does not affect the date you actually have to pay the payroll taxes to the government.

☑ CHECKLIST:

- When you close your books for the year, determine the portion of the year-end payroll and related payroll taxes (FICA and FUTA) properly allocable to the current year.
- Make a book entry to document the accrual. Debit the payroll tax expense account and credit the payroll tax payable account for the amount of the accrual.
- A realistic allocation of the year-end payroll and an accounting entry to document the accrual is all the paperwork you need to support your deduction.

Small Business Fringe Benefits

▼
▼
▼

68 Working Late? Have Your Company Buy You a Deductible Dinner

$ Occasional supper money is 100% deductible.
$ You can provide this benefit for yourself without providing it for other employees.

If you are a partner in a partnership or a shareholder-employee in a regular C or S corporation and you have to work overtime, your company can, on occasion, provide you with dinner. The cost of such a dinner is 100% deductible for your company, and you don't have to pay personal income tax on the value of the meal. On top of this, your company does not have to provide this fringe benefit to other employees who work late.

☞**EXAMPLE:** Ms. Smith is the sole shareholder-employee of Smith Company. To get the company financial records together for the accountant who is preparing the company income tax return, Ms. Smith has to work late into the evening. Several other employees are also working late. Ms. Smith orders dinner for herself and has the company pay for it.

If Ms. Smith is so inclined, she can order dinner for the other employees who are working late. If the company picks up the tab, the cost of their meals would also be deductible. But whether the company pays for the other employees' meals or not, Ms. Smith's meal is tax deductible.

♀PLANNING POINTERS: Your company does not have to pay for the meal directly. Instead, it can provide you with supper money.

For your company to be able to deduct your supper money, the amount you receive must be reasonable. This does not mean that you have to order from the cheapest carryout in the area, but it also doesn't mean you can eat a seven-course dinner at a four-star restaurant. If the IRS determines that the amount of supper money you received is unreasonable, it will consider the entire amount of the supper money—not just the unreasonable excess—to be taxable personal income.

Your company can give you supper money only on an occasional basis, and the only time it can give you the supper money is when you have to work overtime. The supper money is supposed to make it easier for you to finish the work you are doing after hours.

Finally, your company cannot base the amount of supper money it gives you on the number of overtime hours you work. For example, it cannot provide you with $6 in supper money for every hour of overtime you work. Instead, your company should give you a flat amount—no matter how many overtime hours you actually work.

☑ CHECKLIST:

- Have your "employer" company occasionally reimburse you for supper money when you work after hours.
- For bookkeeping and tax preparation purposes, the company payment for supper money should be characterized as a Section 132 "de minimis" fringe benefit. The company payment is 100% deductible.
- Protect the deduction with a note on the company petty cash record or check stub. For example: "$15 payout to J. Smith for supper money. Worked late Feb. 28 to compile records for company accountant."

69 Reward Special Employees (and Yourself) with an Occasional Deductible Ball Game

$ There is a tax-deductible way to see an occasional sporting or theatrical event.

$ This reward must be primarily for the benefit of rank-and-file employees and does not have to benefit all employees.

$ This clearly benefits shareholder-employees of a corporation or partners in a partnership.

$ It probably does not benefit self-employed individuals, but it can be enjoyed by the employees, including spouse or children, of self-employed individuals.

If you are a partner in a partnership or a shareholder-employee of either a regular C corporation or an S corporation, your company can treat you to an occasional ball game, movie, or trip to the opera. To deduct this fringe benefit, your company must also extend it to employees who are not owners or highly compensated employees. That is, the tickets to the ball game or movie must be primarily for the benefit of rank-and-file employees. But this does not mean all your employees must receive a ticket. It just means that more employees than bosses should go to the ball game. And you can choose which employees get to go. So, tickets to an occasional ball game can be a reward for special employees. And of course you get to enjoy the game as well.

Because the reward is only an occasional outing, your company enjoys an income tax deduction, and you and your employees are not required to pay personal income tax on the value of the tickets. On the other hand, if the tickets were not occasional but were seasonal, you would have to pay personal income tax on the value of the tickets.

Another plus: Since the occasional tickets are primarily for the recreation of rank-and-file employees, the cost of the tickets is 100% deductible. The 50% expense disallowance that usually applies to business meals and entertainment does not apply.

☞EXAMPLE: Mr. Smith, the sole shareholder-employee of Smith Company, a construction company with 10 rank-and-file employees, has been working hard and has not taken a day off in some time. Following IRS guidelines, Mrs. Smith, the treasurer and office manager for Smith Company, orders tickets to a ball game for Mr. Smith and three other employees (not related to Mr. Smith). The company pays for the tickets. Upon receipt of the tickets, Mrs. Smith, as office manager, distributes the tickets to Mr. Smith and the other three employees. Smith Company does not give cash directly to Mr. Smith or the other employees to reimburse them for buying the tickets.

Smith Company can deduct 100% of the cost of the tickets. If the company is in the 15% corporate federal income tax bracket, and the tickets cost $80, the company saves $12 in corporate federal income tax.

Assume that Mr. Smith and the three rank-and-file employees are all in the 28% personal federal income tax bracket. If all four had to pay personal income tax on the cost of a ticket, they would each be out $5.60—that's a total of $22.40 for the four of them.

Because the company—rather than Mr. Smith and the three employees—buys the tickets, there is a combined corporate and personal federal income tax savings of $34.40 ($12 plus $22.40). In short, the IRS picks up the tab for 43% of the cost of the tickets.

♀PLANNING POINTERS: The employer must pay for the tickets and then distribute the tickets to the employees. According to IRS regulations, if the employer gives employees cash to pay for the tickets, the cash payments do not qualify as tax-free fringe benefits, even if the payments are actually used to pay for the tickets. The employees have to include the cash value of the benefit in their personal income and pay the related personal income tax.

For this reason, it is especially important to document that the company paid for the tickets and that it never put cash in the hands of the employees. The best bet is to pay with the company checkbook and to have a company "official" pick up the tickets and then distribute them to employees. However, the regulations do not require that the company employee receiving and distributing the tickets be an officer of the company. Your bookkeeper or secretary could qualify as the "ticket distributor" for the company.

Because of this "can't be cash" requirement, it is currently unclear in the IRS regulations whether this deductible benefit is available to a self-employed person. With corporations and partnerships, the employer is always a separate entity from the employees. The company, one entity, buys the tickets and then distributes them to another entity, the employees. This is true even if one of the employees is the controlling shareholder of the company. With a self-employed person, there is by definition only one entity. The IRS could argue that the self-employed person, by definition, always has the option of taking cash or taking the benefit. Thus, it is unclear if a self-employed person can deduct this benefit.

Of course, this applies only if the self-employed person is the recipient of the benefit. Occasional tickets purchased by the self-employed person for his or her employees are clearly deductible fringe benefits. So if your spouse or your children are employed by your self-employed business, you can provide them with occasional tickets and deduct the cost of their tickets as a fringe benefit. But be careful. You can deduct the cost of tickets provided to employees who are family members only if more tickets are provided to unrelated rank-and-file employees. You cannot deduct the cost of tickets provided only to employees who are part of your family.

☑ CHECKLIST:

- Have your "employer" company order and pay for occasional tickets to a sporting or theatrical event for your benefit and the benefit of special rank-and-file employees.
- For bookkeeping and tax preparation purposes, the company payment for the tickets should be characterized as a Section 132 "de minimis" fringe benefit. The payment is 100% deductible.
- The employer company should distribute the tickets to the employees. The employer company should not, under any

circumstances, give cash or a cash equivalent to the employees so that they can purchase the tickets. Taking cash or a cash equivalent from your employer makes the benefit taxable to you.

70   Make Your Daily Parking Costs Tax Free

$ This tip is for shareholder-employees of regular C corporations and S corporations.

$ Your corporation can reimburse you for your daily parking and take a tax deduction.

$ You don't pay personal income tax on the reimbursement.

$ For 1997, you can be reimbursed up to $170 each month.

$ Your corporation can reimburse you without reimbursing other employees.

$ Catch up on previous years' parking costs for big tax savings this year.

If you are a shareholder-employee of either a regular C corporation or an S corporation, your company can deduct your daily parking cost. By picking up the tab for this personal expense, your company can enjoy a tax deduction and you can escape personal income tax on the value of the benefit. Best of all, your company can provide free parking for you without having to provide it for other employees—it is strictly up to your company how many other employees, if any, park for free.

As a "qualified transportation fringe benefit," up to $170 per month (for 1997) can be allocated by your company to pay for your daily parking costs. Your company does not have to pay the maximum $170 per month ($2,040 per year) directly to the parking lot but can reimburse you after you have paid the parking fee.

EXAMPLE: Mr. Smith is the sole shareholder-employer of Smith Company, a regular C corporation that owns and operates a small downtown restaurant without a private parking lot. Every day, Mr. Smith drives to work and pays to park.

At the end of each month, Smith Company reimburses Mr. Smith for his daily parking costs (up to $170 per month for 1997). Since Mr. Smith often works six- and seven-day weeks, his monthly parking costs always total at least $170. Even though Smith Company employs several other individuals who also pay for daily parking, Smith Company is not required to reimburse them for their parking expenses.

If Smith Company is in the 15% corporate federal income tax bracket, an annual deduction of $2,040 saves the corporation $306 in corporate federal income tax. If Mr. Smith is in the 31% personal federal income tax bracket, not having to pay tax on the $2,040 annual benefit saves Mr. Smith $632 in personal federal income tax. The combined corporate and personal federal income tax savings for Smith Company and Mr. Smith is $938. In total, the tax savings pay for 46% ($938 divided by $2,040) of the annual parking cost.

PLANNING POINTERS: You should document your parking costs for your company. Provide your company with copies of documentation such as receipts and canceled checks. This will document that the parking cost was actually incurred and that the company reimbursement was for a bona fide employee parking expense.

Your company cannot deduct reimbursements for parking costs incurred on or near a property that is used by an employee as a residence. Practically speaking, this means that if you operate your company out of your home and you have to pay to park near your home, you and your company cannot use this fringe benefit.

Finally, the Internal Revenue Code section and the related IRS regulations that govern this fringe benefit do not impose any time limitations on the reimbursement for parking costs; that is, your company is not required to make the reimbursements on any fixed schedule. For example, your company is not required to reimburse you for parking costs within 10 days after the end of the month or within three months after the end of the company's taxable year. The only limitation is that this fringe benefit is available for parking costs incurred after December 31, 1992.

Strictly speaking, this means that if you have incurred parking expenses anytime after 1992 and have not been reimbursed for those expenses, you can still be reimbursed for them currently. If you can document previous years' parking expenses from your personal records to account to your company, your company can reimburse you currently for those expenses—up to the applicable monthly limit. In 1993 and 1994, the limit was $155 per month. In 1995, the limit was $160 per month. In 1996, the limit was $165 per month.

It is important to note that a current reimbursement for past years' costs does not require you or your company to file amended income tax returns. Your company simply reimburses you this year for the entire unreimbursed amounts generated in previous years and takes the "cumulative" deduction this year. Similarly, you exclude the entire amount from personal taxable income this year.

Catching up on previous years' unreimbursed parking costs can be a one-time way for your corporation to transfer a large chunk of cash to you in a tax-beneficial manner.

☑ CHECKLIST:

- If you are a shareholder-employee in a regular C corporation or an S corporation and you commute to work and incur daily parking costs, have your company reimburse you up to $170 (for 1997) per month for those parking costs. Be certain to document the parking costs to account to your company.
- If you have incurred unreimbursed parking costs since 1993, account to your company for those previous year's costs and have your company reimburse you this year.
- For bookkeeping and tax preparation purposes, characterize the parking reimbursements as a "Section 132(f) Qualified Transportation Fringe Benefit."

Special
Tax Savings for
the Self-Employed

▼
▼
▼

71 Save Self-Employment Tax When You Rent Your Home Office from Your Spouse

$ This is a home office strategy for saving self-employment tax.

$ It can be used by self-employed persons who own a home jointly with their spouse, file a joint income tax return, and use their home for self-employed business purposes.

$ Shifting from self-employed business income to rental income saves self-employment taxes (Social Security and Medicare).

If you are self-employed and use space in your home for an office or other business purposes, you can save self-employment taxes (Social Security and Medicare) if you rent part of the business-use space from your spouse, even if you file a joint income tax return.

This tax saver was given the go-ahead in a recent Tax Court case. The case involved a self-employed taxpayer who owned a home jointly with his wife and filed a joint income tax return with her. Instead of taking the normal allowable home office deductions on his self-employed business tax form (Form 1040 Schedule C), the taxpayer paid himself rent and then took the rent deduction on his Schedule C. The Tax Court disallowed him this tactic (you can't pay yourself rent). However, the court surprised the IRS by allowing the taxpayer to pay his wife rent on the portion of the home office that belonged to her. Since the husband and wife were joint owners, the wife was presumed to be a half owner, and one-half of the rent was allowed as a deduction on the husband's Schedule C as a business expense.

This tactic won't save you income taxes, because the rent deducted on the self-employed business form Schedule C must be taken into income on the rental income form Schedule E. So for income tax purposes, the rent transaction is a wash. But since deductions on the Schedule C also save self-employment taxes (and no self-employment taxes are due for Schedule E rental income), the shifting from Schedule C to Schedule E (from business expense to rental income) will save self-employment tax.

EXAMPLE: Mr. Smith is a self-employed building contractor who uses one floor of his three-floor house as a home office and workshop space (i.e., one-third of the house space is for business use). He is married and owns the home jointly with his wife. They file their income tax on a joint income tax return. Before taking a deduction for his home office/workshop space, Mr. Smith projects net self-employment earnings of $60,000 for the year.

The total business deductions allocated to the self-employed office/workshop space—including depreciation, one-third of the mortgage interest, one-third of the property taxes, one-third of the property insurance, and one-third of the household utilities—come to $4,000 for the year.

Instead of treating the entire expense as a business expense and deducting the $4,000 from his Schedule C, Mr. Smith checks around and finds that to rent a comparable space for comparable purposes he would have to pay rent of $800 per month. He sets up a rental agreement with his wife and pays her $400 per month rent on half of the business-use portion of the house, which belongs to her as a joint owner.

He is then able to deduct the following on his Schedule C:

- First, he deducts his one-half of the $4,000 workspace business expenses—$2,000. This reflects his half share of the business expenses for the workspace.
- Second, he deducts the $4,800 ($400 per month times 12 months) in rent expense that he paid his wife.

So instead of deducting only $4,000 as a business space expense on his Schedule C, he can deduct $6,800 ($2,000 plus $4,800).

Using the business expense/rent paid combination, he can deduct $2,800 more ($6,800 less $4,000) on his Schedule C. But this does not save income tax. The $4,800 rent he pays to his wife must be included on the rental income tax form Schedule E. From this rent income amount is deducted his wife's half of the $4,000 in workspace business expenses. The gross rent of $4,800 less the related expenses of $2,000 equals net rental income of $2,800 for income tax purposes. The extra $2,800 he was able to deduct on the Schedule C is taken back into income on Schedule E—for an income tax wash.

But Mr. Smith will save on the self-employment tax. Because the increased Schedule C deduction of $2,800 is reducing net self-employment earnings below the Social Security tax cap for the year, Mr. Smith will save 15.3% in self-employment taxes on every dollar he deducts—remember, Mr. Smith's net income before the workspace deduction or rent paid is $60,000. So the extra Schedule C deduction of $2,800, even though it doesn't save anything in income tax, will save Mr. Smith $428 in self-employment tax ($2,800 times 15.3%).

💡**PLANNING POINTERS:** The self-employment tax savings generated by renting from your spouse are greater if your net income from self-employment is below the Social Security tax cap for the year. For 1997, the Social Security tax cap is $65,400. If your net self-employment income is more than this, this rent strategy will save you only the Medicare portion (2.9%) of the self-employment tax.

If your spouse is the sole owner of the home, the full amount of fair rent for the space can be paid and deducted by you on your Schedule C.

Rule of thumb: As long as the allowable fair rent for the space is more than the allocable actual business expense, you can save more in self-employment taxes.

☑ **CHECKLIST:**
- Determine the actual allowable business expenses (such as depreciation, allocated mortgage interest, etc.) for your home business-use space.
- Determine and document the fair rental value for the same business-use space.
- If the fair rental value is more than the actual allowable busi-

ness expenses, it will benefit you in self-employment tax savings to set up a rent agreement with your spouse and take a rent deduction as well as your portion of the actual business-use expenses from your Form 1040 Schedule C.

- Remember to include the rent paid to your spouse as rental income on Form 1040 Schedule E. And remember to offset this rental income with your spouse's portion of the actual business-use expenses.

72 Deduct Your Telephone Expense Even If You Can't Deduct Your Home Office

$ This tip benefits start-up self-employed individuals and "sideline" self-employed individuals who earn minimal self-employment income.

$ Telephone expenses are not subject to home office limitations.

$ Telephone expenses can be deducted without regard to gross income.

According to a recent Tax Court case, if you are self-employed you can deduct your telephone costs, even if your home office expenses are not currently deductible. This is good news for start-up self-employed individuals and "sideline" self-employed individuals who use a home office space but generate little or no gross income from their self-employed business.

The IRS tried to characterize telephone expense as a home office expense, but the Tax Court disagreed. Why is this distinction important? Under the home office deduction rules, deductions for expenses allocable to home office use (such as utilities and insurance) are currently deductible only to the extent of the self-employed business's gross income. And added to this "gross income" limitation is another limitation: Expenses that are otherwise deductible regardless of the level of gross income (such as allocable mortgage interest and property tax) can indirectly limit the deductibility of the other home office expenses.

If the IRS had its way, telephone expense would be treated like utilities and insurance. Your allowable telephone expense would be limited to your gross income from your self-employed business. And if you had enough gross income to deduct your telephone expense, any mortgage interest or property tax you might also deduct could swallow up this gross income. In effect, your deductible mortgage interest or property tax could indirectly disallow your telephone expense.

☞ **EXAMPLE:** Mrs. Smith has started a sideline business this year as a self-employed writer. Her gross income consists of one $500 receipt for a magazine article.

Mrs. Smith has set aside a home office space that she uses regularly and exclusively for her writing business. Her allowable home office expenses are $1,000 for mortgage interest, $200 for property tax, $300 for utilities, and $150 for insurance. Mrs. Smith also has business telephone expenses of $600 (lots of long-distance calls).

According to the IRS, Mrs. Smith should not be allowed to deduct her telephone expenses this year. She can deduct the allowable mortgage interest and property tax, but since these expenses shelter her gross income and then some, the utilities, insurance, and telephone expenses will not be deducted this year. Instead, she will carry these expenses to a future year when she has a gross income from her self-employed business larger than these deductions.

Fortunately, the Tax Court disagrees with the IRS on this issue. In keeping with the decision, Mrs. Smith can deduct the mortgage interest, the property tax, and the telephone expense this year. She is required to carry forward only the utilities and insurance expenses.

If Mrs. Smith is in the 28% federal income tax bracket and 5% state income tax bracket, this $600 telephone expense deduction saves her $198 ($600 times 33%) in current income tax.

💡 **PLANNING POINTERS:** The cost of the basic service of your home phone cannot be allocated to business use. It does not matter how much you use it in your self-employed business. It is best to have a second phone line installed for business use. All the costs associated with this second line are deductible.

If you do not install a second phone line, the following costs of the first line are deductible and should be carefully documented:

- Telephone services you add for business purposes (call waiting, call forwarding, etc.).
- Unit costs for local business telephone calls. Request an itemized list from the telephone company and indicate the business calls on the list.
- Any itemized long-distance business calls on your phone bill.

☑ CHECKLIST:

- If you have a second phone line for your business, or if you have carefully documented the allowable business costs of your only home phone line, deduct these costs currently.
- Deduct these costs on your IRS Form 1040 Schedule C. Do not include your telephone expenses on IRS Form 8829 (Expenses for Business Use of Your Home).

73 Save More Tax When You Deduct Tax Preparation Fees as a Business Expense

$ Deduct tax preparation fees as a self-employed business expense.

$ Business tax preparation expense saves self-employment tax as well as income tax.

$ Business tax preparation fees are not subject to ordinary tax preparation fee limitations.

$ Have your tax preparer itemize the tax preparation bill.

Until a few years ago, the IRS required that all tax preparation fees be deducted as a miscellaneous personal itemized deduction on Schedule

A. It did not matter whether most of the fees were paid for preparing business-related tax forms. Then the IRS changed its position. Taxpayers who are self-employed are now allowed to deduct the portion of their tax preparation expense allocable to business-form preparation as a self-employed business expense on Schedule C.

Why is this important? First, to get a deductible benefit, taxpayers formerly had to itemize deductions. There was no benefit for taxpayers who took the standard deduction. Second, miscellaneous itemized deductions are allowed as a deduction only to the extent they exceed 2% of a taxpayer's adjusted gross income. For many taxpayers, this income limitation kept them from being able to deduct miscellaneous expenses. Finally, even if they were able to deduct the full tax preparation expense as an itemized deduction, they saved income tax only.

Under the new rule, taking a part of your tax preparation expense as a self-employed business expense does not require that you itemize deductions. There is no 2% of adjusted gross income limitation or any other income limitation. And finally, apart from saving income tax, this deduction will also save you self-employment tax (Social Security and Medicare).

If you are self-employed and pay a tax preparer to complete your Form 1040 income tax return, make sure to get an itemized bill that shows the portion of the tax preparation fee allocated to preparing your Schedule C and any other related business tax forms that are attached to your Form 1040. Your accountant should also state separately any charges for consulting with you about business-related matters or for completing business-related services.

☞**EXAMPLE:** Mr. Smith is self-employed. For completing his 1995 Form 1040 in March 1996, his tax preparer charged him $500. Of this, $350 was allocated to Mr. Smith's self-employment tax form preparation.

Mr. Smith itemizes deductions, but since his adjusted gross income is $60,000, he can deduct only miscellaneous itemized deductions that exceed 2% of $60,000 ($1,200). Since his tax prep expense is his only miscellaneous deduction, he would not be able to deduct any of the tax prep expense if he were forced to treat it only as a miscellaneous itemized deduction (his total tax prep expense of $500 does not exceed the $1,200 disallowance amount).

But since $350 has been allocated to his self-employment business, he can deduct this amount on his Schedule C as a business expense. Not only will this save him $98 in federal income tax ($350 times 28% federal income tax), but Mr. Smith will also save $54 in self-employment taxes ($350 times 15.3% self-employment tax).

Because a portion of Mr. Smith's tax preparation bill can be treated as a self-employed business expense, he saves $152 ($98 plus $54). The tax savings generated effectively pay for 30% of Mr. Smith's tax preparation cost.

♀PLANNING POINTERS: It is important that you have your tax preparer give you an itemized bill for the tax preparation service. A canceled check for the entire amount is not enough proof to support allocating a portion of the payment as a self-employed business expense.

Make sure to include this itemized statement in your tax documentation when you return to your tax preparer next year. If you don't include the itemized statement in your paperwork, your paid preparer may not remember that an allocation was made. Including the itemized statement will be a good reminder.

Of course, if you are changing tax preparers, make sure to point out the itemized treatment to your new preparer.

☑ CHECKLIST:

- Include the itemized tax preparation charges in your tax prep documentation for the tax year the tax preparation expense is deductible.
- If you are attempting to do your taxes on your own this year, include on Form 1040 Schedule C any tax preparation fees you paid during the year that are allocable to your self-employed business as an expense.

Replace Nondeductible Business Interest with Deductible Business Interest

$ Replace nondeductible personal interest with deductible business interest.

$ Replace deductible home equity interest with deductible business interest.

$ Compare the difference in interest rates charged, as well as the difference in tax savings.

If you are self-employed, there is no reason for you to pay nondeductible personal interest. Or, at the very least, you should use your self-employed status to minimize your nondeductible personal interest expenditures. You can do this by borrowing to meet your business expense requirements and then using business receipts to pay down or pay off personal debt. Handling it this way, you "replace" nondeductible personal interest expense with deductible business expense.

☞ **EXAMPLE 1:** Mr. Smith is a self-employed construction contractor who just started his business this year. Prior to going into business, he incurred personal credit card debt of $5,000. The interest he must pay on this credit card debt is considered personal interest and is not deductible.

Mr. Smith applies for a second credit card and uses it to charge purchases made for his business—tools, supplies, construction materials, and so on. As he receives business income, he uses the business income to pay off the personal credit card debt and makes only the minimum required payments on the business credit card debt.

By doing this, he erases the personal debt that generates nondeductible interest expense and replaces it with deductible business interest expense.

Bonus: The deductible business interest expense saves Mr. Smith self-employment tax (Social Security and Medicare) as well as income tax.

☞**EXAMPLE 2:** Mr. Smith is a self-employed construction contractor. He wants to buy a new car that will be used only for personal purposes. He knows if he takes out an auto loan, the interest he will pay on the loan will be nondeductible personal interest. For this reason, he has been thinking it would be better to take out a home equity loan. With a home equity loan, he can use the proceeds of the loan to purchase the new car and then write off the interest paid as home equity interest.

Initially, Mr. Smith does take out a home equity loan to purchase the new car. Afterwards, over a period of several months, Mr. Smith uses credit cards to make purchases for his business—tools, supplies, construction materials, and so on. The interest rate he pays on the business credit cards is approximately the same as the home equity loan interest rate. As he receives business income, he uses the business income to pay off the home equity loan and makes only the minimum required payments on the business credit card debt.

Why pay off the home equity debt and in effect replace it with business debt? As long as the interest rates are approximately the same for the home equity debt and the business debt, Mr. Smith will save more by deducting business interest than he will by deducting home equity interest. This is because a home equity interest deduction saves only income tax. On the other hand, a business interest deduction saves self-employment tax (Social Security and Medicare) as well as income tax.

♀**PLANNING POINTERS:** To deduct business interest, the debt must be related to a business purpose, and you must be able to document that purpose. For this reason, it is better to keep business debt separate from other debt. Use a separate credit card exclusively for business purposes. This way, all the interest expense paid on the business credit card is deductible business interest expense. Otherwise, if you use a credit card for different purposes (personal and business) you have to distinguish the business debt from the personal debt, and then allocate the interest paid between deductible business interest and nondeductible personal interest. Obviously, the record keeping will be a lot less painful if you use a separate credit card for business purposes.

When "replacing" one kind of debt with another, first compare the interest rates charged by the different kinds of debt. If a home equity interest rate is quite a bit less than the interest rate you will pay for business indebtedness, it may not make sense to replace home equity debt with business debt, even with the further self-employment tax savings you will enjoy with the interest paid on the business debt. Estimate the economic cost and tax savings of the home equity loan and compare it with the economic cost and tax savings of the business debt. If the business debt interest rate is higher than the home equity loan interest rate, the self-employment tax savings generated by the business interest deduction should justify paying the increased interest rate.

☑ CHECKLIST:

- Pay down or pay off personal debt by "replacing" it with business debt.
- Pay down or pay off home equity debt by "replacing" it with business debt.
- Compare interest rates charged as well as tax savings when "replacing" home equity debt with business debt.
- Be careful to document the business use of funds borrowed for business purposes. To this end, it is better to keep business debt separate from other debt.

75 Deduct Lawn Maintenance, Landscaping, and Driveway Repair Costs

$ This tip is for self-employed taxpayers who deduct expenses for a home office and use the home office to meet with customers on a regular basis.

$ Take a business deduction for lawn maintenance, landscaping, and driveway repair costs.

$ This strategy saves self-employment tax as well as income tax.

$ If you plan to start a self-employed business, delay driveway repairs.

If you run your business out of a home office, you probably already know that you are allowed a business expense deduction for the home office portion of such expenses as mortgage interest, property tax, insurance, utilities, maintenance and repairs, and depreciation. But don't shortchange yourself when it comes to your home office write-offs. If you use your home office on a regular basis to meet with customers, the home office portion of any lawn maintenance, landscaping, and driveway repair cost is also deductible as a home office cost.

☞ **EXAMPLE:** Mrs. Smith uses 33% of her home regularly and exclusively as a home office in her self-employed business. She therefore deducts as a business expense 33% of her mortgage interest expense, 33% of her property tax expense, 33% of her homeowner insurance expense, 33% of her electric bills, and so on.

This year, Mrs. Smith also paid little Joanie Jones $30 per week for 18 weeks to mow, weed, and otherwise care for the two-acre lawn on which her house sits. After sustaining several years' ice damage on the property, Mrs. Smith also spent $1,500 this year to repair both her driveway and the walkway that runs from her driveway to the front door. Between the regular lawn care and the driveway/walkway repairs, Mrs. Smith spent $2,040.

Mrs. Smith is allowed to deduct $673 ($2,040 times 33%) as a home office business expense. If Mrs. Smith is in the 28% federal income tax bracket, 5% state income tax bracket, and 15.3% self-employment tax bracket (Social Security and Medicare), this $673 deduction saves $325 in combined tax.

PLANNING POINTERS: Keeping up necessary business appearances is the justification for being able to deduct the home office portion of your lawn maintenance and driveway repairs. To support the deduction, you should be able to show that you meet with customers in your home office on a regular basis. Entries in your daybook or other similar appointment book indicating that meetings with customers took place on a regular basis at your home office should be sufficient documentation.

Like other deductible home office expenses, the home office portion of the cost of lawn maintenance and driveway repair will save self-employment tax (Social Security and Medicare), as well as federal and state income tax.

If you are planning to start a self-employed business in the near future and will use a home office to meet with customers on a regular basis, you should wait until after you have started the business to have any repairs done on your driveway or walkway. If you make the repairs before you go into business, the entire amount you spend is a nondeductible personal expense. If you wait, you can deduct the home office portion of the expense.

☑ CHECKLIST:

- If you use a home office for your self-employed business and meet with customers in your home office on a regular basis, document all lawn maintenance, landscaping, and driveway repair costs.
- If you pay someone cash to mow your lawn or weed your flower garden, have them sign a receipt when you pay them.
- Use your daybook or other appointment book to document meetings with customers in your home office.
- Deduct the "home office portion" of these expenses on IRS Form 8829 (Expenses for Business Use of Your Home).

76 Hire Your Spouse and Write Off 100% of Your Health Insurance Premiums

$ This loophole is for self-employed taxpayers who are married.
$ It allows self-employed taxpayers to fully deduct the cost of health insurance premiums as a business expense.
$ It saves you more federal income tax.
$ It saves you self-employment tax.

By the year 2007, 100% of annual health insurance premiums paid by self-employed people will be deductible. For several years, lawmakers limited the deduction self-employed people take for health insurance premiums to a percentage of the amount of the premium. However, they are easing the limitation. In 1997, a self-employed individual can take an income tax deduction for 40% of any health insurance premiums paid (subject to certain other limitations). And the deduction will increase every year until 2007.

This is good news, but why wait until 2007? Instead of paying for your family's health insurance and taking this limited, phased-in deduction, why not hire your spouse to work in your self-employed business and pay health insurance premiums on your spouse's behalf as an employee? If you provide health insurance for your spouse as an employee, you have the option to insure your spouse's family as well—including yourself!

By paying health insurance premiums on behalf of your employee-spouse instead of yourself, you can deduct 100% of the premiums as a business deduction. This saves self-employment tax (Social Security and Medicare) as well as income tax.

☞**EXAMPLE:** Mr. Smith is a self-employed construction con-tractor. In 1997, he will pay $4,000 in health insurance premiums for himself and his family. If he pays the premiums directly on his own behalf, he will be allowed an income tax deduction of $1,600 ($4,000 times 40%). If he and his wife file a joint income tax return and are in the 28% federal income tax bracket, the $1,600 deduction will save them $448 in federal income tax.

On the other hand, if Mr. Smith hires his wife to work for his self-employed business, he can contribute the same $4,000 to pay for a health insurance policy in his wife's name that will also cover the members of her family, including Mr. Smith.

Using this indirect method, the entire $4,000 can be deducted as a business expense on Mr. Smith's Form 1040 Schedule C. Assuming the Smiths are in the 28% federal income tax bracket, the increased allowable deduction will save them $1,120 ($4,000 times 28%) in federal income tax. This is $672 more than they would have saved if Mr. Smith had paid the insurance premiums directly.

On top of the income tax savings, Mr. Smith will also save self-employment taxes. Depending on the level of Mr. Smith's net self-employment income, the $4,000 deduction could save him as little as $116 or as much as $565 on top of the income tax savings.

In any case, Mr. Smith will be ahead $672—plus any self-employment tax savings—on the same $4,000 of health insurance premiums. And these are the extra tax savings for only one year. By the end of 2006, Mr. Smith could have accumulated income tax savings of $6,720!

💡**PLANNING POINTERS:** To set up a health insurance bene-fit for a spouse-employee, it is not necessary to cover your other employees. According to the IRS regulations on the subject, an em-ployee health insurance plan "may cover one or more employees, and there may be different plans for different employees or classes of em-ployees." If your spouse is your only employee, you can still deduct the health insurance premiums you pay on your spouse's behalf.

The employee health insurance plan does not have to be in writing, but it is probably a good idea to draw up a written statement outlining your intent to create a health insurance plan benefiting your spouse-employee and your spouse-employee's family.

Be certain to hire your spouse as a bona fide employee. Your spouse should provide services to your business, should be compensated as an employee, and should receive a W-2 at year-end. The amount of money you give your spouse for health insurance premiums should be excluded from your spouse's taxable income and should not be included as part of the taxable income on your spouse's W-2.

☑ CHECKLIST:

- Determine how much you save in income tax by taking the limited income tax deduction for health insurance premiums paid by a self-employed individual.
- Determine how much you could save in income tax and self-employment tax by taking a 100% business deduction for the same health insurance premiums paid on behalf of your spouse-employee and your spouse-employee's family, including yourself.
- If your spouse is not already employed in your self-employed business, hire him or her and create an employee health insurance plan for the benefit of your spouse-employee and family.
- The health insurance policy should be in the name of your spouse-employee and family, and you should make the premium payments on behalf of your spouse-employee.
- Be certain that your spouse-employee provides bona fide services to your self-employed business and is compensated for those services.

77 Deduct the Cost of Parking When You Drive to Work with Your Spouse-Employee

$ This tip is for self-employed workers who employ their spouse.

$ Reimburse your employee-spouse for parking costs and take a tax deduction.

$ For 1997, you can deduct up to $170 per month.

$ You are not required to provide the same benefit to other employees.

If you are self-employed, you cannot deduct the cost of parking as a "qualified transportation fringe benefit" (including partners with net self-employment earnings). But if you are self-employed and your spouse works as an employee in your business, you can avoid this limitation and make your parking costs deductible by simply driving to work with your spouse.

Here's how it works. If you employ your husband or wife as an ordinary employee (so that his or her earnings from the business are employee earnings rather than self-employment earnings), you can give him or her up to $170 each month (for 1997) for parking costs. You can deduct the $170 per month ($2,040 per year) as a business expense, and you do not have to include it in your spouse's taxable income. You do not have to pay for the parking directly from your business checkbook but can reimburse your spouse-employee for his or her parking costs up to the $170 monthly limit. And you do not have to provide this benefit to your other employees—it is strictly up to you how many, if any, of your other employees receive this benefit.

☞**EXAMPLE:** Ms. Smith is a self-employed computer programmer who employs four other programmers. She also employs her husband as the office manager for her business. To save gas, they usually commute to and from work together.

Since Ms. Smith is self-employed, she is unable to deduct her daily parking costs. Because of this limitation, she has her husband pay for the parking out of his own funds and then reimburses him up to the $170 monthly cap out of her business checkbook. As she does not wish to incur any further parking costs, she does not provide this parking reimbursement benefit to any of her other employees.

If Ms. Smith reimburses her husband the full $170 each month ($2,040 for the year) and is in the 31% federal income tax bracket, she will save $632 in personal federal income tax. As the deduction is a self-employed business deduction, she will also save self-employment (FICA/Medicare) tax.

PLANNING POINTERS: Your spouse should pay for the parking out of his or her own funds. Have your spouse pay with his or her own checkbook or charge card. The reimbursement from your business should likewise be payable to your spouse only. It is also wise for you to have your spouse account to your business for the parking costs incurred. Your spouse should provide copies of documents such as receipts and canceled checks showing that the cost was in fact incurred and that the reimbursement by your business was for a bona fide employee parking expense.

Note for self-employed workers who operate out of a home office: You cannot deduct reimbursements to your spouse for parking costs incurred on or near a property used by your spouse-employee as a residence. So if you use office space in your home and also employ your spouse, you cannot deduct parking costs your spouse incurred to park near the home office.

☑ CHECKLIST:

- If you employ your spouse in your self-employed business and you commute to work together, have your spouse pay for the cost of parking out of his or her own funds.
- Reimburse your spouse for these parking costs on a monthly basis (up to $170 per month in 1997). Have your spouse-employee account to your business for the parking cost.
- For bookkeeping and tax preparation purposes, characterize the parking reimbursements as a "Section 132(f) Qualified Transportation Fringe Benefit."

---

78 | Take a Travel Deduction Without Taking a Home Office Deduction

$ This tip is for taxpayers who use a home office regularly but are not allowed to take a home office income tax deduction.

$ Travel between the regular home office and outside worksites is deductible.

$ Make sure you know what you can deduct and how to defend it.

Self-employed taxpayers can deduct the cost of traveling from their home office to other work locations, even if their home office does not qualify for a home office deduction. So said the Tax Court in a recent ruling.

In an earlier case, the Tax Court had ruled favorably for a taxpayer, but the IRS declined to accept the verdict and disallowed the travel deduction for another taxpayer (who also ended up taking the IRS to Tax Court).

According to IRS thinking, no home office deduction also means no travel deduction. To take a home office deduction as a self-employed, your home office must be used regularly and exclusively for business purposes. Also, either it must be your principal place of business or you must use it to meet regularly with clients.

To determine whether a home office is your principal place of business, the IRS applies a "time spent" test. Thus, taxpayers who spend more time working away from their home office than working at their home office and who do not meet regularly with clients in their home office are not allowed to take a home office deduction. But according to the Tax Court, just because you cannot take a home office deduction does not mean you cannot deduct your travel cost.

☞ **EXAMPLE:** Mr. Smith is a self-employed computer consultant. He works out of a home office, but, because of the nature of his work, he spends more time working at client locations than he does at home. On average, he spends about seven hours per week in his home office. The rest of the time he is at client locations.

Even though Mr. Smith cannot take a home office income tax deduction, he can deduct the cost of traveling from his home office to an outside worksite, from an outside worksite to another outside worksite, and from an outside worksite back to his home office.

If Mr. Smith's travel expenses come to $5,000 per year and he is in the 28% federal income tax bracket, he could save $1,400 each year in federal income tax.

Because Mr. Smith is self-employed, he will also save self-employment tax as a result of this deduction. Assuming he has $5,000 in deductible travel expenses each year, depending on the level of his net self-employment income, this could mean an annual self-employment tax savings of as little as $145 or as much as $706.

💡**PLANNING POINTERS:** If you are audited, and the IRS attempts to disallow your travel deduction based on its interpretation of the law, do not accept the disallowance. If the IRS auditor won't budge, take it up with the IRS appeals officer. Let both the auditor and the appeals officer know that you will proceed—if necessary—to Tax Court. If the appeals officer refuses to allow the deduction, head for Tax Court. If you have to go to Tax Court, be sure to ask for every allowable reimbursement of legal and accounting fees you incurred as a result of the IRS disallowance. In short, let the government pay for the lawyers.

Even if the IRS decides to accept the Tax Court's interpretation of the law, it can still disallow the travel deduction based on fact. To defend against this possibility, be certain you carefully document two items:

- First, be able to show that you use the home office on a regular basis—even if you are unable to take a home office income tax deduction. Keep a log or a time sheet indicating the regular weekly home office usage. In one of the above-mentioned Tax Court cases, the taxpayer used his home office as little as seven hours per week and was still able to take the travel deduction.
- Second, document the travel expenses themselves.

If you use public transportation, you can deduct the entire cost of bus tickets, train tickets, and subway tokens.

If you use your car, you must keep a mileage record that indicates the business miles driven, the business destination, and the business purpose. If you don't keep a special mileage log (which is ideal), an entry in your appointment book that says, for example, "65 miles round-trip to Jones Company to work on computer network" would be sufficient.

If you use your car for business travel, you can use either the "standard mileage method" or the "actual expense method." With the standard mileage rate method, you apply a cents-per-mile rate (established by the government) to the number of business miles driven. This is the easier method to use but does not always generate the largest possible deduction.

With the actual expense method, you keep track of your business mileage for the year as a percentage of the total mileage (business and personal) driven for the year. This business percentage is then applied to all the actual expenses, such as gas, repairs, and insurance. You can also depreciate your vehicle based on the same business-use percentage.

☑ CHECKLIST:

- Document your regular home office use, even if you are unable to take a home office deduction.
- Document business travel from your home office to outside worksites and the return trip.
- If you use your car, use either the standard mileage method or the actual expense method to determine the deductible travel expense.
- As a self-employed person, deduct the travel expense on your Form 1040 Schedule C.
- If you have failed to take the deduction in previous years and have proper documentation for both regular home office use and the travel expense, amend your previous years' income tax returns using Form 1040X. You generally have three years to file an amended income tax return for a refund of overpaid income and self-employment taxes.

Running
Your Business as
a Regular
C Corporation

▼
▼
▼

79 Don't Wait for a Refund If You Have Overpaid Your Estimated Income Tax

$ This tip is for regular C corporations that make quarterly estimated income tax payments.
$ You can get a quick refund when your corporation has overpaid quarterly estimates.

When you sat down to crunch your corporation's projected income for the year, did you overestimate? If you did, don't give the use of your money to the government. File for a quick refund.

Projecting income accurately (so that you can make the required quarterly estimated income tax payments to the IRS) is a lot more difficult than it should be. Since your corporation is not considered large—it had less than $1 million in taxable income in each of the last three tax years—you can either (1) estimate this year's income tax using last year's total income tax due, (2) try to calculate exactly what this year's income tax will be and pay it in the four quarterly installments, or (3) use one of the more complicated "annualized income" methods to figure the required estimated payments.

Using any of these methods, it is quite common for a corporation to overpay estimated income taxes during the year. For example, if you used last year's tax as the basis of calculation and then have a drop in income for this year, you will have overpaid.

If you have overpaid your estimates, don't wait until you file the final income tax return for the year to receive your refund. Your corporation is eligible for a quick refund of the overpaid amount within 45 days of filing the proper IRS form. For you to receive a corporate quick refund, the overpayment has to exceed the new total estimate for the year by at least 10% and the overpaid amount must be at least $500.

☞EXAMPLE 1: At the beginning of the year, Mr. Smith of Smith Company projected a taxable corporate income of $85,000 for 1997. Per the corporate income tax rates, this taxable income would generate a corporate income tax liability for 1997 of $17,150. Based on these calculations, Mr. Smith has made four quarterly corporate estimated income tax payments of $4,288 ($17,150 divided by 4).

At year-end, Mr. Smith realizes that because of a bonus paid to himself as well as other previously unaccounted expenses, Smith Company will in fact have a taxable income of only $45,000 for 1997. Per the corporate income tax rates, this corrected taxable income will generate a corporate income tax liability for 1997 of $6,750.

Smith Company has overpaid its estimated income taxes for 1997 by $10,400. Since this overpayment exceeds 10% of the revised estimate—it is more than $6,750 times 10%—and since the overpayment is more than $500, Smith Company can file for a quick refund. Mr. Smith files for a quick refund on January 1 and has his $10,400 back by the middle of February.

☞EXAMPLE 2: Mr. Jones of Jones Company is in the same situation as Mr. Smith of Example 1. Mr. Jones does not file for a quick refund. Instead, he files for a refund when he files the corporate income tax return on March 15, and he receives his $10,400 refund by the end of April or beginning of May. If he had extended the filing of the corporate income tax returns until September 15, he would have had to wait another six months—on top of what he had already waited—to receive the corporate refund.

♀PLANNING POINTERS: Corporations must apply for a quick refund by filing IRS Form 4466 after the close of the corporation's tax year and before the 15th day of the third month after the end of the tax year. For calendar-year corporations, this means Form 4466 must be filed between January 1 and March 15. The sooner your corporation files, the quicker you get your refund.

You should file for a quick refund even if you have to make estimated tax payments for the following year. In the first example, Smith Company received its refund by the middle of February, while its first quarterly estimate for 1998 will not be due until April 15. Even if Smith Company has to make a first-quarter estimate for 1998 that equals or exceeds the refund amount, it still has had the use of the funds and the related interest earnings for the two months between the middle of February and the middle of April.

☑ CHECKLIST:

- At year-end, calculate your corporation's actual taxable income and corporate income tax generated for the year.
- Compare this revised tax liability with the total estimated income taxes actually paid during the year.
- If the corporate estimated taxes have been overpaid and the overpayment is more than $500 and also more than 10% of the corrected total tax liability for the year, file IRS Form 4466 for a quick refund of the overpaid estimated taxes.

80 Act Fast and Use Next Year's Losses to Cut This Year's Income Tax

$ This strategy uses next year's corporate losses to save on this year's income tax.

$ Current income tax savings means positive corporate cash flow.

$ IRS charges tax-deductible interest when you use this method.

$ IRS interest rates compare favorably with commercial loan interest rates.

$ There are other options if you don't use this method.

If your regular C corporation has generated taxable income this year and you either expect or can create a net operating loss (NOL) next year, you can "carry back" next year's NOL and save corporate income tax this year. This course of action allows your corporation to use next year's tax losses to save cash immediately.

You have to be quick, because you can use this strategy only if you still have unpaid corporate income taxes due for this year. If you've already made corporate estimated tax payments for all the income tax due this year, it's too late to improve your corporate cash flow by means of this strategy.

There are only two steps your corporation has to take:

1. First, your corporation must file IRS Form 1138. This is an extension form that automatically allows your corporation to extend the time of payment for the balance due on this year's income tax. The automatic extension lasts until after the end of next year, when it is possible to calculate the actual amount of the NOL for next year. This IRS Form 1138 automatic extension must be filed before the final payment of any tax due for this year.

2. Second, after the end of next year, when you can calculate next year's actual NOL, your corporation must file a "carryback refund claim" on IRS Form 1139. This carryback of next year's NOL is used to satisfy this year's unpaid income tax liability.

☞**EXAMPLE:** Smith Company, a calendar-year regular C corporation, has determined that its net taxable income for 1997 will be $60,000, generating a total federal corporate income tax due of $10,000. So far this year, the company has made three corporate estimated tax payments totaling $3,000. These payments leave a balance due of $7,000 ($10,000 total tax less $3,000 estimated tax payments made to date), which will have to be paid by March 15, 1998, the due date for filing the corporate income tax return for 1997.

Smith Company also projects that it will have a $35,000 net operating loss in 1998. If operations are better than expected in 1998, Mr. Smith, the sole shareholder-employee of Smith Company, will pay himself a salary and make contributions to the company retirement plan large enough to reduce any net profit to a $35,000 net operating loss.

Smith Company can use its expected 1998 $35,000 NOL to reduce its 1997 net taxable income. With a further $35,000 deduction for 1997, Smith Company will have a net taxable income of $25,000 ($60,000 net taxable income less $35,000 NOL carryback). This $25,000 of income would generate a corporate federal income tax of $3,750. Since Smith Company has already paid $3,000 in estimated income tax payments, it will have to pay a balance due of only $750 ($3,750 less $3,000) by March 15, 1998.

By using next year's projected NOL this year, Smith Company keeps an extra $6,250 in its pocket ($7,000 that it would have had to pay without the NOL carryback less the adjusted balance due of $750 after the NOL carryback).

Before making the final payment due for the year, Smith Company will have filed IRS Form 1138, extending the payment due date for 1997 until after the close of 1998 (sometime early in 1999). When the actual NOL for 1998 is determined in early 1999, Smith Company will file IRS Form 1139, carrying back the 1998 NOL to 1997.

♀PLANNING POINTERS: There is a price for using this strategy. The IRS will charge your corporation interest on the up-front tax savings. If the NOL actually occurs as planned, the interest stops running on the due date for filing the income tax return for the actual loss year. In plain English, this means you'll pay one year's worth of interest at the going IRS rate.

In the example, where $6,250 was saved by using the NOL carryback, if the IRS interest rate is 9% per year, Smith Company will have to pay about $563 in interest charges. But this is less than what the company would pay for a commercial business loan, and the IRS interest paid is tax deductible.

Before using this one-year advance NOL carryback, you should also consider the benefits of waiting until after the NOL actually occurs. Under the 1997 tax act, if you wait, you can carry the NOL either back 2 years or forward 20 years. If your company is in a higher corporate federal income tax bracket in one of these "carry" years, you will save more in taxes waiting to use the NOL than if you use it prior to its occurrence. Furthermore, by waiting, your corporation will not have to pay the IRS interest. You have to decide whether your corporation needs more available cash now or potentially higher income tax savings later.

☑ CHECKLIST:

- Determine next year's projected NOL before paying the balance of any income tax due for this year.
- File Form 1138 to extend the payment due date for this year until after the close of next year. File this IRS form before paying the balance of any income tax due for this year—once you pay, you can't use the carryback to get the money back. You can file Form 1138 separately or as an attachment to Form 7004 (corporate automatic filing extension). *Note:* Filing Form 1138 is a payment extension, not a filing extension. You must still file Form 1120 (corporate income tax return) for the year. Note on Form 1120 that the unpaid balance of tax due is being extended per Form 1138.
- After the close of next year, determine the actual NOL for next year. File IRS Form 1139 to apply next year's actual NOL to this year. File Form 1139 only after filing next year's Form 1120 (corporate income tax return).

81 Keep Out of the Corporate Estimated Tax Trap, Earn Interest, and Avoid IRS Underpayment Penalties

- \$ This tip is for regular C corporations required to make quarterly estimated income tax payments.
- \$ Instead of a zero-tax year, generate a small-tax year.
- \$ This allows the corporation to make minimum estimated income tax payments the following year.
- \$ It helps you avoid IRS underpayment penalties.

$ Compare the benefit of recouping previous years' taxes with a net operating loss carryback to the benefit of paying minimum estimated taxes.

One way your corporation can pay quarterly estimated income tax payments is to base this year's estimated tax payments on 100% of last year's tax. This is a good strategy for a growing corporation. Even though your corporation's taxable income (and the related income tax) will be more this year than last year, you can defer paying the increase in tax until year-end. During the year, your corporation can stash the tax money that will be due at year-end in a savings account. Your corporation can then earn interest without having to pay estimated-tax underpayment penalties.

But this strategy applies only if your corporation paid income tax the previous year. A zero-tax year does not allow you zero estimated quarterly payments the next year. On the contrary, a zero-tax year forces you to make quarterly estimated payments the next year equal to 100% of the tax that will be due that year. If you have a zero-tax year, you lose the benefit of a "growth year tax deferral." For this reason, it is sometimes better to pay a small corporate income tax rather than no income tax at all.

☞**EXAMPLE:** Mr. Smith is the sole shareholder-employee of Smith Company, a first-year business operating on a calendar tax year. At the end of 1997, Mr. Smith plans to take a salary large enough to reduce his corporation's taxable income to zero. But if he does this, he will not be able to base the corporation's 1998 quarterly estimated income tax payments on the 1997 zero tax. Instead, Smith Company will be required to pay, in four quarterly installments, 100% of the corporate income tax that will be due in 1998.

Mr. Smith projects that the corporate income tax for 1998—after salary deductions—could be as high as $10,000. If Smith Company has a zero-tax year in 1997, it will have to make 1998 quarterly estimated tax payments of $2,500 each and will not be able to defer any of the corporate income tax due until year-end.

Instead of paying himself a salary large enough to reduce Smith Company's 1997 taxable income to zero, Mr. Smith takes a salary that reduces the company's taxable income to $26. On this $26 in corporate taxable income, the company will pay $4 in federal income tax.

Because the company pays income tax in 1997, it is now only required to make four quarterly installments in 1998 of 1997's total tax. So instead of having to make four quarterly installments of $2,500 each, Smith Company is required to make four quarterly installments of only $1 each. Smith Company will not have to pay the 1998 balance due of $9,996 until March 15, 1999 (the due date for filing the 1998 corporate income tax return). During 1998, Smith Company can bank the $9,996 and earn interest. Even if it earns only 3% on the $9,996, that's an extra $300 in Smith Company's pocket. This is obviously a good return on a $4 tax payment.

♀ **PLANNING POINTERS:** Generating a small taxable income in the first year of business is a good idea for a company that plans to grow in the second year. By doing this, the corporation minimizes the required corporate estimated income tax installments for the second year.

A zero-tax year can also occur in a net-operating-loss year. In this case, you may want to carry back the corporate net operating loss to an earlier year to recoup previously paid income tax. If the net operating loss is small and will not recoup much in previous years' income taxes, it may be wiser to reduce the loss and show a small profit. You should do this if the benefit of making small quarterly estimated payments the following year outweighs the amount of tax you will recoup by carrying back a net operating loss from a zero-tax year.

There is another problem with a zero-tax year. If you are forced to make quarterly estimated income tax payments that equal 100% of the current year's tax, you will probably end up overpaying the estimates. This is because it is generally impossible to know a year ahead of time the exact amount of income tax that will be due for the year. So you have a choice: Either overpay the estimated payments and lose interest earnings (to avoid IRS underpayment penalties) or underpay the estimated tax payments and earn more interest (and risk paying IRS underpayment penalties). Since the amount of the underpayment penalties is probably more than what you can earn in interest, you are forced to overpay your estimates. This is another reason for avoiding a zero-tax year. After a "small"-tax year, you know exactly how much has to be paid in estimated quarterly installments the following year.

☑ CHECKLIST:

- Instead of having your corporation generate zero taxable income, have it generate a "small" amount of taxable income.
- You can base next year's required quarterly income tax installments on this year's small income tax, deferring the bulk of next year's income tax due until year-end.
- If your corporation has zero taxable income for this year, it is required to make quarterly estimated income tax payments next year based on 100% of next year's actual tax.
- In a net-operating-loss year, measure the benefit of the net operating loss carryback. The amount of tax the net operating loss carryback can recoup should outweigh the disadvantage of having to pay estimated taxes the following year that equal 100% of the tax due for that year.

82 Earn a Larger After-Tax Return on Your Investments

$ Shift dividend income to business corporation by transferring stock shares to corporation.

$ Avoid personal income tax on dividend income.

$ Enjoy preferential tax treatment as corporate dividend income.

$ This tip is ideal for sole shareholders of business corporations who also have a personal stock portfolio.

If you are considering incorporating your business or already have a business and run it as a regular C corporation (not as an S corporation), don't overlook the benefit you could reap if your corporation were to own some or all of your personal investment stock portfolio. It could mean big income tax savings, and that would translate into a larger return on your investment.

As an individual investor, you have to pay income tax on all the dividends you earn from your stock investments. But this is not true for a corporate investor. A regular C corporation can deduct part of the dividends it earns from any domestic U.S. stock it owns.

How much your corporation can deduct depends on how much stock it owns. If your corporation owns less than 20% of another company's stock, it can deduct 70% of the dividends received. If your corporation owns 20–80% of another company's stock, it can deduct 80% of the dividends received. And if your corporation owns more than 80% of another company's stock, it can deduct 100% of the dividends received.

The idea is to transfer personally owned shares of stock in other domestic U.S. companies to your corporation in exchange for shares of your corporation's stock. By doing this, you shift your personal dividend earnings to your corporation and save on income taxes.

But is there a tax bite involved in this transfer? Do you have to recognize taxable gain on the shares before they reach your corporation? The answer is no, not if you are transferring the shares to your business corporation and you meet a few other requirements. You must exchange the shares only for shares of your business corporation. You must own at least 80% of your business corporation after you have transferred the shares. These requirements make this strategy ideal for sole shareholders who own and operate their own business using the regular corporate form.

☞**EXAMPLE:** Mr. Smith owns shares of stock in several domestic blue chip companies. He earns about $3,000 a year in dividends from these stocks. Since he is in the 31% federal personal income tax bracket, he pays $930 ($3,000 times 31%) each year in federal income taxes on the dividend earnings.

Mr. Smith is also the sole owner of a small manufacturing company, Smith Company, which he incorporated some years ago as a regular C company (not as an S corporation). After paying Mr.

Smith's salary, Smith Company usually shows about $60,000 in annual taxable earnings. This puts the company in the 25% corporate federal income tax bracket.

If Mr. Smith transfers his personally owned shares of domestic stock to Smith Company in exchange for shares of Smith Company stock, he will not have to pay any capital gains income tax on the transfer. Since all the shares of blue chip stock represent a very small percentage of ownership in the blue chip companies, Smith Company will obviously own less than 20% of those companies after the transfer. Smith Company will be limited to deducting 70% of the dividends earned.

But even though the company will be allowed only the smallest possible deduction for the dividends it will receive, the tax savings will be big. In the first place, 70% of the dividends received are deductible. This means Smith Company will have to pay income tax on only 30% of the $3,000 annual dividend earnings, $900 ($3,000 times 30%). And at the 25% corporate federal income tax bracket, instead of Mr. Smith's 31% personal federal income tax bracket, Smith Company will have to pay only $225 ($900 times 25%) in federal corporate income taxes.

By Mr. Smith transferring his shares of stock to his corporation, the annual federal tax bill on the $3,000 in dividend earnings drops from $930 to $225.

♀PLANNING POINTERS: To take advantage of the dividends-received deduction for the first year of the transfer, the corporation must own the stock for a minimum number of days during the year. You can't wait until the last day of the corporation's tax year, transfer the shares, and benefit from the dividends-received deduction. For dividends paid after September 5, 1997, the '97 tax act complicates the corporation's holding period requirements. The corporation must hold dividend paying common stock at least 46 days during the 90-day period that begins 45 days before the stock's ex-dividend date. Under the new rules, you have to plan the corporation's holding period around the ex-dividend date (the day the corporation becomes entitled to the dividend) in order to take the dividends-received deduction.

- Compare your personal income tax bite on dividend income with what your corporation would pay after taking the dividends-received deduction.
- Check to make sure you meet the requirements for a tax-free transfer of your stock shares to your corporation.
- Make the transfer of your investment shares of stock in exchange for shares of stock in your business corporation in a timely fashion. Keep your eye on the ex-dividend date.

83 Use Your Corporation to Take a Big Charitable Deduction for Donated Inventory

$ This loophole involves corporate charitable deductions of business inventory items.

$ It allows for a corporate tax deduction greater than the cost of the gifted items.

$ Participating employees also receive a deductible charitable contribution on their personal income tax returns.

$ Donated inventory can indirectly benefit family members of employees who make contributions.

Your regular C corporation is usually allowed to deduct the cost of inventory donated to a charity. But because of a special rule in the tax laws and recent guidance from the IRS, your corporation can also establish an employee product gift program and write off more than the cost of the donated items. And not only does your corporation get a charitable deduction, but you and your employees can get a charitable deduction on your own personal income tax returns.

The tax law allows for a special deduction for corporations that donate inventory to qualified organizations—inventory that will be used in caring for infants, the needy, and the ill. In its recent guidance, the IRS considers infants to be children under the age of 18. Qualified organizations include schools, hospitals, nursing homes, food banks, museums, and other organizations that are tax-exempt charitable organizations under IRC Section 501(c)(3). The IRS makes it clear, however, that public schools do not qualify as recipients of this special benefit.

Using this special tax rule, your corporation can write off the cost of the donated item and in addition write off one-half the difference between the item's cost and the item's selling price (limited to 200% of the cost).

On top of this increased charitable corporate deduction, the IRS will allow employees to personally deduct the expense of any item they purchased at cost and then donated to a qualifying organization. The employees choose the qualifying organization from a list of organizations provided by their corporate employer.

One more plus: The recent IRS guidance says that the IRS will not disallow these charitable donations if the children of donating corporate employees benefit indirectly from the donations. That is, even if the benefit is specifically enjoyed by the children of the donating employees, it is still deductible.

☞**EXAMPLE:** Mr. Smith is an employee and the sole shareholder of Smith Company, a retail computer hardware outlet. Mr. Smith's daughter attends a nonpublic school that qualifies as a tax-exempt organization under IRC Section 501(c)(3). Mr. Smith selects a computer from his inventory at work and contributes it to the school. Even though his daughter will be able to use it along with the other students and thereby will benefit from it indirectly, the IRS will still allow the charitable contribution.

The computer has a selling price of $1,000. Mr. Smith pays Smith Company $250 for a share of the computer (25% of the selling price), which then enables him to take a personal income tax deduction for the $250.

The cost to Smith Company for the computer is $400, and the company's charitable deduction—according to the IRS guidance—is figured in this way:

1. First, Smith Company calculates its "profit" from Mr. Smith's $250 contribution. From the $250, it subtracted $100 (which is 25% of the $400 cost to Smith Company). The resulting $150 is Smith Company's profit.

2. Next, Smith Company calculates the value of its deduction without taking into account the money it received from its employee. It has a corporate charitable deduction of $600 calculated in this way: It can deduct the remaining 75% of the $400 cost ($300) plus 50% of the difference between the item's cost and the item's selling price. The difference between the item's cost and selling price is $600 ($1,000 less $400), and 50% of this difference is $300. So, $300 plus $300 equals the $600 corporate charitable deduction.

3. Finally, Smith Company has to reduce its charitable deduction by the amount of profit it received from its employee. When Smith Company subtracts the $150 profit from the charitable deduction of $600, it has a tax-deductible contribution of $450. So instead of the corporation receiving a corporate charitable tax deduction of $400 (the cost of the donated inventory), it receives a $450 corporate charitable tax deduction. In addition, Mr. Smith gets a deduction on his personal income tax return for $250. That's $700 in combined corporate and personal income tax deductions, instead of only a $400 corporate charitable tax deduction.

♀**PLANNING POINTERS:** The IRS guidance on an employee product gift program does not mention any requirement for a specific written plan; however, corporations should outline their charitable intent in their corporate minutes. They should also be careful to keep records of the costs and the selling prices of donated inventory items. Also, they should request letters from the recipient organization affirming that the gifts will be used to help fulfill the organization's tax-exempt purpose (not sold for the cash).

If you do not know which charitable organizations qualify, contact the National Association for the Exchange of Industrial Resources ▾

▾

▾

at (800) 562-0955. NAEIR is a nonprofit clearinghouse for charitable donations of inventory.

☑ CHECKLIST:

- Your corporation should document your charitable intent in the corporate minutes.
- Establish a list of various qualifying organizations from which the employees can choose to make a charitable gift.
- Establish a list of inventory items that can be donated by the employees, along with a cost/sales price list for those items.
- For single donations with a value of more than $250, the recipient tax-exempt organization should provide a letter verifying the receipt of the gift.
- Employees should deduct their personal charitable contribution of a portion of the inventory item on their Form 1040 Schedule A.

84 Have Your Corporation Pay You Rent Instead of Salary

$ This loophole is for taxpayers who are shareholder-employees of a regular C corporation.

$ Making rent payments instead of salary payments saves payroll tax.

$ You must determine and document the "fair rent" amount.

$ Discount the rent you charge your corporation for your personal use of the same space.

$ Enter into a written lease agreement with your corporation, specifying all the terms.

If you are a shareholder-employee in a regular C corporation, you should take cash out of your corporation in the least tax-expensive way possible. Paying salary is one way to take cash out of your corporation. But a less expensive way is for your corporation to pay you rent.

With a salary, your corporation takes a corporate income tax deduction for the salary paid, and you pay personal income tax on the salary received. This is certainly less expensive than having your corporation pay you dividends. With a dividend payment, the corporation does not get a corporate income tax deduction, and you still have to pay personal income tax on the dividends you receive.

But having your corporation pay you rent rather than salary saves you even more because your corporation is not required to pay payroll taxes (Social Security and Medicare) on the rent it pays to you.

☞ **EXAMPLE:** Mr. Smith is a shareholder-employee of Smith Company. He uses an office at home to do corporate paperwork and also uses his garage to store corporate materials. Mr. Smith checks around and discovers that to rent similar space, Smith Company would have to pay a third party $600 per month.

Mr. Smith enters into a written lease agreement with Smith Company. Because the office space and garage space are not used regularly and exclusively for company business, and to charge a fair rent, Mr. Smith discounts the monthly rent to $500. The discount—and the reason for it—are noted in the written lease agreement.

Mr. Smith had planned for Smith Company to pay him a salary of $50,000 for 1997. Since Smith Company pays him annual rent of $6,000 ($500 times 12 months), Mr. Smith has the company reduce his salary from $50,000 to $44,000. Mr. Smith still receives $50,000 for the year, and Smith Company still has a $50,000 corporate income tax deduction. But the difference is that no payroll tax is due on the $6,000 paid in rent.

The company saves $459 ($6,000 times 7.65%) that it would have had to pay on $6,000 in salary, and Mr. Smith saves $459 ($6,000 times 7.65%) that would have been withheld from his salary for Social Security and Medicare. By paying $6,000 in rent (instead of salary), a total of $918 is saved each year.

PLANNING POINTERS: The amount of rent you charge must be "fair rent." Before entering into the lease agreement, you should document the rent charged for similar space by outside third parties. Keep the fair rental documentation in case of a tax audit. If you don't document the fairness of the rent, the IRS may attempt to recharacterize the "unreasonable" portion of the rent as a nondeductible dividend payment. This means your corporation could lose an income tax deduction and end up paying more corporate income tax. One way to avoid IRS recharacterization of the deductible rent paid as a nondeductible dividend payment is to set up a hedge agreement with your corporation. See Loophole 89 "Keep the IRS Out of Your Pocket with a Hedge Agreement (page 279).

In determining the amount of "fair rent" charged to your corporation, be certain to discount the amount of rent for any personal use of the space your corporation uses for business purposes. Note this discount and the reason for it (the personal use of the same space) in the lease agreement.

In other circumstances, not using the space regularly and exclusively for business purposes keeps you from taking a tax deduction for depreciation and other related expenses, such as insurance and utilities. However, since 1987, if you rent space in your principal residence to your corporation, you can no longer deduct these items anyway. You are limited to deducting items you are already able to deduct without the rent income: mortgage interest, property taxes, and casualty losses.

So if you rent out space in your principal residence for your corporation to use regularly and exclusively for business, you won't increase the deductions on your personal income tax return. Renting out the space (at a discount) and using it for both business and personal purposes will not disallow potential tax breaks on the future sale of your principal residence.

☑ CHECKLIST:

- Rent space in your principal residence to your corporation and reduce your corporate salary by the amount of the rent paid.

- Document that the rent you charge to your corporation is a fair rent.
- It is not necessary to use the rented space regularly and exclusively for business purposes. Use it for personal purposes as well as business purposes, and document the personal use.
- Enter into a written lease agreement with your corporation that outlines the fair rent for the space and the discount reducing the fair rent (due to your use of the rented space for personal purposes).

85 Use Your Company's Growth to Help Fund Your Child's College Education

$ This strategy is best for a company that is about to grow.

$ Give shares of your company's stock to your young child.

$ When your child reaches college age, your company redeems all of the child's shares.

$ You get the benefit of tax deferral and long-term capital gains treatment, and you avoid "kiddie tax" treatment.

If you have just incorporated a business and plan for it to grow, here is way you can use some of your company's growth to fund your child's college education. Just give your child some shares in the company. When your child reaches college age, he or she can redeem all the shares and pay income tax on the redemption using the favorable long-term capital gains tax rates. In the meantime, the appreciation on the shares of stock goes untaxed, so you do not have to worry about the so-called kiddie tax rules.

EXAMPLE: Mr. Smith has just started Smith Company, a software development company. Mr. Smith capitalized the company by contributing $10,000 for 100 shares of stock. At the time of the initial capitalization, Mr. Smith gifted 10 shares of stock (from the initial capitalization of 100 shares) to his baby daughter. The value of this gift was $1,000.

Mr. Smith expects the company to grow. Assume that by the time Mr. Smith's daughter is ready to attend college, the value of the 100 shares of stock has risen to $500,000. Mr. Smith's daughter's stock will be worth $50,000. She can redeem all 10 of her shares and will have to pay income tax on the gain of $49,000 ($50,000 redemption proceeds less initial value of $1,000), but she can use the long-term capital gains tax rates.

PLANNING POINTERS: To receive the benefit of using the long-term capital gains rate, your company will have to redeem all the shares of stock that your child owns. The redemption cannot be for only some of the shares.

Also, your child will have to stay out of the affairs of your company for at least 10 years after the redemption. So if you plan for your children to follow you in your business, you should consider this carefully before your company makes the redemption and your child treats the profit from the redemption as a long-term capital gain.

If you want your child to be able to stay involved in the business, the worst-case scenario is that the redemption of the shares will be treated as dividend income and taxed at ordinary income tax rates. Your child—and you—will still have enjoyed a deferral of the tax until the redemption occurs.

This deferral is important. Under the so-called kiddie tax rules, children under age 14 who earn investment income in excess of $1,300 (for 1997) must pay income tax on the excess income using their parents' higher income tax rates. By using the growth of your company, your child can defer recognizing taxable income until he or she is old enough to be taxed without reference to your higher income tax bracket. So even if your child ultimately has to pay the tax using the ordinary income tax rates, he or she will still pay less than if he or she had to pay the tax under the kiddie tax rules.

☑ CHECKLIST:

- Give your child shares of stock in your company before the company's growth increases the value of the shares.
- When your child reaches college age, have your company redeem all the shares so that your child can pay income tax on the taxable gain using the favorable long-term capital gains tax rates.

86	Cut Your Tax in Half When You Invest in Your Child's Corporation

$ If your child's company qualifies, you can invest in it and pay tax on only one-half of your profit.

$ Any tax you do pay is limited to a maximum of 14% of the entire profit.

$ To reap this benefit, the company must meet certain requirements, and you must hold your investment in the company for more than five years.

You can invest in your child's business and receive favorable tax treatment from the government—if your child's business is set up as a regular C corporation, you invest by purchasing stock in the business, and the business is eligible to issue "qualified small business stock." Then, as long as you hold the stock for more than five years, only 50% of your profit from its sale will be taxed.

Unfortunately, the new capital gains tax rates of 10% or 20% will not apply when you sell your shares of qualified small business stock. Depending on your level of taxable income in the year you sell the stock, the old capital gains tax rates of either 15% or 28% will apply.

But this is not as bad as it sounds. Because you can exclude 50% of the gain from taxable income, your effective capital gains tax rate on the entire gain will be either 7.5% (15% times 50%) or 14% (28% times 50%).

☞**EXAMPLE:** Mr. Smith's son John is starting a small manufacturing company with good prospects. Because of the size and nature of the business (see Planning Pointers below), the company is eligible to issue "qualified small business stock."

Mr. Smith invests in the company by purchasing shares of stock worth $50,000 on November 1, 1997. He holds the stock until December 1, 2002 (more than five years), and then allows the company to redeem the stock for $100,000.

On the profit of $50,000 ($100,000 sales price less $50,000 original investment), Mr. Smith will be able to exclude one-half the gain ($25,000) from his taxable income. If Mr. Smith is in the 28% (or higher) ordinary income tax bracket, he will have to pay $7,000 in capital gains tax ($25,000 times 28% capital gains tax). On his entire gain of $50,000, Mr. Smith is effectively paying only a 14% capital gains tax ($7,000 divided by $50,000).

♀**PLANNING POINTERS:** For a corporation to qualify to issue this tax-saving stock, it must be a regular C corporation with gross assets of less than $50 million. Obviously, this gross assets test will not be a limitation to most start-up small businesses.

To qualify for this special tax treatment, the stock must be issued after August 10, 1993, which makes it ideal for new businesses. The shares of stock must be issued to the shareholder by the corporation. Shares of stock purchased from another shareholder do not qualify.

For the entire period that the shareholder owns the shares of stock (five years plus), at least 80% of the corporation's assets must be used in the "qualified trade or business" of the corporation. The new rules that allow this tax-saving benefit do not say what a qualifying trade or business is—they only define what a qualifying trade or business is not. Qualifying trades or businesses are businesses other than the following:

- any trades or businesses that perform services in the fields of health, law, accounting, actuarial science, architecture, athletics, brokerage services, consulting, engineering, financial services, performing arts, or any trades or businesses where the principal asset is the reputation or skill of one or more of its employees
- any banking, insurance, financing, investing, leasing, or similar businesses
- any farming business, including the business of raising or harvesting trees
- any business involved in extracting or producing a natural resource that is able to take a deduction for percentage depletion
- any business of operating a hotel, motel, restaurant, or similar business

So, if your child is starting, for example, a law practice, an insurance business, a hotel, or a farm, it is clear that you are denied the privilege of excluding 50% of the gain on your investment. On the other hand, a trucking company, a manufacturing company, a construction company, or a computer software company all seem to qualify.

☑ CHECKLIST:

- If you are considering investing in your child's new C corporation, determine whether the corporation's business is a "qualified trade or business" for the purpose of taking the 50% exclusion from income benefit.
- If the corporation qualifies, request that there be written corporate minutes stating that the stock sale to you qualifies as IRC Section 1202 stock. This is not currently required but it will help to document the future tax-beneficial tax treatment for the stock.
- While you hold the stock, be certain to review company financial data on a regular basis to confirm that at least 80% of the company assets are being used at all times in the qualified trade or business.
- When you finally sell the stock (after at least five years), be

certain to exclude 50% of the gain you recognize from taxable income. The applicable tax rate on the taxable portion of the gain will be either 15% or 28%, depending on your total taxable income for the year.

87 Define Your Corporate Fiscal Year with an Eye Toward Personal Income Tax Deferral

$ This tip is for corporations that use the accrual method of accounting and have shareholder-employees who own less than 50% of the corporation.

$ Corporation takes an income tax deduction now and pays shareholder-employees later.

$ Shareholder-employees defer personal income tax until next calendar year, when they receive the cash.

$ This is especially beneficial when the corporation will have a lean year after a profitable year.

If you are incorporating your current business or a new business as a regular C corporation, you should define your corporate fiscal year with an eye toward personal income tax deferral. If this is properly handled, your corporation can deduct a salary paid to you at the end of your fiscal year, but you won't have to pay personal income tax on that salary until the next calendar year.

You can use this method of personal income tax deferral if your corporation uses the accrual method of accounting and you and the other corporation shareholder-employees do not each own more than 50% of the outstanding shares of stock in the company (either directly or indirectly). You "create" the deferral by operating your corporation either on a calendar year basis or with a fiscal year that ends October 31 or November 30.

A company using the accrual method of accounting can take a

deduction for an expense it has not actually paid—that is, even if the expense deducted is still only a "payable." To deduct unpaid expenses for tax purposes, you must have completed all the actions necessary to establish the payable, you must have determined the amount of the payable accurately, and your corporation must have met a special tax requirement called "economic performance."

The first two requirements for an "accrued" corporate salary deduction are pretty straightforward: You create the salary expense and you determine the amount of the salary expense. The third requirement, however, complicates matters and necessitates that you base your business on the calendar year or on a fiscal calendar with an October or November year-end.

"Economic performance" means that your corporation must actually pay the deducted expense within two and a half months after the close of the corporation's tax year. For example, if your corporate year ends October 31 and the corporation accrues and deducts a shareholder salary, the corporation must actually make the salary payment by January 15.

By using an October 31 fiscal year-end, your corporation has an income tax deduction in the current year for the salary expense, while you, as a cash-basis/calendar-year individual taxpayer, defer taking the salary into income until the next calendar year (when it is actually received).

Once you meet this third requirement, your corporation has a tax deduction in the current fiscal year for the salary and you do not have to pay personal income tax on the salary until your next calendar year.

☞**EXAMPLE:** Mr. Smith is one of three unrelated shareholder-employees in the Smith Shoe Company. Each of the three shareholder-employees owns one-third of the company (no one shareholder-employee owns more than 50%). Because the Smith Shoe Company has an inventory, it is required by the IRS to operate with an accrual accounting method. The company fiscal year ends November 30.

During November 1997, while evaluating year-to-date operations, Mr. Smith notes that the projected current fiscal year's net income for the corporation will be $95,000, much more than previously expected. Per the corporate federal income tax rates, the corporation will owe a total federal income tax of $20,550 on this income. On top of this, because Smith Shoe Company has seriously underestimated its required quarterly estimated income tax payments, it will owe underpayment penalties as well.

Instead of settling for this hefty corporate income tax liability and its related underpayment penalties, Mr. Smith and the other two shareholder-employees elect to accrue a salary bonus of $15,000 for each shareholder-employee. As a result, Smith Shoe Company gains an additional income tax deduction of $45,000 ($15,000 times 3), thereby reducing the corporation's net taxable income for the fiscal year to $50,000 ($95,000 less $45,000). The additional deduction also reduces the corporation's total federal income tax liability to $7,500 and results in a current corporate federal income tax savings of $13,050. Likewise, as a result of its reduced corporate federal income tax liability, the Smith Shoe Company can greatly reduce its underpayment penalties.

In keeping with the "economic performance" rules, Smith Shoe Company actually pays the salary bonuses to the three shareholder-employees on February 14, 1998 (within two and a half months after the close of the fiscal year). Since all three shareholder-employees are cash-basis/calendar-year individual taxpayers (almost all individual taxpayers are cash-basis/calendar-year taxpayers), they do not have to take the salary and pay the income tax on it until 1998. And even though they receive the salary payments in February 1998, they can have federal income tax withheld at any time during the year (right up until December 31, 1998) and still avoid underpayment penalties on their personal income tax returns for 1998.

If all three shareholder-employees are in the 28% personal federal income tax bracket, the government would take $12,600 in personal federal income tax from them for the $45,000 in salary bonuses their company paid them. But this is almost equal to the $13,050 the corporation saved in taxes by deducting the $45,000. What the corporation really gains is the use of this money for two and a half months. The three shareholder-employees gain from the deferral by getting use of the money for another nine and a half months. Between the corporation and the shareholder-employees, the one-year deferral at a 5% earnings rate generates about $650, money that stays in the pockets of the company and shareholder-employees.

♀PLANNING POINTERS: This deferral strategy is especially effective when your corporation expects a lean year after a profitable year. If your corporation takes a tax deduction at the end of the profitable year, it will save more in income tax than if it waits to deduct the salary payment in the following lean year, when it will be in a lower income tax bracket. Because of the drop in corporate business during the lean year to come, your shareholder-employee salary may have to be reduced. In such a case, the additional deferred salary will not push you up into a higher personal income tax bracket but instead will replace money you lost in the lean-year salary reduction.

You should formally establish the amount of any salary bonus before the end of the corporate tax year. You should draw up corporate minutes to establish the corporation's liability for the salary—a book entry is not enough. You do not have to know the exact dollar amount of the accrued salary bonus—it can be based on a percentage of profits or some other formula. If you use such a formula, you must adopt the formula before the end of the corporate fiscal year, and it should be documented formally in your corporate minutes.

You should also ensure that shareholder-employees do not have "constructive receipt" of the salary bonuses before they receive them. That is, the bonuses must not be available to the shareholder-employees until the next calendar year. There should be no power in the corporate by-laws (or anywhere else) allowing a shareholder-employee to compel the corporation to pay the bonus at an earlier date. The corporate minutes should state that the salary bonuses are unavailable—absolutely and without qualification—until the agreed-upon date in the next calendar year.

Making sure that your corporation has insufficient funds to pay the cash bonuses at the time of their accrual will also help to protect you against an IRS determination of constructive receipt. Clearly, documenting the planned use of any money on hand at the time of the accrual will help in this regard. So long as you can show that the corporate funds on hand were needed or may have been needed for other purposes, you should be able to defend the corporation against an IRS determination of constructive receipt.

If you fail to protect yourself against an IRS determination of constructive receipt, the IRS might, as a result, force you and your corporate shareholder-employees to include your salary bonuses in your personal income in the current calendar year instead of the next calendar year. In short, constructive receipt kills the deferral.

Again, this deferral strategy can be used only for shareholder-employees who own no more than 50% of the company. Note also that the strategy is unavailable to personal service corporations, no matter how much of the company stock each shareholder-employee owns.

Finally, there is a way to extend the two-and-a-half-month corporation payment period. The IRS will allow the company to make the actual payment of the salary bonus at a later date if it is impractical (either administratively or economically) to make the actual payment at the end of the two-and-a-half-month period and such impracticability could not have been foreseen.

The IRS specifically states that the lack of funds with which to make the payment is a justified excuse for extending the actual payment date, as long as the lack of funds was unforeseen.

If you wish to extend the date of payment past the two-and-a-half-month deadline, be careful to document the reason for the delay, and be able to show that this delay could not have been foreseen when you originally accrued the salary bonuses at the end of the corporate fiscal year.

☑ CHECKLIST:

- If your corporation will operate on the accrual method of accounting and there are shareholder-employees in the company who do not own more than 50% of the company, establish either a calendar tax year or a fiscal tax year ending on October 31 or November 30.
- Determine the benefit of a salary bonus deferral. Calculate the current corporate income tax savings as well as the deferred personal income tax liabilities.
- Formally establish the amount of the bonus—whether it be an exact dollar amount or based on some formula—by including the amount of the bonus in the corporate minutes prior to the corporate tax year-end.
- Avoid potential IRS recharacterization of the bonus as constructively received by the shareholder-employees in the earlier calendar year.

- If the corporation is unable to make the actual bonus payment within the two-and-a-half-month period, be careful to document why it was impractical for the corporation to make the payment in a timely manner and why this impracticability could not have been foreseen when the salary bonus was originally accrued and deducted by the corporation.

88 Be Tax Ready for Success and Failure

$ Capitalize your corporation with regard to both success and failure.

$ Capitalize with a shareholder loan as well as a stock purchase.

$ A successful corporation makes deductible corporate interest payments as well as nondeductible dividend payments.

$ Before the business fails, exchange shareholder loan for stock.

$ When the business fails, you benefit from a larger first-year personal income tax deduction.

If you can, why not have it both ways? Properly capitalize your closely held corporation in the beginning, keep your eyes open along the way, and enjoy tax savings whether your small business corporation succeeds or fails. The only requirement is that you are careful with your corporate capitalization—otherwise, you may lose one of your options and your tax benefits will no longer be guaranteed, regardless of your corporation's success or failure.

The best way to capitalize a success-bound corporation is for the company shareholders to both buy stock in the company and make loans to the company.

With a part stock/part loan capitalization, a successful corporation will be able to do more than pay dividends to its shareholders on the shares of stock they hold. The corporation will also be able to pay interest to the shareholders on the shareholder loans. This is important because the corporation cannot deduct from its taxes the dividends it pays its shareholders. The interest it pays on the shareholder loans, however, is tax deductible. Of course, the shareholders must include both the dividends and the interest they receive in their computation of personal income, but at least the corporation has a tax deduction for the interest payments.

The best way for a failed corporation to be capitalized is for the company shareholders to own shares of stock only. If a failed corporation qualifies as a "small business corporation" (generally, a corporation with less than $1 million in capitalization), the shareholders can deduct their losses on the corporate stock. Shareholders who are married and file jointly can deduct up to $100,000 each year ($50,000 for others not filing jointly) for these so-called Section 1244 losses.

So what is it to be? Bet on success, or have a safety net in case of failure? Should your shareholders make loans to your corporation, or should they only purchase shares of stock in the corporation?

If you are careful, you do not have to choose. You can benefit either way. Initially, you should capitalize your corporation partly with a loan and partly with a purchase of stock. If you see that the corporation is heading for failure (but before it actually does fail), have the corporation issue shares of stock for the cancellation of the shareholder loan. As long as the debt is not a "security" (e.g., a corporate bond) and as long as the debt is not owed to the shareholder for personal services, the stock issued for the shareholder loan can qualify for the tax-beneficial Section 1244 loss treatment when the corporation fails.

EXAMPLE: Smith Company has operated successfully for five years. When Mr. Smith, the sole shareholder, set up the company, he capitalized it by purchasing $15,000 in shares of stock and loaning the company $45,000. The company has had to pay Mr. Smith some nondeductible dividends on his stock ownership, but most of his return on investment has come from deductible interest paid by the company for the shareholder loan.

For various reasons, business has taken a turn for the worse, and it looks as if the company may go belly up very soon. Mr. Smith has the company issue him shares of stock in exchange for canceling the balance of his outstanding shareholder loan—say, $35,000—to the company ($10,000 of the original loan has been paid back to Mr. Smith over the five-year period). These shares of stock qualify as Section 1244 stock. When the business finally does fail, instead of deducting only $15,000 Mr. Smith will be able to deduct $50,000 ($15,000 plus $35,000) on his personal income tax return for the year the business fails.

If Mr. Smith had not exchanged the shareholder loan for stock, the loan would have to be treated as a nonbusiness bad debt. Since nonbusiness bad debts are accorded only short-term capital loss treatment, if Mr. Smith had no capital gains to offset by the "bad debt" capital loss, he would be limited to deducting only $3,000 of these losses per year. At that rate, it would take him up to 12 years to deduct the same $35,000 as a nonbusiness bad debt.

$\textbf{PLANNING POINTERS:}$ Be careful when you capitalize your corporation. Do not capitalize too "thinly." A thin capitalization occurs when too much of the capitalization is a shareholder loan and not a stock purchase. When this happens, the IRS considers part of the loan to be "disguised equity." Exchanging this disguised equity for shares of stock will not qualify for Section 1244 deductible treatment.

To avoid this backfire and ensure the Section 1244 deduction, the ratio of shareholder loan to shareholder equity should not be more than 3 to 1. In the example, the ratio is $45,000 to $15,000, or 3 to 1, so there should be no problem with the shareholder loan being treated as disguised equity. Thus, the cancellation of the shareholder debt in exchange for stock would still qualify for deductible Section 1244 treatment.

The IRS will not accord a Section 1244 loss for stock that is exchanged for a shareholder loan when the shareholder loan has already become worthless. That's why it is important that you make the switch before the business actually goes belly up—as far ahead as possible of your corporation's board of directors' vote to dissolve the corporation.

Note the following requirements for Section 1244 treatment:

- Section 1244 stock is issued by a "small business corporation." The total money and property it receives from its shareholders for the corporation's stock, contributions to capital, and any paid-in surplus cannot exceed $1,000,000.

- For the corporation's stock to qualify for Section 1244 treatment, in the year of the corporation's demise more than 50% of the corporation's gross receipts for the five preceding years (all the preceding years if the corporation has been in existence less than five years) must be from sources other than interest, dividends, annuities, royalties, rents, and the sale of stock or securities. In other words, the bulk of the corporate receipts must be from active business and not investments.

- Section 1244 ordinary loss treatment can be used only by the person to whom the stock was originally issued. If the stock has changed hands since the original sale, Section 1244 treatment is not an option for the new shareholder.

- Shareholders must contribute money or property for the Section 1244 stock. An exchange for services, securities, or other stock will not qualify.

- Stock issued after July 18, 1984, can be common or preferred stock and still qualify for Section 1244 treatment.

☑ CHECKLIST:

- Capitalize your corporation partly with a loan and partly with a stock purchase. Do not make the loan portion too large (i.e., avoid "thin" capitalization).

- While the business is successful, the corporation pays you deductible interest on your loan as well as nondeductible dividends on your stock.

- When you see that the business may fail but before it actually does fail, have your corporation issue you stock in exchange for forgiving your shareholder loan.

- In the year the corporation fails, deduct the cost of all your corporate stock from your other ordinary income as a Section 1244 loss (subject to annual $100,000 deduction limit if married filing jointly; $50,000 if filing otherwise).

89 Keep the IRS Out of Your Pocket with a Hedge Agreement

$ This is a corporate audit safety net.
$ It is especially beneficial for closely held corporations.
$ It defends the corporation and shareholder-employees from having payments made to shareholder-employees recharacterized by the IRS as dividend payments.
$ You avoid the double tax associated with dividend payments.

The best way for your closely held corporation to avoid an IRS hassle over the deduction of the reasonable reimbursement of employee expenditures is to create a hedge agreement between your corporation and any shareholder-employees, including yourself.

What you think is reasonable and what the IRS thinks is reasonable can often be stormy oceans apart. When the IRS audits your closely held corporation's tax return, chances are good that it will attempt to recharacterize the payments made to you, the shareholder-employee.

These recharacterized payments can include what are considered unreasonable salary payments, unreasonable rent payments, unreasonably reimbursed travel and entertainment expenses, unreasonably reimbursed legal expenses incurred on behalf of the corporation, and other unreasonable expenses reimbursed by the corporation.

By regarding these payments as unreasonable, the IRS is trying to transform them into corporate dividend payments made to you. In this way, deductible corporate expenditures become nondeductible, and the IRS benefits from the double tax that a dividend payment carries—one tax from your corporation and one tax from you personally. A tactic you thought was saving you money ends up costing you a whole lot more.

However, with a hedge agreement, the double tax can be avoided. All that is required is that you, the shareholder-employee, agree to repay the corporation for any payments disallowed by the IRS. The corporation loses the deduction, but you personally deduct the repayment. The hedge effectively brings everything back to the beginning, prior to your corporation's deduction of the payment and your inclusion of the payment in personal income. The treatment of expense as dividend can be avoided by either of the following: The cash comes back to the corporation as "payback" or the corporation reduces payments made to the shareholder-employee in the future.

The following resolution, taken from a corporation's by-laws, is one example of a hedge agreement allowed by the IRS: "Any payments made to an officer of the Corporation such as a salary, commission, bonus, interest, or rent, or entertainment expense incurred by him, which shall be disallowed in whole or in part as a deductible expense by the Internal Revenue Service, shall be reimbursed by such officer to the Corporation to the full extent of such disallowance. It shall be the duty of the Directors, as a Board, to enforce payment of each such amount disallowed. In lieu of payment by the officer, subject to the determination of the Directors, proportionate amounts may be withheld from his future compensation payments until the amount owed to the corporation has been recovered."

☞ **EXAMPLE:** In an audit of Smith Company's tax return, the IRS has determined that an unreasonable rent payment of $5,000 has been paid to Ms. Smith, an employee and the sole shareholder of the company. The company deducted the payment and, falling in the 34% corporate federal income tax bracket, saved $1,700 ($5,000 times 34%). Ms. Smith, in the 31% personal federal income tax bracket, declared the payment on her personal income tax return and paid $1,550 ($5,000 times 31%) in personal income taxes. The combined transaction generated a tax savings of $150 ($1,700 saved by the corporation less $1,550 paid by Ms. Smith).

Unfortunately, the IRS wants to recharacterize the payment as a dividend payment. As such, Ms. Smith would still pay the personal income taxes of $1,550 but the corporation would no longer have tax savings of $1,700 because dividend payments are not deductible by the corporation. Instead of a combined tax savings of $150, the combined tax liability on the $5,000 payment would be $3,250 ($1,700 from the corporation and $1,550 from Ms. Smith).

Fortunately, Smith Company has a hedge agreement resolution in its by-laws. Ms. Smith must repay the company the $5,000, but everything goes back to the way it was before the original payment was made: Smith Company does not get a deduction for the $5,000, and Ms. Smith can reduce her personal income for that amount so that the $1,550 in personal taxes she had to pay comes back to her. In short, the combined tax savings of $150 on the original transaction is lost, but this is a lot better than having to pay combined taxes of $3,250 on the $5,000 payment.

PLANNING POINTERS: To establish the hedge agreement, shareholder-employees must (prior to receiving any payment) contract with the corporation that they will repay any money disallowed by the IRS.

The disallowed amounts do not necessarily have to be repaid to the corporation in cash to be deducted by the shareholder-employee. Once it is established that the amount must be "repaid," the amount can be characterized as a loan from the corporation to the shareholder-employee. Shareholder-employees can take the deduction on their personal income tax return for the "repayment," even though there has been no cash repayment. The corporation, then, offsets the loan amount by reducing future cash payments to the shareholder-employee.

As for the "future reduced payments," the shareholder-employee must still claim as personal income the full unreduced amount, even though the payments revert to the corporation to repay the recharacterized "loan."

Check your own state law. If a resolution in the by-laws is not legally binding, you should make the resolution part of an employment contract that is legally binding in your state. If you are audited, it may be wise to let the auditor know (in a subtle fashion) that you have such a resolution in your by-laws. Faced with the realization that the recharacterization of corporate payments will not bear any dividend fruit, the auditor may be deterred from even starting in that direction.

☑ CHECKLIST:

- Check with your state law to see whether a hedge agreement in your by-laws is legally binding.
- If it is, include a hedge agreement resolution in your by-laws or amend your by-laws prior to making payments to the shareholder-employees.
- If a hedge agreement is not legally binding in your state, make the hedge agreement part of an employment agreement that is legally binding in your state.

Running
Your Business as
an S Corporation

▼
▼
▼

90   Treat Your Employee Business Expenses as a Contribution to Capital for the Largest Deductible Benefit

$ S corporation employees can treat unreimbursed employee business expenses to avoid the 2% miscellaneous itemized deduction limitation.

$ This treatment also allows you to avoid complete disallowance of unreimbursed employee business expenses in years when the owner-employee fails to take a salary from the corporation.

$ This strategy is ideal for S corporations with one owner-employee but can be used when there is more than one.

If you are the sole owner-employee of an S corporation, here is a way to get the largest deductible benefit for your unreimbursed employee business expenses, even in years you don't take a salary from your corporation. With a little planning, an S corporation owner-employee can avoid the deduction limitations that most employees have to face.

Any employee with unreimbursed business expenses deducts those expenses as a miscellaneous itemized deduction on Form 1040 Schedule A, subject to the 2% limitation rule. According to this rule, certain miscellaneous deductions (including unreimbursed employee expenses) equal to 2% of a taxpayer's adjusted gross income for the year, are not allowed. For many taxpayers whose miscellaneous deductions consist mainly of unreimbursed employee expenses, this can be quite costly.

While the 2% limitation generally applies to most miscellaneous deductions, another deduction limitation, applicable specifically to S corporation owner-employees, is the result of a Tax Court ruling. In this ruling, it was decided that S corporation owner-employees who were not paid a salary by their S corporation for a particular tax year could not deduct unreimbursed employee expenses paid for that year. According to the court, no salary meant no employee status, which in turn meant no deductible unreimbursed employee business expenses.

The best way for an S corporation owner-employee to avoid these limitations is to treat the unreimbursed employee expenses as contributions to capital. In this way, the S corporation deducts the expenses in full and passes this deductible benefit to the shareholder in the form of reduced S corporation net income.

It is also important to note that the contributions to capital do not necessarily have to be treated as a purchase of corporate stock. A portion of the contributions can be characterized as a loan to the corporation that the corporation can repay to the owner-employee over a period of time.

By treating the expenses in this way, the S corporation owner-employee avoids the 2% limitation rule. And in years when the owner-employee does not take a salary (for whatever reason) from the corporation, business employee expenses can still be deducted.

☞ **EXAMPLE:** Mr. Smith is the sole owner-employee of Smith Company, an S corporation. During the tax year, he has $1,500 in various employee business expenses that are not reimbursed by his company. Because of large outlays for equipment, he forgoes a salary for the year. However, because he does not take a salary, he cannot use the unreimbursed business expenses as a miscellaneous deduction on his Form 1040 Schedule A. If he had taken a salary, these business expenses (together with any other miscellaneous expenses he had) would be deductible only to the extent of 2% of his adjusted gross income.

Instead of treating these expenses as unreimbursed employee expenses, he characterizes them as contributions to capital. The S corporation directly deducts the $1,500 as S corporation expense; as a result, reduced S corporation net income is passed to Mr. Smith's Form 1040. Because the deduction is taken in this way, the 2% limitation is avoided. In effect, Mr. Smith "deducts" 100% of the expense.

The contribution to capital increases Mr. Smith's basis in the company, and he treats $1,000 of the contribution as a loan to the company and $500 as a purchase of stock. In this way, the $1,000 can be returned to him in the form of a loan repayment.

♀**PLANNING POINTERS:** This strategy works best when there is only one owner–employee. When there are two or more owner–employees, disproportionate business expense amounts can create disproportionate capital contribution amounts, as well as disproportionate tax deductions. In situations where there are multiple owner–employees, care should be taken to "even up" the business expense amounts.

☑ **CHECKLIST:**

- Add a resolution to the corporate by-laws that all owner–employee unreimbursed employee business expenses are to be treated as contributions to capital.
- Owner–employees should carefully document the expenses and account for them to the corporation.
- The corporate books and tax returns should reflect the treatment as capital contributions.

91 Match Year-End Salary to Deductible Losses

$ Reduce your year-end S corporation salary for best use of S corporation loss.

$ You save personal income tax.

$ You and your S corporation also save FICA tax.

If your S corporation will operate at a loss this year, plan your year-end salary with respect to the loss. Limit your total annual salary as a shareholder-employee to the amount of S corporation loss the IRS will allow you to deduct on your personal income tax return. How much of the S corporation loss can you deduct? You can deduct the loss to the extent of your tax basis in the S corporation. By limiting your salary to the amount of S corporation losses you are allowed to deduct, you can minimize the amount of current income tax you have to pay, and you and your S corporation can also save payroll taxes.

☞**EXAMPLE:** Ms. Smith is the sole shareholder-employee of Smith Company, an S corporation. She has a tax basis of $30,000 in the corporation, and she plans for Smith Company to make her a year-end salary payment of $30,000. This will bring her total salary for the year to $50,000. Smith Company has already paid Ms. Smith $20,000 for the year to date. After paying her salary, Ms. Smith estimates that the corporation will have an operating loss of $65,000 for the year.

The problem with this plan is that Ms. Smith will not be able to deduct the full $65,000 S corporation loss on her current personal income tax return. The loss that is deductible is limited to her $30,000 basis in the S corporation. She will be able to deduct only $30,000 of the $65,000 total loss. The unused $35,000 loss must be "suspended" until a year in which Ms. Smith has increased her tax basis in the S corporation.

By handling her year-end salary this way, Ms. Smith will have to include her full $50,000 salary into her personal taxable income for the year and will be able to deduct only $30,000 in S corporation loss from that salary. As a result, she will end up with $20,000 in taxable personal income.

On the other hand, if Ms. Smith limits her year-end salary to $10,000, her total salary for the year will be only $30,000. And after making this reduced salary payment, the S corporation will have a reduced operating loss of $45,000 for the year.

By doing it this way, Ms. Smith will limit her total salary income for the year to $30,000. This salary will be completely sheltered by her allowable deductible S corporation loss of $30,000. As a result, she will have zero in personal income from the S corporation. And, instead of having $35,000 in "suspended" losses, she will have only $15,000 ($45,000 in loss less $30,000 allowable deduction) on hold until she increases her tax basis in Smith Company.

On top of the personal income tax savings for Ms. Smith, she and her S corporation will also save payroll taxes. By taking $20,000 less in salary before year-end, the combined personal and company FICA tax of 15.3% will be saved. This will mean an extra $3,060 ($20,000 times 15.3%) that can stay in the company's pocket for a while longer.

PLANNING POINTERS: If you need the cash from a year-end salary payment, you should attempt to delay your cash requirements until the day after the close of the year. In this way, you will be able to receive the cash almost at year-end but can still delay the tax treatment into next year.

✓ CHECKLIST:

- Before your S corporation makes your final salary payment for the year, determine your tax basis in the S corporation.
- Project the amount of S corporation loss for the year after deducting your year-end salary amount.
- With an eye to your tax basis in the S corporation, determine how much of the S corporation loss you will be able to deduct against your salary income on your personal income tax return.
- If your combined salary income less allowable deductible S corporation loss results in taxable personal income for the year, have the corporation reduce the amount of your year-end salary payment.

92 Don't Shortchange Your S Corporation When It Comes to Fringe Benefits

$ Certain deductible fringe benefits are available for all S corporation employees.

$ Establish employee benefit plans that benefit you as well as your employees.

$ Use benefit plans to attract new employees for less-than-going-rate salaries.

$ Save payroll taxes on benefit plan payments.

Your company doesn't have to be a regular C corporation for you and your employees to enjoy tax-deductible fringe benefits. The trick with an S corporation is to know which fringe benefits are available to only rank-and-file employees and which are available to all employees, including shareholder-employees. Once you know the difference, you can offer only those benefits which you, as well as your employees, will be able to use.

The most important benefits that an S corporation can provide for all its employees, even shareholder-employees, are dependent-care assistance and pension and profit-sharing plans. Health plans are also big items. Shareholder-employees who own more than 2% of their S corporation can deduct from their taxes a portion of their payments to an employee health plan. If you are a "2% shareholder-employee" in 1997, you can deduct 40% of the health insurance premiums the S corporation paid on your behalf. According to the 1997 tax law, this deductible percentage will be increased each year until it reaches 100% in the year 2007.

In addition to the more important benefits, 2% shareholder-employees can also enjoy the fruits of company group legal service plans, qualified employee discounts, working condition fringe benefits, and de minimis fringe benefits.

The fringe benefits that are not available to 2% shareholder-employees—without having to pay taxes on them—are group-term life insurance coverage up to $50,000, medical reimbursement plans, accident and health plans (except for the 40% deduction), disability plans, meals and lodging furnished for the convenience of the employer, and cafeteria plans.

☞**EXAMPLE:** Mr. Smith is the sole shareholder-employee of Smith Company, an S corporation. Knowing that benefit plans are an important employee incentive and wanting to share in these tax-beneficial incentives, Mr. Smith decides to implement a profit-sharing retirement plan, a dependent-care assistance plan, and an employee health plan.

Mr. Smith, as well as his employees, will get both the retirement plan and the dependent assistance plan tax free. Mr. Smith will be able to deduct only 40% of the health insurance premiums the corporation paid on his behalf for 1997, but this deductible benefit will increase each year until 2007, when he will be able to deduct 100%.

♀PLANNING POINTERS: You can benefit in other ways by establishing fringe benefit plans. Your S corporation may be able to hire new employees for less than the going rate because they are willing to accept less pay to enjoy the benefits. This saves the payroll taxes your company would have otherwise had to pay on higher employee salaries.

For most employee benefit plans, the government exempts payments made on behalf of all employees from payroll tax (FICA and FUTA tax). This applies to pension and profit-sharing plans that are not salary reduction plans, dependent-care assistance plans, and certain employee health plans.

☑ CHECKLIST:
- Determine which available fringe benefit plans you would like to enjoy.
- Establish these fringe benefit plans for the employees, including yourself, of your S corporation.
- When interviewing for new employees, use the available benefits to make a less-than-going-rate salary seem attractive.
- Be careful to save payroll tax on applicable employee benefit plan payments.

The Limited Liability Company— New Kid on the Block

▼
▼
▼

A Note About Limited Liability Companies

A new way to form your business is as a limited liability company (LLC). It is a mixed business form—part corporation and part partnership. An LLC enjoys the corporate advantage of limited liability while being treated as a partnership for federal income tax purposes. It is an ideal business form for two or more business owners who wish to have the corporate advantage of limited liability but prefer to have the tax benefits of a partnership rather than those of an S corporation.

To be treated as a partnership for federal income tax purposes, an LLC cannot have more than two of the four characteristics of a corporation: (1) limited liability, (2) continuity of life, (3) centralized management, and (4) free transferability of ownership. Most states allow you to choose which two corporate characteristics your LLC will have. A few states require your LLC to have specific corporate characteristics. As a practical matter, most LLCs will have limited liability (that's usually the main reason for having an LLC form) and centralized management because of its efficiency. Therefore, it is ordinarily the continuity of life and the free transferability of ownership that LLC creators avoid.

Before setting up an LLC, you should carefully consider the four corporate characteristics and decide whether you can do business without two of these characteristics. If you live in a state that requires your LLC to have specific corporate characteristics, you should be certain you can do without the characteristics your state prohibits.

Note the following considerations:

- *Limited liability*. This means that only the business's assets are subject to the liabilities of the business. Your risk is ordinarily limited to your investment in the business. Your other personal assets are safe from risk.
- *Continuity of life*. This means that the business continues when the ownership of the business changes. You can dispense with

this corporate characteristic if the LLC agreement requires that the LLC dissolve when any LLC member-owner dies, goes insane, retires, or is removed from the LLC by the other member-owners. In some states, if a majority of member-owners agree to continue the LLC, an LLC can avoid this corporate characteristic without dissolving the LLC. In other states, unanimous agreement is required among the remaining member-owners to continue as an LLC.

- *Centralized management.* This occurs when some of the owners do not participate in the management of the day-to-day affairs of the business. You can avoid this corporate characteristic if all the member-owners engage in the management of the day-to-day affairs. Usually, management authority in an LLC is allocated in accord with each member-owner's contribution of capital.
- *Free transferability of ownership.* This characteristic allows you to freely transfer your ownership of the business to a third party. In some states, to avoid this characterization, a majority of LLC member-owners must agree to the transfer of an owner's interest. In other states, all member-owners must consent.

☞**EXAMPLE:** Mr. Smith and Mr. Jones are considering establishing an LLC for their new business. They want to be able to borrow against the assets of the business and distribute the proceeds to themselves personally. Doing this with a corporation would result in a taxable transaction, so an LLC seems like the best bet. The state in which they live allows them to choose which corporate characteristics the LLC will not have.

First, they decide that the business must have limited liability to protect their personal assets.

Second, since they will be the only member-owners and both will actively manage the business, they will avoid the corporate characteristic of centralized management.

Third, they agree to dissolve the LLC when either of them dies, goes insane, retires, or is expelled by the other member-owners. By doing this, they can avoid the corporate characteristic of continuity of life.

Fourth, they agree that all member-owners must consent before one member-owner can transfer an interest in the business to a third party. In doing so, they can avoid the corporate characteristic of free transferability of ownership.

Because they will have only one of the four corporate characteristics, they will be allowed to treat their business as an LLC.

♀ PLANNING POINTERS: If you are starting a business, you can easily establish an LLC. Contact your state corporations office for any filing and registration requirements. Check to see whether there are any limitations on which corporate characteristics your business can have.

Apart from state filing requirements, you must also create an LLC membership agreement. An LLC membership agreement defines the rules and membership rights in the LLC (similar to the partnership agreement or by-laws of a corporation).

Existing partnerships that are already doing business do not have to liquidate their assets to become an LLC. Consequently, the changes in business forms are fairly straightforward. Unfortunately, existing S corporations must liquidate and pay any related taxes before becoming LLCs. Existing regular C corporations can avoid this liquidation requirement by establishing LLCs for new or expanded lines of business and then acting as the parent company, or brother-sister company, for the new LLCs.

☑ CHECKLIST:

- Determine whether you have a good tax reason for creating an LLC rather than a partnership, a regular C corporation, or an S corporation.
- If so, check with your state corporations office to see whether your state requires LLCs to have certain corporate characteristics.
- If you are able to comply with your state's LLC corporate characteristic requirements or if your state has no specific requirements, determine whether you can operate your business without the other corporate characteristics. Remember, your LLC can have no more than two of the four corporate

characteristics, including the ones your state may require your LLC to have.

- If you decide to establish your business as an LLC, file the necessary registration documents required by your state. Also draw up an LLC membership agreement.

93 Shift Income to Family Members and Distribute Cash Tax Free with an LLC

$ An LLC is an ideal vehicle for shifting ownership interest in a business or in other appreciating assets to family members.

$ Shift income to family members.

$ An LLC can borrow against LLC assets and distribute loan proceeds to family members without current income tax.

$ Annual gifts of LLC membership interests can avoid gift tax liability.

A limited liability company is a business form that protects your personal assets with the "limited liability" characteristic of a regular corporation. Only the assets of the LLC, not your personal assets, are subject to the claims of the LLC's creditors. At the same time, an LLC is treated like a partnership for federal income tax purposes. Income, loss, and other tax items pass from the LLC to the member-owner's personal income tax return.

The combination of limited liability and partnership tax treatment make the LLC an ideal vehicle for shifting income between LLC member-owners who are also family members. And because an LLC is not treated as a corporation for tax purposes, it is also an ideal vehicle for making tax-free distributions of cash.

☞**EXAMPLE:** The Smiths have an LLC. Mr. Smith owns 75%, Mr. Smith's son owns 20%, and Mr. Smith's grandson owns 5%. When Mr. Smith and his son established their business as an LLC, Mr. Smith contributed two commercial rental properties to the company.

Mr. Smith and his wife file a joint income tax return. Consequently, they can make gifts of $20,000 each year to as many recipients as they choose without having to pay gift taxes. For a few years, Mr. Smith has been donating LLC membership interests valued at $20,000 to his son. This year he gave his grandson a membership in the LLC valued at $20,000. By doing this, Mr. Smith still retains control of the LLC, but he can shift more taxable income from the LLC to his son and grandson in proportion to their LLC ownership. More taxable income to his son and grandson means less taxable income to himself. And less taxable income means less income tax.

On top of this, Smith Co. LLC has borrowed $100,000 against the two commercial rental properties. Mr. Smith, his son, and his grandson are personally liable for the loan. From this $100,000, Mr. Smith gives $20,000 ($100,000 times 20%) to his son and $5,000 ($100,000 times 5%) to his grandson. Unlike a regular C corporation distribution, these distributed LLC funds are tax free. Mr. Smith's son and daughter-in-law can donate their $20,000 to Mr. Smith's grandson without gift tax liability. Mr. Smith's grandson can use this $20,000 gift from his parents, along with the $5,000 he received from the LLC loan proceeds, to help defray college costs without incurring a current income tax liability.

💡**PLANNING POINTERS:** You don't have to use an LLC just for business purposes. You may want to set up a family LLC to hold real estate that you own. Over time, you can use the LLC to transfer ownership and related income without incurring gift taxes. At the same time, you can borrow against the properties and use the LLC to distribute the cash to family LLC members, without a current income tax bite on the cash distributions.

☑ **CHECKLIST:**
- Contact your state corporations office for registration requirements for an LLC.

- Establish a schedule of annual LLC membership gifts to family members. Be careful not to gift away your controlling interest.
- Be certain to allow for gifts of membership interests in your LLC membership agreement.

94 Use Your LLC to Convert Nondeductible Personal Interest into Deductible Business Interest

$ This loophole is for member-owners of an LLC who also have personal debt on which they are paying nondeductible personal interest.

$ Convert such nondeductible interest as car loan interest and credit card interest into deductible business interest.

$ Distributions from an LLC are currently tax free.

$ Deductible LLC business interest expense can save self-employment tax as well as income tax.

For several years, the government has not allowed you to deduct so-called personal interest on your individual income tax return. If you have taken out a car loan or paid interest on credit cards, you have been unable to deduct the interest you paid. But you can use your LLC to transform this nondeductible personal interest into fully tax-deductible business interest.

How is it done? Just have your LLC take out a loan that equals the amount of your personal debts. Next, have the LLC "indirectly" distribute the proceeds of the loan to you and then use the proceeds to pay off your personal debts. The interest your LLC pays on its loan is tax deductible as business interest. And since an LLC is a "conduit" business entity (the LLC's income and expenses flow to your personal income tax return), you can enjoy the deductible benefit of the LLC's "business interest expense."

EXAMPLE: Ms. Smith and Ms. Jones are member-owners of an LLC. Ms. Smith currently has a car loan with a $10,000 balance outstanding and has unpaid credit card charges of $4,000. Ms. Jones currently has a car loan with a $15,000 balance outstanding.

Since Ms. Smith and Ms. Jones are 50/50 owners in the LLC, they wish to keep everything on an equal footing. If $15,000 is to be distributed to Ms. Jones, then $15,000 must also be distributed to Ms. Smith, even though she needs only $14,000 to cover her personal debt.

The LLC borrows $30,000 and uses the loan proceeds for such direct business purposes as payroll, office rent, and business advertising. Since business needs do not require the entire $30,000 immediately, the LLC keeps the unused portion of the loan proceeds as working capital. The LLC is careful to document that loan proceeds are used directly for business purposes.

At the same time, the LLC distributes business receipts to Ms. Smith and Ms. Jones. These business receipts ordinarily would have been used to pay business expenses, but since the loan proceeds are covering the business expenses, the business receipts are available to distribute.

The LLC gives $15,000 each to Ms. Smith and Ms. Jones, so that both can pay off their personal debts. The LLC deducts the interest on the $30,000 loan as business interest, and the benefit of the deduction "flows through" 50/50 to the personal income tax returns of Ms. Smith and Ms. Jones.

Even though the LLC itself (not Ms. Smith and Ms. Jones) has taken out the loan, each has her tax basis in the LLC increased by the amount of the loan. Each tax basis increases by $15,000 (their proportionate share of the LLC loan). When they receive the $15,000 cash distributions from the LLC, each tax basis is reduced by the same amount. But because each has her tax basis increased by the LLC loan before it is decreased by the cash distribution, the cash given to the two member-owners is not currently taxable. In effect, they are able to pay off personal debts with money that is untaxed.

PLANNING POINTERS: It is important to document that the proceeds of the LLC loan are used for business purposes. The easiest way to do this is to deposit the loan proceeds into a separate LLC business checking account. By separating the loan proceeds in this way and then writing business checks from the separated loan proceeds, the business use of the loan funds is clearly indicated.

When an LLC takes out a loan, the individual tax basis of each of the member-owners is increased by his or her proportionate share of the LLC's loan. As a result, when the LLC loan proceeds are "indirectly" distributed to the member-owners, the distributions are not currently taxed.

This is an important difference between an LLC and an S corporation. When an S corporation takes out a loan, the tax basis of each S corporation shareholder is not increased by the amount of the S corporation loan. Depending on the tax basis of each of an S corporation's shareholders, an "indirect" distribution to them of the S corporation's loan proceeds may be taxable, nontaxable, or partially taxable.

Finally, an LLC business interest deduction can save self-employment tax (Social Security and Medicare) as well as federal and state personal income tax. If you are in the 28% federal personal income tax bracket, 5% state income tax bracket, and the 15.3% self-employment tax bracket, a $1,000 business interest deduction allocated to you will save you $483 in combined taxes.

☑ CHECKLIST:

- Determine the total amount of personal debt for which you are currently paying nondeductible interest.
- Have the other member-owners of your LLC make the same personal debt determination.
- Have the LLC take out a loan that will be indirectly distributed to the member-owners in proportion to their ownership interest in the LLC.
- Deposit the LLC loan proceeds in a separate checking account and use them for business purposes.
- Use other LLC business receipts to make proportionate distributions to the member-owners to the extent of their proportionate share of the LLC loan.
- Use the cash distributions from the LLC to pay off personal

debt on which you are currently paying nondeductible interest.

- Take a tax deduction for your share of the deductible business interest paid by the LLC on the LLC loan.

95 Consider the Tax Advantages of an LLC Over Those of an S Corporation

$ Due to changes resulting from the '96 tax act, S corporations are now more attractive; however, an LLC still has at least three additional tax privileges.

$ LLC owners can take tax losses based on LLC loans.

$ LLCs can make special allocation of profits and losses.

$ LLCs can distribute appreciated property without current income tax to the LLC or LLC owner.

While the Small Business Act of 1996 expanded the use of an S corporation as a business form, a limited liability company is still allowed at least three tax privileges that are denied to an S corporation:

- The LLC member-owners can include LLC liabilities in their tax bases when calculating their allowable current tax losses. Liabilities incurred by an S corporation cannot be included in the S corporation shareholders' tax basis. This difference allows LLC member-owners to claim larger current tax losses than S corporation shareholders.
- An LLC has more flexibility than an S corporation in allocating income and loss between its member-owners. This privilege enables you to create tax incentives with which to entice potential member-owners to join your LLC. S corporation owners do not have this option.

■ Generally, an LLC can distribute appreciated property tax free to its member-owners. However, when an S corporation distributes appreciated property to shareholders, a current taxable transaction occurs.

☞EXAMPLE 1: Smith Company has two owner-employees who materially participate (i.e., work regularly) in the business and each contribute $20,000 to the capital of the business at start-up. To help finance the business, Smith Company borrows $100,000. During the first year of business, Smith Company generates a loss of $140,000.

If Smith Company is an S corporation, the loss would be passed equally to each of the two owners—$70,000 each. However, according to S corporation rules, since each owner's current tax loss is limited to his or her current tax basis, each owner would be able to deduct only a $20,000 loss. The extra $50,000 each of their unused losses would have to be suspended until a later year when the shareholders would be able to increase their tax basis. If they were in the 31% federal income tax bracket and 5% state income tax bracket, a $20,000 loss would save income taxes of $7,200.

If, on the other hand, Smith Company is an LLC, things would look better. According to the LLC rules, the member-owners' tax basis could be increased by the $100,000 their LLC borrowed. If they were equal members, each member would have a $70,000 basis ($20,000 original capital contribution plus one-half of LLC loan) and each would be allowed to claim a $70,000 loss on their current tax return. For someone in the 31% federal income tax bracket and 5% state income tax bracket, a $70,000 loss would save income taxes of $25,200.

Because of the privilege of an increased tax basis, operating the business as an LLC rather than an S corporation would save each of the two member-owners $18,000 more in first-year income taxes.

☞EXAMPLE 2: Smith Company has two owner-employees who materially participate (i.e., work regularly) in the business and are 50/50 owners, each having contributed $30,000 to the capital of the business. During the first year, Smith Company generates a loss of $20,000.

If Smith Company is an S corporation, the loss would have to be split between the two owners 50/50—each would receive a $10,000 loss. This is because S corporations are allowed to have only a single class of stock. With a single class of stock, income and loss of the S corporation must be allocated in proportion to the ownership of the stock. A 50% shareholder must receive 50% of income or loss. Changing this allocation would create a second class of S corporation stock, automatically ending S corporation status.

If Smith Company is an LLC, a special allocation of income and loss could be made in the membership agreement, so long as the special tax benefits were tied to economic benefits. With an LLC, for example, one member-owner could receive 100% of the losses—$20,000 in this case—and then 100% of the profits, until the member-owner's profits equaled the previous losses. After that, the profits could be shared equally by all the member-owners.

For a start-up company expecting losses in the early years, this tax privilege creates a tax-deferral strategy that could be offered as an incentive to a new and needed LLC member-owner. The new member-owner would take the entire company loss for the first year. Later, all the LLC profits would be allocated to this member until the previous losses were netted out. This new member-owner would enjoy current tax savings from the losses and would not have to "return" these income tax savings until profits were generated.

☞**EXAMPLE 3:** Smith Company distributes an acre of raw land to an owner. The property has a basis of $10,000 and a current fair market value of $25,000.

If Smith Company is an S corporation, it must recognize a capital gain of $15,000 ($25,000 less $10,000) and pass it to the shareholders' personal income tax returns in proportion to their percentage of ownership in the company. If Mr. Smith and Mr. Jones were 50% shareholders, they would each have a capital gain of $7,500 ($15,000 times 50%). At the current maximum capital gains tax rate of 20%, each would have a federal income tax liability of $1,500. That's $3,000 in total income taxes paid between the two of them because of the distribution of the land.

If Smith Company is an LLC and distributes the same piece of property, neither the LLC nor the LLC member-owner receiving the property would need to recognize a taxable gain, even if the value of the property were to exceed the LLC member-owner's tax basis in the LLC.

The only exception to this rule is when one LLC member-owner contributes appreciated property to the LLC and the LLC then distributes this property to another member-owner within seven years. In this case, the LLC member who contributed the appreciated property to the LLC would have to pay tax on the appreciation in value that occurred prior to the time the property was given to the LLC.

♀PLANNING POINTERS: Before choosing between an S corporation and an LLC format for your new business, you should carefully consider all the advantages and disadvantages of both business forms. List the advantages of both business forms and determine which are priorities for your particular business. Most new business owners will find that the benefits of an LLC far outweigh the benefits of an S corporation—even so, it is still important to evaluate each benefit with regard to the particular requirements of your business.

☑ CHECKLIST:

- Before deciding on S corporation or LLC status for your business, determine whether the business will be borrowing and how this will affect the recognition of any tax losses (Example 1).
- Before deciding on S corporation or LLC status for your business, determine whether a special allocation of profit and loss could be an incentive to enlist needed business owners (Example 2).
- Before deciding on S corporation or LLC status for your business, consider whether distributions of appreciated property will be part of future transactions with owners (Example 3).

Up Against
the IRS

▼
▼
▼

96 Take the IRS to Tax Court to Determine Independent Contractor Status

$ A new procedure allows you to keep your cash until your case is heard.

$ For disputes involving less than $10,000 per calendar quarter, use the informal small case division of the U.S. Tax Court.

$ Attorney and other professional fees can also be reimbursed if you prevail.

The Taxpayer Relief Act of 1997 gives small business employers an important new procedure to use against the IRS when it attempts to reclassify independent contractors as employees. Beginning August 5, 1997, employers can petition the U.S. Tax Court to decide worker classification disputes. If the amount of disputed employment taxes is less than $10,000 for each calendar quarter in question, employers can use the small case division of the Tax Court to have their case heard.

This is an important change for taxpayers who own businesses and use the services of independent contractors as well as employees. Previously, in a worker classification dispute with the IRS, an employer was forced to pay at least a portion of the disputed employment tax and then had to sue the IRS for a refund in either a federal District Court or the U.S. Claims Court. The whole process could become tedious and expensive, in many cases forcing employers to settle with the IRS just to avoid the drawn-out hassle and expense.

Now, a small business employer can take the IRS to Tax Court. No portion of the tax has to be paid until the Tax Court renders a decision in the case. In addition, if the disputed amount is small enough and the employer is confident in the position he or she has taken, the employer can utilize the small case division of the Tax

Court without having to use the services of an attorney. The small case division of the Tax Court hears cases on an informal basis, and the usual rules of evidence are relaxed. Unlike with other courts, however, the decision of the small case Tax Court is final and cannot be appealed.

Finally, if attorney or other professional fees are incurred by the taxpayer and the taxpayer prevails over the IRS, the taxpayer can petition the Tax Court for reimbursement of all or a portion of the attorney fees (subject to a $110 per hour cap).

☞EXAMPLE: Mr. Smith is the owner of Smith Company. He employs two persons for whom he is required to pay federal payroll taxes (FICA/Medicare and FUTA). He also utilizes the services of four independent contractors, for whom he does not pay federal payroll taxes.

In late 1997, Smith Company is audited, and all four independent contractors are reclassified by the IRS auditor as employees. The auditor assesses back payroll taxes, interest, and penalty charges.

Previously, Mr. Smith would have been forced to pay at least a portion of the payroll tax assessment and then sue for a refund in federal District Court or the U.S. Claims Court. But because of the new tax law change, Mr. Smith can appeal the assessment with the appeals division of the IRS. If he is not successful in the appeals division, he can then petition the U.S. Tax Court. He can avail himself of this process without paying any portion of the assessment up front.

♀PLANNING POINTERS: This new audit procedure is helpful, but the best defense in a worker classification dispute still involves the fact that certain persons are in fact independent contractors rather than employees. Generally, an independent contractor is someone who produces a result for an employer without the employer controlling the means the independent contractor uses to accomplish the result. An employee is someone who is controlled by the employer both as to the desired results and the means to those desired results.

Various practices indicate whether an individual is an independent contractor or an employer. For example, if the employer provides a place of work, determines a set schedule of work hours, and provides supplies for a worker, the worker is an employee. On the other hand, if a worker provides his own place of work, sets his own hours, and provides his own supplies, the individual is an independent contractor.

Employers should be careful to document independent contractor status. The best way to do this is to establish a written contract with the independent contractor, detailing all the indicators of independent contractor status. The employer should then document as best as possible that the terms of the contract are actually met. A written contract is important for documenting intent, but what is outlined in the contract must actually occur and be documented.

☑ CHECKLIST:

- If independent contractors are reclassified as employees during an audit of your business, appeal the related payroll tax assessment to the appeals division of the IRS.
- If you do not prevail with the appeals division, petition the U.S. Tax Court. You can do this without having to pay any part of the payroll tax assessment before your case is heard.
- If the disputed payroll tax is less than $10,000 for any calendar quarter, consider using the more informal and relaxed small case division of the Tax Court.
- Be careful to document that the workers in question are in fact independent contractors and not employees.

97 Take the IRS to Court Without an Attorney

$ Use small tax case procedure when tax dispute is $10,000 or less.
$ Rules of evidence are relaxed.
$ Hearing is informal and final.
$ Hearing can be held close to your home.

Often when you have a dispute with the IRS, you have a choice between paying the IRS and paying an attorney to fight the IRS. Heads you lose, tails you lose. But it doesn't have to be that way if your tax dispute involves $10,000 or less. You can use the small tax case procedure and take the IRS to the U.S. Tax Court without an attorney.

If you believe you are right and the IRS is wrong, you can have an informal hearing at the Tax Court and represent yourself. With this procedure, the usual Tax Court rules of evidence are relaxed. Neither you nor the IRS is required to file legal briefs. The good news is that you can handle the case without having to gamble the cost of legal expertise. The bad news is that the decision of the court is final. If you lose, you cannot appeal the decision.

To be heard in court, you must file a simplified petition form with the Tax Court and pay a $60 filing fee. This simplified petition form must be completed and mailed within 90 days of the mailing date on the Notice of Deficiency sent to you by the IRS. The 90-day rule is strictly applied, so it is important that you file your petition in a timely fashion. Your petition can be filed only after receiving the IRS Notice of Deficiency.

For a copy of the simplified petition form, instructions, and a copy of a request for place of trial form, write to: Clerk of the Court, United States Tax Court, 400 Second St., N.W., Washington, D.C. 20217. Make sure to note that these forms are for the small tax case procedure.

Once you have received the petition forms, completing them is a straightforward process. On the form, you must include your name and Social Security number, the year or years the IRS claims you have a tax deficiency, the disputed amount of the deficiency, the city and state of the IRS office that issued the Notice of Deficiency, and a brief statement spelling out what the IRS is assessing and why you do not agree. When you file the petition, attach a copy of the IRS Notice of Deficiency.

☞ **EXAMPLE:** Mr. Smith, a self-employed taxpayer, is audited by the IRS for tax year 1995. During 1995, Mr. Smith deducted the standard mileage rate for all business driven to and from his home office, even though he is not allowed to take a tax deduction for his home office use. The IRS disallows the deduction for business travel from the home office to the first business stop each day and the return trip home from the last business stop each day. The IRS treats the daily first and last trip as nondeductible commuting.

Mr. Smith argues that the Tax Court has allowed the deductibility of this daily first and last trip, even though the taxpayer is not able to take a deduction for a home office. But the IRS won't budge. Since the amount of income and self-employment tax generated by the disallowed deduction comes to $2,500 (less than $10,000), Mr. Smith can take the IRS to Tax Court and use the small tax case procedure. Mr. Smith can do this without having to pay a lawyer as much as he is trying to save in tax.

♀PLANNING POINTERS: When you go to court, be as organized as possible. If you want to win, you must tell your side of the story in the best possible manner. Bring receipts, canceled checks, and any other documentation (including copies of tax rules) that you think prove your case. After the hearing, the judge will prepare a summary giving his reasons for the decision in the case.

You do not have to travel to Washington, D.C., to have the case heard. The Tax Court convenes at several locations around the country. When you send for a copy of the simplified petition form, also request a "place of trial" form. Request the closest available location for the hearing.

☑ CHECKLIST:
- If you are expecting a Notice of Deficiency from the IRS, don't wait until it arrives to get the blank forms from the Tax Court. Order them right away so you have them handy when the IRS Notice of Deficiency arrives.
- Once the Notice of Deficiency arrives, file the petition as soon as possible. If you take too much time and miss the 90-day period for filing the petition, you won't be able to take advantage of this procedure.
- Mail your completed small tax case petition by certified mail

for proof of timely mailing. Use the U.S. Post Office to mail the petition.

■ The Tax Court will notify you of the place and time for the hearing.

98 Stop the Interest Charges on the Extra Taxes Due

$ This tip is for taxpayers being audited.
$ If it looks like you'll owe more tax, make a cash deposit.
$ A deposit stops IRS interest charges.
$ Be careful not to overdeposit.

Additional tax is not the only thing an IRS audit might cost you. Once a further tax is assessed, there are other additions to the tax as well. Most significant, you become liable for penalties and interest on the increased tax. But you can stop the running of interest and cut your audit out-of-pocket expense by making a cash deposit to the IRS before the increased tax is assessed.

It usually takes the IRS a few years after you have filed an income tax return to invite you to an audit. It is even possible to receive an audit notice as late as a few months before the tax year in question "closes" (is no longer subject to audit). But regardless of the time of the audit, if the IRS ultimately assesses a further tax against you, not only will you owe the further tax, you will also owe interest on the tax—interest calculated from the due date of the original tax return. So if it takes the IRS three years to assess the tax increase, you will automatically owe three years of interest on the tax assessed.

If during an audit you find that you agree with some of the IRS auditor's tax increases though you disagree with others, you will want to minimize the interest on the tax you know you will have to pay. To do so, all you have to do is make a deposit with the IRS for the amount of that tax before it sends you a Notice of Deficiency.

☞EXAMPLE: In 1997, Mr. Smith's 1994 income tax return is audited by the IRS. Early in the audit, the IRS auditor disallows $3,000 in business expenses for which Mr. Smith has no documentation. The IRS auditor is also planning to disallow the rollover of the gain on the sale of Mr. Smith's principal residence.

Mr. Smith is unable to locate the documentation for the business expenses and feels that he will ultimately have to pay additional tax because of this. At the same time, he disagrees with the disallowance of the rollover of the gain on his principal residence and plans to appeal this assessment. He plans, if necessary, to take the issue to Tax Court small claims.

He calculates that the tax due on the $3,000 in disallowed business expenses—including an increase in the self-employment tax (Social Security and Medicare)—will come to approximately $1,235. The approximate interest on this amount at an estimated rate of 9% for the two-year period since the due date of the original income tax return is $225 (IRS interest rates can change every three months, so you have to approximate).

Before the audit proceeds any further and before Mr. Smith receives a Notice of Deficiency from the IRS, he makes a cash deposit with the IRS for $1,460 ($1,235 approximate tax due plus $225 approximate interest due). Mr. Smith notes on the check to the IRS that the payment is a "deposit in the nature of a cash bond."

♀PLANNING POINTERS: There are two important advantages to making a cash deposit with the IRS. First, assuming the deposit is large enough, the deposit stops the running of interest on the tax you might owe. If a tax increase is ultimately assessed, you will have minimized the interest charges.

Second, by making a cash deposit, you don't give up your right to go to Tax Court. You can go to Tax Court only if you owe a tax. If you are assessed a further tax and pay that tax, you can't go to Tax Court to sue for a refund. Instead, you are limited to suing for a refund in District Court or Claims Court. But by making a cash deposit, you have technically not paid the tax, so you can still go to Tax Court to argue your case.

The downside to a cash deposit is that it does not earn interest while it is held by the IRS. So if you end up not owing tax and the deposit is returned to you, it will be returned without interest. For this reason, it is important that you do not make a deposit that is larger than necessary. The idea is to walk the line between underdepositing and overdepositing. If you deposit too little, you will owe more in interest to the IRS. But if you deposit too much, you will lose interest earnings on the extra money you deposited. Before you make the cash deposit, carefully estimate how much will ultimately be due in additional tax and interest. It is almost impossible to be exact, so approximate as best you can.

If you do make a deposit and then decide you want the deposit back, you can request that all or a part of the deposit be returned. But you must do this before the IRS is entitled to assess the tax. The IRS will return the deposit unless you owe other taxes or unless the IRS determines that a tax will be due and that you will be unlikely to pay it. If you owe other taxes (say, for an earlier year), the IRS will apply your deposit to those taxes first. So if you owe other taxes, you should think twice before making a cash deposit.

Once the IRS assesses a further tax due, you can do one of two things. You can agree to the assessment, in which case your deposit will be applied to the assessment due and any overdeposit will be refunded to you. Or, you can disagree with the assessment and proceed to the appeals division of the IRS and, if necessary, to the Tax Court.

If there is an additional tax due and you disagree, the IRS will issue a Notice of Deficiency, the so-called 90-day letter. Once this notice is issued, you will have 90 days to file a petition with the Tax Court. During this 90-day period, you must also request to the IRS in writing that your deposit continue to be treated as a deposit. This request must be in writing, and you should send it by certified mail for proof of timely mailing. If you fail to make this written request, your deposit will be treated as a tax payment, and you will not be able to seek a refund in Tax Court. Instead, you will have to go to District Court or Claims Court and sue for a refund.

☑ CHECKLIST:

- During a tax audit, realistically approximate the potential tax increase and related interest charges.
- Make a cash deposit for the estimated amount of potential tax

and interest due. This will stop interest running on the amount deposited.

- Be as exact as possible with your estimates. An overdeposit will be refunded to you, but without earning interest.
- If you make a deposit and then disagree with the IRS auditor's assessment, be certain to make a written request that your deposit continue to be treated as a deposit. Make this written request to the IRS during the 90-day period after the IRS issues the Notice of Deficiency.

99 Recover More in Attorney Fees When You Take the IRS to Court

$ With this tip, you can recoup more in legal and accounting fees when you beat the IRS in court.

$ Exhaust all possible administrative remedies before taking the IRS to court.

$ Keep careful records of legal and accounting fees tax issue by tax issue.

The new Taxpayer Bill of Rights has increased the amount you can recoup in legal fees when you prevail against the IRS in court. You can now recover up to $110 per hour—this is up from $75 per hour. And beginning in 1997, the allowable hourly rate will be increased annually for inflation.

To recover legal fees, you must prevail against the IRS in court. "Prevail" means to win substantially with respect to the disputed tax amount or the tax issues presented in the case. The legal fees include fees paid to persons authorized to practice before the Tax Court or the IRS: attorneys, enrolled nonattorneys, enrolled agents, and CPAs. Remember, you have to beat the IRS in court to be reimbursed for these attorney and accountant fees.

In addition to winning in court, you must also exhaust all administrative remedies before going to court. You cannot lose patience in the initial audit and then proceed straight to Tax Court. If you do, you won't be reimbursed for legal fees, even if you win in court.

You have to let the audit take its course. If you can't get satisfaction for an issue with the initial IRS auditor, do not give in. At the end of that first audit, request a meeting with the auditor's supervisor. If you cannot resolve the conflict with the auditor's supervisor, hold out. After the audit has been completed, request an appointment with the appeals office of the IRS. If after meeting with the appeals officer you still cannot resolve the conflict, then you should petition the Tax Court.

EXAMPLE: Ms. Smith is being audited by the IRS for tax year 1995. She hires the enrolled agent who prepared her income tax return for the audit year to represent her in the audit. Her agent and the auditor discuss and settle favorably a variety of issues. Unfortunately, the IRS auditor is very stubborn about one issue.

Prior to selling her principal residence, Ms. Smith converted some business-use space to personal-use space. By making this conversion, she avoided a current capital gains income tax on that portion of the house which had previously been used for business. Although Ms. Smith complied with the Internal Revenue Code section governing this issue, and even complied with a more restrictive IRS revenue ruling on the subject, the IRS auditor is unwilling to settle the issue in Ms. Smith's favor.

If Ms. Smith storms off to Tax Court, she may win the case but will be unable to recover any of the enrolled agent's fees or any other legal fees she might incur as a result of the court dispute.

Consequently, Ms. Smith's enrolled agent will request a meeting with the auditor's supervisor. If this meeting fails to resolve the conflict, it will be on to the IRS appeals office. If there is no satisfaction with the appeals officer, then Ms. Smith will file a petition with the Tax Court. In this way, Ms. Smith will protect her recovery of legal fees.

PLANNING POINTERS: During the audit process, instruct your hired representative—whether it be your enrolled agent from the initial audit and appeals meetings or your attorney during the sessions in Tax Court—to keep careful records of the time spent on each tax issue. At the beginning of an audit, it is difficult to determine which issues will be settled without dispute and which issues you will have to wrangle over. A careful record showing which legal or accounting fees resulted from which issues will help you recoup as much of the cost as possible should any of those issues take you to court.

☑ CHECKLIST:

- Exhaust all administrative remedies with the IRS before proceeding to court. See the audit through, meet with the auditor's supervisor, and appeal the issue.
- Keep careful records of professional fees (legal and accounting) incurred during a tax audit for all separate tax issues.

100   Shortcut a Tax Audit and Still Recover Attorney Fees

$ This is a tax audit strategy.
$ Declining to extend the IRS tax assessment period will not count against you in recovering audit-related legal fees.
$ You should make certain considerations before declining to extend the IRS tax assessment time period.

The new Taxpayer Bill of Rights allows a shortcut around the IRS audit process that allows the recovery of attorney and accountant fees. If your dispute with the IRS concerns only one issue, you may want to consider using this option.

Ordinarily, to recover legal and accounting fees that result from a dispute with the IRS during a tax audit, you have to exhaust all the administrative remedies before proceeding to court. The process usually entails finishing the initial audit, meeting with the auditor's supervisor about the disputed item, and then, if necessary, meeting with an IRS appeals officer. Sometimes this process can take years.

But if the IRS is auditing a tax year that is about to "close" (generally three years previous), the auditor will ordinarily ask you to sign an extension of the limitations period. This means the IRS will get your permission to extend the legal allowable time in which it can assess your tax for the year being audited.

Generally, the IRS has argued that if a taxpayer refused to extend the limitations period, that taxpayer was not exhausting all administrative remedies. According to the IRS reasoning, if the taxpayer then went to court and won the tax dispute, the taxpayer ought to be ineligible to collect attorney and accounting fees.

The new Taxpayer Bill of Rights makes it clear that this is not the case. As long as you exhaust all other administrative remedies, refusing to extend the limitations period will not disqualify you from collecting attorney and accountant fees you incur during the audit—assuming you ultimately prevail over the IRS in court.

If you refuse to extend the limitations period, the IRS is forced to issue a Notice of Deficiency—a so-called 90-day letter. Once this notice is issued, you have 90 days from the date on the Notice of Deficiency to file a petition with the Tax Court. Going straight to court will save the time you would normally have to spend meeting with the IRS auditor's supervisor and going through the IRS appeals process.

EXAMPLE: Mr. Smith is being audited by the IRS. The IRS auditor checked Mr. Smith's income tax return for the last two years but found no discrepancies. When he checked Mr. Smith's income tax return from three years ago, he found something he thought might possibly lead to a tax assessment.

Mr. Smith had sold his principal residence that year. Prior to selling the residence, Mr. Smith had converted his business-use space to personal-use space. This allowed Mr. Smith to roll over the entire gain on the residence and thereby avoid current capital gains income tax. Even though Mr. Smith complied with both the governing Internal Revenue Code section and a more restrictive IRS revenue ruling on the subject, the IRS auditor thinks that a tax should be assessed on the previous business-use portion.

The IRS auditor wants to take more time to evaluate the issue, but the closing of the assessment period for that year is fast approaching. The IRS auditor asks Mr. Smith to sign an extension of the limitation period. If Mr. Smith declines to sign the extension, the IRS will have to either issue a 90-day letter assessing a tax due or drop the assessment.

If the IRS issues a 90-day letter, Mr. Smith is required to file a petition to the Tax Court within 90 days of the date on the 90-day letter. Furthermore, by declining to sign the extension of the limitation period, he will not be prevented from collecting the audit-related attorney and accountant fees, assuming he ultimately prevails over the IRS in court.

♀PLANNING POINTERS: If you are disputing only one item with the IRS and are confident your tax position is the correct one, you should consider declining an extension of the limitations period. This will speed up the process of getting the IRS to court and won't deny you the chance to recover the audit-related legal and accounting fees.

On the other hand, if several issues are in dispute and you are unsure about them, you may want to extend the limitations period. This will give you a chance to settle many of the issues in the normal audit process. Maybe you won't even have to go to court, or, if you do, it will concern fewer issues.

☑ CHECKLIST:

- Before declining to extend the limitations period, carefully evaluate the merits of your position with regard to all the tax issues that could be assessed if you decline to sign.
- If you are confident as to the merits of your position on all the issues, don't sign the extension and shortcut the tax audit process.
- Keep careful records of professional fees (legal and accounting) incurred during the tax audit for all separate tax issues. In this way, if you ultimately prevail against the IRS on the bulk

of the issues, you will be able to properly justify the legal and accounting fees incurred to support your position on those issues and to recover those fees.

101 T.A.M. the IRS

$ Don't get mad—get correct.
$ If the auditor disputes items on your tax return, request a T.A.M.
$ Issues are put on hold and tax audit cannot be completed until T.A.M. is either denied or provided.

A tax audit is rarely smooth sailing. As it audits your income tax return, the IRS may dispute the way you handled specific items, disallowing your treatment and assessing you further income tax. To support the IRS position, the auditor may rely on tax rules or court cases that are not on point, dismissing as irrelevant your justifications for the position you have taken. If this happens, don't get mad—get correct. Request a technical advice memoranda (T.A.M.) from the IRS National Office.

The IRS encourages taxpayers to request technical assistance when the treatment of a tax issue is inconsistent or when the tax issue is unusual or complex. So take it up on its offer. Request a T.A.M. on each tax issue in dispute.

When you request a T.A.M., the IRS auditor can deny the request. But if that happens, you can appeal to the chief, examination division, or the chief, appeals office. If the chief in turn denies your request, you cannot appeal the decision but you can request a review of the decision by the assistant commissioner, examination, or the national director of appeals.

The worst that can happen is that your request for technical advice will ultimately be denied. Keep copies of the denied requests. These documents will help show that you attempted to "exhaust all administrative remedies" before going to Tax Court. If you prevail in Tax Court, the exhaustion of all administrative remedies is one of the requirements you must meet to recover the legal and accounting fees you incurred during the tax audit.

And what happens if the IRS okays your request for technical assistance? If the National Office decides in your favor, your tax auditor is bound by the decision. However, even if the National Office decides against you, you can still dispute the finding—first with the IRS appeals office and then in court.

EXAMPLE: Ms. Smith is being audited by the IRS for tax year 1995. During 1995, she sold her principal residence and rolled over the gain into the purchase of a new residence, avoiding the current capital gains tax on the sale. Prior to making the sale, Ms. Smith converted her business-use space in her home to personal-use space.

Although Ms. Smith complied with the Internal Revenue Code section governing this issue and even complied with a more restrictive IRS revenue ruling on the subject, the IRS auditor is unwilling to settle the issue in Ms. Smith's favor.

The auditor points to a court case in which a taxpayer was required to pay capital gains tax on the portion of the gain allocated to the business-use of the house. Even though Ms. Smith points out that this case was different because the business-use space was not converted to personal-use space prior to the sale, the IRS auditor refuses to budge.

Ms. Smith then requests a T.A.M. The IRS auditor denies the request. Ms. Smith then appeals to the chief, examination division. The chief, examination division, okays the request, and it is forwarded to the National Office.

PLANNING POINTERS: As soon as a T.A.M. is requested, the disputed issue must be put on hold until the T.A.M. request and any appeals for the request are ultimately denied or the National Office provides the technical advice. This means the tax auditor cannot close your case until the T.A.M. situation is resolved one way or the other.

Even if the request is ultimately denied, two or three months can pass before the initial request, the appeal for the request, and the review of the appeal is complete. And if the IRS National Office accepts the request, the process can take a year—maybe more—depending on how backed up the IRS National Office is.

As everyone should know, IRS tax auditors are not evaluated according to the amount of revenue they generate from the audits they are assigned but on the number of cases they close. Tell the IRS auditor that you are considering a T.A.M. request. Perhaps this will motivate the auditor to take a more broad-minded look at your analysis of the issue.

This is not to say that you should use a T.A.M. request as a stalling tactic with which to gain leverage with the tax auditor. This would not be proper. As the mission of the IRS is to assess the proper tax—not to generate revenues—your purpose in requesting a T.A.M. should be to resolve the disputed tax issue correctly, not to stall the IRS process.

☑ CHECKLIST:

- If the IRS tax auditor disputes your basis for the treatment of an item on your tax return, request a T.A.M.
- Retain copies of requests for a T.A.M. whether or not the requests are okayed. If you ultimately prevail in court against the IRS, use this documentation to support the position that you attempted to exhaust all administrative remedies before proceeding to court. Exhausting all administrative remedies is required to recover the legal costs of a tax case.

Index

money purchase plan, 147, 148
for owners of two or more
businesses, 141–44
profit-sharing plan, 147, 148, 149–50
timing for funding, 27–30, 137–39
Kiddie tax rules, 265, 266–67

Landscaping expenses, 236–38
Lawn maintenance expenses, 236–38
Leasehold improvements, 189–91
Leases, *see* Rentals and rents
Letters of credit, irrevocable, 20–22
Life expectancy tables, IRS, 132, 134,
155
Lifetime learning credit:
for business-related education
expenses, 5–8
for child's education, 2–5
Limited liability companies (LLCs),
292–303
distinctions from S corporation, 299,
300–303
making tax-free distributions with,
295–96
overview of, 292–95
requirements, 292–95
shifting income to family members,
295–97
state law, compliance under, 292–95
Lump sum distributions taken before
year 2000, 144–47

Medicaid payments, deduction of
friend's personal exemption and,
15–16
Medicare payments, deduction of
friend's personal exemption and,
15–16
Modified Accelerated Cost Recovery
System (MACRS), 174–76
Mortgage interest deduction, 37
for paying family-member's
mortgage, 63–65
prepaying extra month at year-end,
38–41
Mortgages:

children's, paying, 63–65
co-signing, 63, 64
wraparound, 60–63
see also Home equity loans; Mortgage
interest deduction
Mutual funds:
accurate record keeping, 117–20
basis averaging methods, 119
with check-writing privileges, 120–
23
FIFO method, 118–19
planning when selling at a loss, 114–
17
specific share method, 117–20

National Association for the Exchange
of Industrial Resources, 261–62
New business:
accrual method of accounting, 211–
14
buying a, 192–94
payroll tax deduction before actual
payment of taxes, 211–13
underpayment penalties, avoiding,
253–56
Non-home-equity loan election, 42–45

Older taxpayers:
IRA penalty-free distributions for
those over 50, 131–34
lump sum retirement plan
distributions, 144–47
parents, *see* Elderly parents
Roth IRAs for, 126–28
with SEP plans, strategies for, 154–
57
unused capital losses, 101–104
Overpayment of taxes:
C corporation estimated taxes, 248–
50
interest on refunds of, 78–80
Parking costs, 176, 221–23, 241–43
Partners:
entertainment benefits, 218–21
overtime supper money, 216–17

ABOUT THE AUTHOR

SEAN M. SMITH, a practicing tax accountant for fifteen years, is an Enrolled Agent licensed by the federal government to represent taxpayers in audits. He is a contributing editor of the *Tax Reduction Report,* a newsletter published by the National Institute of Business Management, and lives in Washington, D.C.